Medtech

Pierre-Yves Donzé

Medtech

The Formation and Growth of a Global Industry, 1960–2020

palgrave
macmillan

Pierre-Yves Donzé
Graduate School of Economics
Osaka University
Toyonaka, Japan

ISBN 978-981-16-7173-9 ISBN 978-981-16-7174-6 (eBook)
https://doi.org/10.1007/978-981-16-7174-6

This Palgrave Macmillan imprint is published by the registered company Springer Nature Singapore Pte Ltd.
The registered company address is: 152 Beach Road, #21-01/04 Gateway East, Singapore 189721, Singapore

Acknowledgements

This book would not have been possible without the generous support of several institutions and boundless assistance of various colleagues and friends. First, I would like to thank the Japanese Society for the Promotion of Science (JSPS), which funded this research through two grants (Grants-in-Aid for Scientific Research C 17K03839 and B 19H01512). The creation and analysis of the medtech patent database was accomplished with the support of a grant-in-aid from Zengin Foundation for Studies on Economics and Finance.

The data and discussion on medtech patents presented in Chap. 2 have already been published in part in a separate article (Pierre-Yves Donzé & Raphaël Imer, "Innovation in the global medtech industry: An empirical analysis of patent applications, 1960–2014", *Osaka Economic Papers*, vol. 69, no. 4, 2020, pp. 18–42). Moreover, some tables and figures in Chap. 6 appear in Pierre-Yves Donzé, "The Postwar Medtech Industry in Japan: A Business History Perspective", in Susanne Brucksch and Kaori Sasaki (eds.), *Humans and Devices in Medical Contexts; Case Studies from Japan*, Singapore: Palgrave Macmillan, 2021, pp. 199–224.

Although this book is single-authored, I benefited from comments and constructive criticism offered by many fellow business historians. Since 2017, I have presented several sections of the book at various seminars, workshops and conferences in Boston, Cartagena, Denver, Nagoya, Sheffield, and Tokyo. I thank all the participants of these meetings for their fruitful discussions and contributions to the development of this book. In particular, I extend my sincere gratitude to Raphaël Imer, Chief Operating Officer at Enovating SA, a market intelligence company based in Neuchâtel, Switzerland, that specializes in the analysis of intellectual property data. Without his support, I would not have been able to build a patent database to discuss medtech innovation since the 1960s. I would also like to thank Qing Xia, PhD student at Osaka University, for her countless and effective searches for scholarly works and data on the Chinese medtech industry. The information and discussion on this industry presented in Chap. 9 owe much to her support. I would also like to express my gratitude to Paloma Fernández Pérez, professor at the University of Barcelona, with whom I have been collaborating for several years in developing a business history of health. Our rich intellectual exchanges have contributed to the realization of this book. Finally, I also benefited from the friendly and insightful advice of Takafumi Kurosawa, professor at Kyoto University, for some parts of the book. The author, of course, is solely responsible for any errors and interpretations made in the following pages.

Osaka
August 2021

Contents

List of Figures

List of Tables

CHAPTER 1

Introduction

In July 2000, Intuitive Surgical, a NASDAQ-listed company founded five years earlier, received Food and Drug Administration (FDA) clearance for laparoscopic surgery applications of its Da Vinci Surgical system, one of the world's first surgical robots. It had been co-developed by a group of engineers and entrepreneurs, supported by venture capital, and conducting joint research with IBM and MIT (DiMaio et al., 2011). As of December 31, 2020, Intuitive Surgical had installed nearly 6000 Da Vinci systems worldwide, primarily in the US. The company has grown from a small firm with gross sales of only 52 million USD in 2001 to a large enterprise generating over 4 billion USD in sales in 2020.[1]

This example embodies two major characteristics of today's medical device industry (hereafter "medtech industry"). First, it is an industry based on the application of high-tech knowledge to medical practice. Micromechanics, electronics, material science, information and communication technologies are used to develop new devices, equipment and instruments for patient care. The medtech industry consists mainly of hardware for medical use, although it also includes orthopedical appliances and implants, which are derived from the application of similar technologies (mechanics and material science). However, it does not comprise low-tech medical supplies (masks, gloves, bandages, etc.), nor pharmaceuticals, which are manufactured by different companies, using different

[1] Intuitive Surgical, Annual Report, 2005 and 2020.

P.-Y. Donzé, *Medtech*,
https://doi.org/10.1007/978-981-16-7174-6_1

technologies.[2] Second, the medtech industry is a fast-growing sector dominated by many large enterprises. In the late 1980s, only a handful of firms had sales of more than one billion USD in the medtech sector. Three decades later, more than 60 companies exceeded that mark—Intuitive Surgical being one of them. They exert a strong dominance over this industry (see Chap. 3). The example of Intuitive Surgical suggests that startups are at the origin of the tremendous growth of this industry. This book will analyze in depth the actors of innovation in the medtech sector and the respective roles of the various types of firms, including old companies, in order to show that not all innovation results from startups alone.

Defining the medtech industry

The expression "medtech industry" includes such a broad range of products that its definition varies according to the criteria that analysists, consultants, and scholars adopt. Moreover, the evolution of innovation since the 1960s has had an impact on the boundaries of this industry, especially with the advent of electronics and ICT. A restrictive definition encompasses only instruments and devices and excludes medical imaging equipment and healthcare IT (e.g., Frost & Sullivan, 2017). In the US, the Census of Manufacturers does not include ophthalmic products. As for academic researchers, most do not explicitly define "medtech industry". However, the prevailing approach is not to include pharmaceutical goods. Drugs and medicine belong to another industry, with (mostly) different actors, although the goods are sold in the same market. Moreover, the recent advent of biotechnology challenges the differentiation between "medtech" and "pharma," as drugs and devices tend to become increasingly integrated.

Three general and internationally accepted indicators help establish a proper definition of "medtech industry." First, the Standard Industrial Classification (SIC) identifies industries with a four-digit code. Category 384 includes "Surgical, Medical, and Dental

(*continued*)

[2] Few pharmaceutical companies, however, have entered the medtech industry through a diversification process, as will be discussed throughout this book.

(continued)

Instruments and Supplies," with five codes (3841, 3842, 3843, 3844 and 3845). These codes have most notably been used to identify the cases of M&A in the Thomson One database, accessed in April and May 2018. However, these are the codes used today. Their scope has changed over time, which is what makes research from a historical perspective challenging. Second, the International Patent Classification (IPC) has a code (A61) referred to as "Medical or Veterinary Science; Hygiene." The category is broad and includes products for dental hygiene, drugs, and transportation devices (among others). For this book, we use subcategory A61B for "Diagnosis, Surgery, Identification," which represents the core of the medtech industry and includes all its major actors. Third, HS commodities for trade statistics have three codes for medtech products (9018 for general medical and surgical instruments, 9021 for orthopedic appliances, and 9022 for X-ray apparatus). These categories have also changed over time. Detailed data on the foreign trade of medtech goods prior to 1990 is largely incomplete.

Consequently, these three major indicators do not cover exactly a similar scope. It is therefore not possible to compare the numbers and values from databases perfectly. Thus, being aware of this methodological bias, the figures given in this book should be considered as orders of magnitude and trends, rather than an exact representation of reality.

Where did the medtech industry originate? How was it formed and how did it evolve into a big business that is organized globally? These are the major questions addressed by this book. Developing and manufacturing medical instruments is an old activity and some scholars offer narratives explaining their gradual evolution since the early modern period until today (David, 1978; Reiser, 1978; Jones, 2018). Others argue that the development of the X-ray machine and of the electrocardiograph (ECG) were turning points in the formation of the growing medical device industry during the interwar years (Gelijns & Rosenberg, 1999; Blume, 2003). However, until the 1970s, medical device and equipment manufacturers were deeply specialized. Multinational enterprises (MNEs) of electric appliances such as General Electric (GE), Siemens, Philips, and Toshiba dominated the medical imaging market, while there were numerous firms—mostly small- and medium-size enterprises (SMEs)—focusing on a narrow range of products, like laboratory equipment, patient monitoring devices, orthopedic implants, pacemakers, and surgical instruments. Moreover, most of these companies were predominantly focused on their national market. The various producers of medical devices did not compete with each other outside of their field of specialization. Thus, at the same time, there was a wide variety of small industries specializing in particular medical devices, mostly organized locally, but there was no market integration. The only exception was the producers of X-ray machines and CT scanners, which were essentially MNEs since the beginning of the twentieth century. However, these were companies in the general electric machinery industry, which were not particularly focused on medical technology. Consequently, a medtech industry per se did not exist.

Half a century later, however, the production and sales of medtech goods are controlled by large corporations, organized globally, and with a diversified portfolio of medical devices. They compete intensively with each other on world markets. The medtech industry was therefore formed through a process of diversification, which is analyzed in detail in this book. It emerged in the 1970s and began its rapid growth during the decades that followed. Data from Google Books (see Fig. 1.1) aptly illustrates that the expressions "medical device industry" and "medtech" were

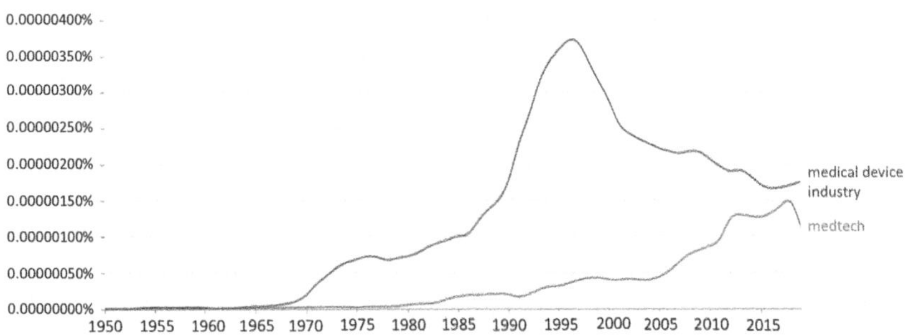

Fig. 1.1 "Medical device industry" and "medtech" in Google Books, 1950–2019. (Source: Google Books, https://books.google.com/ngrams (accessed 2 June 2020))

essentially not in use in the 1950s and 1960s because the industry itself did not yet exist. At that time, companies that manufactured medical devices focused on the production of specific devices. In addition, the largest of these companies were firms that manufactured a broad range of products other than medical devices, so they were not characterized as "medical device manufacturers". Therefore, there was no concept or statistics to classify these companies together. The expression "medical device industry" appeared in the 1970s and its use grew rapidly in the following decades, becoming a buzzword in the late 1990s, followed by "medtech," which emerged seamlessly in the late 1980s. The latter was first mentioned in the *Financial Times* in 1985, when the newspaper discussed the development of a research center belonging to Johnson & Johnson.[3] Of course, this discussion is based solely on English books digitalized by Google and is not representative of scientific evidence. This does give some indication, however, that the 1970s and 1980s were a turning point in the formation and emergence of a medtech industry.

This booming expansion has resulted from both an increase in healthcare expenses, which represents a major incentive for medtech companies, and a high level of investment R&D. Between 1970 and 2019, total expenditures on health as a proportion of GDP increased from 5.7% to 11.7% for Germany, from 4.4% to 11.1% for Japan, and from 6.2% to 17% for the US.[4] This expansion provided an opportunity for numerous firms to invest heavily in R&D. For example, in the US in 2002, the medtech industry had one of the highest proportions of R&D to gross sales (11.4%), second only to the pharmaceutical industry (12.9%) but far higher than the automotive (4.1%), electronics (3.9%), and aerospace-defense (3.1%) industries (Panescu, 2006). It thus stands as a high value-added industry, an attractive target for future economic growth policies for most governments in developed countries (Foray, 2014).

Despite this economic and technological significance, however, the medtech industry remains largely unknown. The questions of who are its main actors, where do they come from, and how did they grow form a major piece in properly understanding the dynamics of the industry—but the lack of investigation on a global scale makes the corresponding answers difficult to come by. A broad variety of actors, ranging from individuals

[3] *Financial Times*, 6 December 1985.

[4] Organization for Economic Co-operation and Development (OECD), Health expenditure and financing, https://stats.oecd.org/ (accessed 27 May 2021).

(medical doctors, engineers and mechanics) to organizations (startups, government agencies, universities, small family firms, and large multinationals) are involved in this industry. Some scholars have demonstrated a trend toward concentration. According to Kruger and Kruger (2005, p. 437), the concentration ratio in the global medtech industry (the market share controlled by the top 10 companies) increased from 45% in 1995 to 62% in 2009. Since the 1990s, M&A efforts have enabled the largest companies to strengthen their dominance. Still, the medtech industry is a truly diverse sector that includes a broad range of actors. According to the American magazine *Medical Design & Outsourcing* (2016), the top-100 ranking of the largest medtech companies worldwide in 2014 was home to large corporations like Medtronic (92,000 employees) and Boston Scientific (25,000 employees) but also numerous startups (e.g., Insulet, 650 employees) and university spin-offs (e.g., Abiomed, 150 employees).

A second characteristic is the overwhelming domination of this industry by US companies, with Japanese and German firms, along with a handful of companies from other European countries, lagging far behind. *Medical Design & Outsourcing*'s ranking of the top 100 largest companies includes a total of 57 companies from the US. The second highest-ranking nation is Japan, with only 15 companies, and the third Germany, at six firms. Other countries have fewer than five firms. Moreover, in the US, the medtech industry is clustered in a few large urban states and cities with competitive universities and R&D research facilities, like California, Boston, New York, Massachusetts, Illinois, and Minnesota (Clayton Matthews, 2001).

Consequently, the diversity of actors makes it difficult to attain a general, comprehensive view of the conditions of development of this high-tech industry and the evolution of these conditions over time. Much of the existing research focuses on specific actors (medical doctors, small firms, large corporations, and universities), specific countries, or specific regions. Hence, although the medtech industry has attracted the attention of numerous scholars in management, economics, and business history, there is a lack of studies addressing it at the global level. The general dynamics of the sector thus remain largely unknown, unlike other high-tech industries such as electronics, ICT, and automobiles. Works on the medtech industry tend to fall into four general categories, as described in the following sections.

1 The Domination of Multinational Enterprises

The presence of large global companies is a major characteristic of the medtech industry. For example, Maresova and Kuca (2014) showed that the 10 largest firms in the sector accumulated revenues of more than seven billion USD in 2012 and 2013. Two types of explanations help clarify this feature. First, some economists have argued that, on the basis of research on X-ray and electromedical equipment, a handful of multinational enterprises has dominated the industry since the interwar years due to continuous and accumulated investments in core technology. Gelijns and Rosenberg (1999) emphasized the first-mover advantage as a major determinant. They also showed that path-dependency investments in innovation have strengthened the positions of large multinationals. Focusing on the example of Johnson & Johnson, Christensen and Raynor (2013) argued that these big firms were able to overcome the so-called "innovator's dilemma" (Christensen, 2013) through the acquisition of disruptive startups.

Second, several scholars have found that large medtech firms result largely from waves of mergers and acquisitions (M&As), another important feature of the industry. With the high-margin, high-growth-potential nature of its business, medtech attracts newcomers from low-growth manufacturing sectors that reorient their resources. Usually, these types of companies enter the medtech industry through the acquisition of small companies specializing in simple devices and then use their own technological resources to upgrade the equipment (Lawyer & Alford, 2005). Representative cases include Tyco International and its subsidiary Tyco Healthcare Group (Covidien since 2007), Danaher Co., OSI Systems Inc., and Smiths Group PLC. According to Boston Consulting Group, the number of medtech companies with more than one billion USD in gross sales increased from 23 in 1994 to 37 in 2004 (Lawyer & Alford, 2005). However, new entrants' diversification toward medical devices is not the only cause of growth among medtech firms. Some medtech companies also developed through diversification within the industry. Wu (2013) tackled the case of the US cardiovascular medical device industry since 1976 and showed that firms used their technological capabilities for product diversification in order to cope with changes in demand.

2 Clusters of SMEs and Spin-Off Chains

Besides the presence a few large companies, the existence of numerous SMEs is another specificity of the medtech industry that has attracted substantial attention among researchers. Moreover, medtech SMEs tend to gather in regional clusters throughout the world, owing to the industry's "long value chain [that requires] different competencies and is highly innovative" (Steinle et al., 2007). According to Shaw (1998), a consequence of such an industrial structure is the potential for innovation via a learning process between various actors (e.g., entrepreneurs, doctors, and patients). That constitution leads to an endless innovation process (development, purchase, feedback, re-innovation, diffusion of new innovation, and so on), benefiting from a dense network of actors.

Most of the medtech clusters that have been subject to scholarly investigations are organized on a national, and sometimes regional, level (Clayton Matthews, 2001; Burfitt et al., 2007). In Germany, for example, Steinle et al. (2007) considered the national medtech industry a single cluster with more than 100 actors (e.g., enterprises, universities, research centers) in the mid-2000s, of which almost 60% formed after 1990. That German cluster also carries out its own innovation and does not depend on outsiders for technology; on the contrary, it attracts US multinational enterprises such as GE Healthcare, which invests in the country to acquire German knowledge. Steinle et al. (2007) did not, however, consider the global organization of Siemens and its impact on the domestic cluster.

A major characteristic of medtech clusters is the importance of spin-off chains for the creation of new SMEs. In the US, for example, many employees of large medical device companies (e.g., Johnson & Johnson, Medtronic, Boston Scientific, Abbott, and St. Jude) founded their own firms, aiming to develop innovative new ideas. Orange County (California) is a particularly important cluster, sprouting many spin-off chains since the beginnings of the medtech industry (de Vet & Scott, 1992). The first important companies appeared during the 1950s, with Bechman Instruments and Edwards Laboratories specializing in mechanical heart valves. Don Shiley, chief engineer at Edwards Laboratories, developed a new artificial heart valve and established his own company in 1963 (Shirley Laboratories). Later, other employees left Edwards to found Bentley Laboratories (1964) and Hancock Laboratories (1967). Then, in the 1970s and 1980s, several shifts in the academic and political environment (the growth of the medical school at the University of California, development of the local airport, and decreases in public spending for defense contracts, for instance) led engineers in electronics to look for new businesses—and medtech was a promising one. Tens of spin-offs were launched during these decades. The profitability of such spin-offs in comparison with the respective parent companies at which their founders previously worked is an important point to address. Chatterji (2009) used financial data (Dow Jones statistics) to investigate this issue, showing that technology itself was not the sole determinant of profitability of a newly created spin-off. The non-technological knowledge at large companies (e.g., expertise in marketing, regulatory affairs, and the identification of entrepreneurial opportunities) is also a major factor in the creation of a new SME. In the United Kingdom (UK), Craven et al. (2012) argued that most medtech SMEs are headed by engineers who lack knowledge in management and health economics. That shortcoming has a negative effect in terms of profitability.

Moreover, SMEs in medtech clusters face two major problems. First, access to the global market is difficult due to limited resources. Analyzing the internationalization of German medtech SMEs, Heiss (2017) demonstrated that firms essentially focused on the domestic and European markets but were underrepresented in overseas markets and emerging countries. This weakness is one of the reasons behind the takeovers by large multinational enterprises that have the resources to provide SMEs' promising technologies with access to the global market. The significant presence of foreign MNEs in a cluster can also benefit the internationalization of local SMEs. This was the case of the French medtech industry, for example, where foreign-owned companies had an 80% share of exports and a 75% share of turnover in the early 2010s. Andersson et al. (2013) showed that for some SMEs, proximity to foreign MNEs is an opportunity to internationalize through M&A or joint ventures.

Second, the domination of foreign-owned companies in some clusters can also have some negative effects in terms of technological development. When local SMEs become subsidiaries of global firms, moving up in the value chain is often a major challenge. In Ireland, the medtech industry centers on manufacturing operations and not R&D due to the considerable weight of foreign MNEs. In 1999, while the share of R&D expenses in the industry averaged 7% of gross sales on a global basis, it was only 1.5% in Ireland (Fennelly & Cormican, 2006).

3 Networks Connecting Medical Doctors and Firms

Research on the history of science and technology, as well as studies on the social history of medicine, have demonstrated the major role played by social networks in the adoption of innovations made by medical doctors and small mechanic workshops. Hospitals, medical associations, and manufacturers connect innovators to users and contribute to the diffusion of new devices and techniques (Schlich & Tröhler, 2006; Timmermann & Anderson, 2006; Rabier, 2013). Some scholars have looked beyond the role of individuals and highlighted the growing importance of large companies as innovators since the last decades of the twentieth century, as has been the case in the US breast prostheses industry (Gardner, 2000). However, no studies have explored in detail the nature of the relations between medical doctors and large companies. Harrington (1988) showed that in the 1950s and 1960s incremental innovation occurred in hospitals and operation rooms, with surgeons developing step-by-step instruments for scoliosis treatment. When the medical procedure reached a stable state, doctors approached a manufacturing company (Zimmer) to standardize and mass-produce instruments and attended academic conferences to publicize the new process. Schlich (2002) demonstrated similar findings using the case of osteosynthesis, which occurred in the same period. Swiss surgeons used both a manufacturing company and international medical conferences for the diffusion of their innovations.

Cooperation between medical doctors and firms has also been approached through an analysis of patents. Shah and Robinson (2007) have shown that, in the US, physicians were involved in 19.3% of the patents filed for medical devices between 1990 and 1996; moreover, approximately 60% of those doctors were physicians in practice (users of technology) but only 14% worked in hospitals. The researchers thus emphasized the importance of involving users (doctors and physicians) in developing medical technology. Chatterji et al. (2008) argued that patents with physicians as co-applicants are of a better quality in that they have more citations than patents not involving physicians. Donzé (2018) showed that Japanese companies that co-developed medical equipment together with doctors increased their competitiveness against foreign MNEs.

In addition to examining individual doctors, some scholars have investigated the roles of hospitals and universities in medtech clusters. Using the case of Berne in Switzerland, Weigel (2011) concludes that the hospital is "the main functional source of medical device innovation" (p. 43). In particular, hospital physicians play central roles as co-developers of technology, users of devices, and diffusers of innovation. However, technology spin-offs from hospitals are rare in Europe, unlike in the US. For example, the roots of Medtronic, a leading medical device company that began with cardiac and neurological technology, go back to open-heart surgery at the University of Minnesota during the 1950s (Llobrera et al., 2000). Gelijns and Thier (2002), meanwhile, argued that the flows of technology transfers between universities and industry should go in both directions to achieve a high level of innovation in the medtech industry. For the US, they stressed the key importance of the Bayh–Dole Act (1980), which allows universities to hold patents. As Mowery and Rosenberg (1998) and Mowery and Sampat (2001) have emphasized, however, university and industry relations have a longer history. In particular, the Research Corporation, founded in 1912, was the interface between university research and industry until its decline in the 1980s, precipitated by a new legislative environment (Bayh–Dole Act).

Recent research has also underscored the dangers of overestimating the impact of medical doctors, hospitals, and universities on innovation in the medtech industry. According to Rosenberg (2009), the most important discoveries in medical science since the late nineteenth century actually emerged from areas outside medicine (physics, computer science, and biology) and found applications in medicine, such as X-rays in the 1890s. His argument is that institutional innovations (the implementation of medical schools at university campuses) in the UK and US promoted these transfers over academic boundaries. For example, MRI technology was developed by physicists. Medical equipment makers invested in MRI business through the employment of PhDs in physics. The paper does not discuss the corresponding implications for the medtech industry directly, but it shows the importance of connections to research outside medicine. Similarly, based on the Swiss case, Coffano, Foray and Pezzoni (2017) argued that innovation in the medtech industry benefits considerably from the presence of inventors specializing in complementary technology—in other words, connecting regional clusters to external knowledge is vital. Their regression analysis of patents showed that the presence of academic inventors has not had any particular effect on innovation.

4 The State and Regulation

Finally, the regulation of healthcare has a major impact on innovation and the diffusion of new medical technology (Romeo et al., 1984; Rossiter & Wilensky, 1984; Slade & Anderson, 2001). The variety of technical directives and legal frameworks, first of all, has an influence on the organization of the global medtech industry (Estrin, 1990; Teixeira, 2013). In the US, for example, the FDA introduced premarket clearance for medtech devices in 1976 after a spate of accidents involving devices such as pacemakers (Panescu, 2006). Due to a lack of international standards, companies need organizational capabilities to apply for certification in foreign markets, which can be a hurdle for SMEs (Heiss, 2017). Safety regulation is also largely used as a non-tariff barrier by some countries, including Japan. According to Foote and Mitchell (1989), measures adopted by Japanese authorities in the 1970s and 1980s (import approval, price fixing by the Ministry, and non-recognition of foreign safety tests and information) led to a trade deficit for the US medtech industry from the mid-1980s onwards and gave way to an FDI strategy in sectors where American companies had cemented their technological leadership, like pacemakers. Consequently, regulation has been discussed primarily as a factor affecting trade and market expansion, not innovation or localization. I will also analyze in this book how companies have had to adapt their equipment and technology to specific local institutions, like US X-ray machines and MRI equipment in Japan (see Chap. 5).

5 A Business History of the Global Medtech Industry

This literature review introduced the most important works related to the medtech industry, its organization, and its conditions of innovation. However, many publications lack a proper historical contextualization—a factor that leads to some apparent contradictions between different studies. The basis of competitiveness for large companies (path-dependency investments or takeovers of innovative SMEs), the nature of relations between SMEs and MNEs, and the roles of medical doctors in innovations represent major issues in the literature that are without consensus. Yet an evolutionist perspective that emphasizes the historical context can offer a general overview of the dynamics of the global medtech industry since 1960, and that grasp can contribute to a better understanding of the major issues in the literature.

In this book, I offer an analysis that follows the methodology of business history and of industry studies. For business history, I use the classical approach developed most notably by Chandler (1990), which involves identifying the main enterprises in an industry and explaining the development of their competitive advantages over the years. The discussion is consequently focused on the main firms, as the objective is to offer an understanding about the general dynamics of this global industry—not to identify and explain exceptional cases. As for industry studies, my work builds on the conceptual model proposed by Kurosawa (2018), which demonstrated that each industry has its own specificities that impact on the conditions of firms' competitiveness. In the case of the medtech industry, one can emphasize first the broad variety of products for which the common point is supporting healthcare; second, the fast expansion of markets due to the ageing population and increasing healthcare expenses; and, third, the importance of R&D and innovation. These characteristics explain the growth of firms through acquisitions and in-house research, which is driven by a growing demand. In particular, this book discusses the formation of medtech as an industry to understand the competitive advantages of the firms that dominate this sector in the twenty-first century. In the case of the industrial gases industry, Stokes and Blanken (2016) demonstrated that innovation and mergers led small firms not only to become larger, but also to move out of their original fields of specialization and to encounter competitors. This process led to the formation of a new industry. However, the industrial gases industry has remained diverse in the sense that not all companies in this sector produce an identical set of goods. They retain a significant degree of specialization and are therefore not all in direct competition with each other. This model can be applied to explain the formation of the medtech industry.

This business history of the global medtech industry begins with two general chapters that provide an overview. Chapter 2 uses statistical data (foreign trade, patents, and M&As) to present the general dynamics of the industry at the global level since the 1960s. This makes it possible to emphasize in particular the domination of the US, the importance of Germany and Japan, and the emergence of China. Next, Chap. 3 focuses on companies. Based on the various rankings of the world's largest firms since the 1980s, Chap. 3 discusses the trend towards industrial concentration and the conditions of growth among large firms. The six chapters that follow tackle the formation and development of the medtech industry in various nations: the three largest manufacturers and exporters (US, Germany, and Japan), one European country competitive in a particular niche of the medtech industry (Switzerland), one European country that failed to develop a medtech industry (France), and one of the largest emerging countries (China). All these national case studies follow a similar structure, with data on national production (if available), foreign trade, M&A, innovation, and a detailed analysis of representative firms. They highlight not only the dynamics of each of these major countries, but also the evolution of their position in the global market. The book finishes with Chap. 10, which provides a discussion the results and proposes an explanation for the formation process of the global medtech industry.

References

Books and Academic Articles

Andersson, S., Evers, N., & Griot, C. (2013). Local and International Networks in Small Firm Internationalization: Cases from the Rhône-Alpes Medical Technology Regional Cluster. *Entrepreneurship & Regional Development, 25*(9–10), 867–888.

Blume, S. (2003). Medicine, Technology and Industry. In R. Cooter & J. Pickstone (Eds.), *Companion to Medicine in the Twentieth Century* (pp. 171–185). Routledge.

Burfitt, A., Macneill, S., & Gibney, J. (2007). The Dilemmas of Operationalizing Cluster Policy: The Medical Technology Cluster in the West Midlands. *European Planning Studies, 15*(9), 1273–1290.

Chandler, A. D. (1990). *Scale and Scope: The Dynamics of Industrial Capitalism.* The Belknap Press of Harvard University Press.

Chatterji, A. K. (2009). Spawned with a Silver Spoon? Entrepreneurial Performance and Innovation in the Medical Device Industry. *Strategic Management Journal, 30*(2), 185–206.

Chatterji, A. K., Fabrizio, K. R., Mitchell, W., & Schulman, K. A. (2008). Physician-Industry Cooperation in the Medical Device Industry. *Health Affairs, 27*(6), 1532–1543.

Christensen, C. (2013). *The Innovator's Dilemma: When New Technologies Cause Great Firms to Fail.* Harvard Business Review Press.

Christensen, C., & Raynor, M. (2013). *The Innovator's Solution: Creating and Sustaining Successful Growth.* Harvard Business Review Press.

Clayton-Matthews, A. (2001). *The Medical Device Industry in Massachusetts.* University of Massachusetts, Donahue Institute.

Coffano, M., Foray, D., & Pezzoni, M. (2017). Does Inventor Centrality Foster Regional Innovation? The Case of the Swiss Medical Devices Sector. *Regional Studies, 51*(8), 1206–1218.

Craven, M. P., Allsop, M. J., Morgan, S. P., & Martin, J. L. (2012). Engaging with Economic Evaluation Methods: Insights from Small and Medium Enterprises in the UK Medical Devices Industry After Training Workshops. *Health Research Policy and Systems, 10*(1), 29.

Davis, A. B. (1978). Historical Studies of Medical Instruments. *History of Science, 16*(2), 107–133.

DiMaio, S., Hanuschik, M., & Kreaden, U. (2011). The da Vinci Surgical System. In J. Rosen, B. Hannaford, & R. M. Satava (Eds.), *Surgical Robotics* (pp. 199–217). Springer.

Donzé, P. Y. (2018). *Making Medicine a Business: X-ray Technology, Global Competition, and the Transformation of the Japanese Medical System, 1895–1945.* Springer.

Estrin, N. F. (Ed.). (1990). *The Medical Device Industry: Science: Technology, and Regulation in a Competitive Environment.* CRC Press.

Fennelly, D., & Cormican, K. (2006). Value Chain Migration from Production to Product Centred Operations: An Analysis of the Irish Medical Device Industry. *Technovation, 26*(1), 86–94.

Foote, S. B., & Mitchell, W. (1989). Selling American Medical Equipment in Japan. *California Management Review, 31*(4), 146–161.

Foray, D. (2014). *Smart Specialisation: Opportunities and Challenges for Regional Innovation Policy.* Routledge.

Frost & Sullivan. (2017). *Global Medical Device Industry Snapshot.* Retrieved October 31, 2018, from https://store.frost.com/

Gardner, K. E. (2000). Hiding the Scars: A History of Post-Mastectomy Breast Prostheses, 1945–2000. *Enterprise & Society, 1*(3), 565–590.

Gelijns, A. C., & Rosenberg, N. (1999). Diagnostic Devices: An Analysis of Comparative Advantages. In D. C. Mowery & R. R. Nelson (Eds.), *Sources of Industrial Leadership: Studies of Seven Industries* (pp. 312–358). Cambridge University Press.

Gelijns, A. C., & Thier, S. O. (2002). Medical Innovation and Institutional Interdependence: Rethinking University-Industry Connections. *Jama, 287*(1), 72–77.

Harrington, P. R. (1988). The History and Development of Harrington Instrumentation. *Clinical Orthopaedics and Related Research, 227*, 3–5.

Heiss, G. (2017). Influencing Factors and the Effect of Organizational Capabilities on Internationalization Strategies for German SMEs in the MedTech Industry. *Management, 5*(4), 263–277.

Jones, C. L. (2018). Surgical Instruments: History and Historiography. In *The Palgrave Handbook of the History of Surgery* (pp. 235–257).

Kruger, K., & Kruger, M. (2005). The Medical Device Sector. *The Business of Healthcare Innovation*, 271–321.

Kurosawa, T. (2018). Industry History: Its Concepts and Methods. In B. Bouwens, P.-Y. Donzé, & T. Kurosawa (Eds.), *Industries and Global Competition: A History of Business Beyond Borders* (pp. 1–24). Routledge.

Lawyer, P., & Alford, R. (2005). Industrial Revolution: The New Medical Device Acquirers. *In Vivo-New York Then Norwalk, 23*(6), 47.

Llobrera, J. T., Meyer, D. R., & Nammacher, G. (2000). Trajectories of Industrial Districts: Impact of Strategic Intervention in Medical Districts. *Economic Geography, 76*(1), 68–98.

Maresova, P., & Kuca, K. (2014). Porters Five Forces on Medical Device Industry in Europe. *Military Medical Science Letters, 83*(4), 134–144.

Mowery, D. C., & Rosenberg, N. (1998). *Paths of innovation: Technological change in 20th-century America.* Cambridge University Press.

Mowery, D. C., & Sampat, B. N. (2001). Patenting and Licensing University Inventions: Lessons from the History of the Research Corporation. *Industrial and Corporate Change, 10*(2), 317–355.
Panescu, D. (2006). Medical Device Industry. In *Wiley Encyclopedia of Biomedical Engineering*.
Rabier, C. (2013). Introduction: The Crafting of Medicine in the Early Industrial Age. *Technology and Culture, 54*(3), 437–459.
Reiser, S. J. (1978). *Medicine and the Reign of Technology*. Cambridge University Press.
Romeo, A. A., Wagner, J. L., & Lee, R. H. (1984). Prospective Reimbursement and the Diffusion of New Technologies in Hospitals. *Journal of Health Economics, 3*(1), 1–24.
Rosenberg, N. (2009). Some Critical Episodes in the Progress of Medical Innovation: An Anglo-American Perspective. *Research Policy, 38*(2), 234–242.
Rossiter, L. F., & Wilensky, G. R. (1984). Identification of Physician-Induced Demand. *Journal of Human Resources*, 231–244.
Schlich, T. (2002). *Surgery, Science and Industry*. Palgrave Macmillan.
Schlich, T., & Tröhler, U. (Eds.). (2006). *The Risks of Medical Innovation: Risk Perception and Assessment in Historical Context*. Routledge.
Shah, S. G. S., & Robinson, I. (2007). Benefits of and Barriers to Involving Users in Medical Device Technology Development and Evaluation. *International Journal of Technology Assessment in Health Care, 23*(1), 131–137.
Shaw, B. (1998). Innovation and New Product Development in the UK Medical Equipment Industry. *International Journal of Technology Management, 15*(3–5), 433–445.
Slade, E. P., & Anderson, G. F. (2001). The Relationship Between Per Capita Income and Diffusion of Medical Technologies. *Health Policy, 58*(1), 1–14.
Steinle, C., Schiele, H., & Mietzner, K. (2007). Merging a Firm-Centred and a Regional Policy Perspective for the Assessment of Regional Clusters: Concept and Application of a "dual" Approach to a Medical Technology Cluster. *European Planning Studies, 15*(2), 235–251.
Stokes, R., & Blanken, R. (2016). *Building on Air*. Cambridge University Press.
Teixeira, M. B. (2013). *Design Controls for the Medical Device Industry*. CRC Press.
Timmermann, C., & Anderson, J. (Eds.). (2006). *Devices and Designs: Medical Technologies in Historical Perspective*. Palgrave Macmillan.
de Vet, J. M., & Scott, A. J. (1992). The Southern Californian Medical Device Industry: Innovation, New Firm Formation, and Location. *Research Policy, 21*(2), 145–161.
Wu, B. (2013). Opportunity Costs, Industry Dynamics, and Corporate Diversification: Evidence from the Cardiovascular Medical Device Industry, 1976–2004. *Strategic Management Journal, 34*(11), 1265–1287.
Weigel, S. (2011). Medical Technology's Source of Innovation. *European Planning Studies, 19*(1), 43–61.

CHAPTER 2

The Dynamics of the Global Medtech Industry

1 Introduction

This chapter offers a general overview of the global medtech industry from various perspectives based on three different sets of data: world exports, patent applications, and mergers and acquisitions (M&As). As the introduction noted, however, medtech is a new industry that formed and developed during the second part of the twentieth century. It includes a broad range of instruments, devices, and equipment that were originally not considered as belonging to a single industry. Consequently, although databases are available to measure world exports (United Nations and COMTRADE), patent applications (PATSTAT), and M&As (Thomson One), only recently have the boundaries of medtech been defined. It is thus impossible to carry out the type of precise, long-term analysis that one can conduct on larger, older industries like automobiles, chemicals, or electronics. Aggregate data for medtech is only available since the 1970s or the 1980s, and shortcomings resulting from methodological difficulties, which I discuss below, abound. This is probably the reason why no scholars have yet done any formal studies on the historical development of the global medtech industry. Therefore, the numbers given in this chapter are not absolute representations of the real world of medtech in wholly precise terms; rather, they are general indicators that help shed light on the dynamics of the global medtech industry.

P.-Y. Donzé, *Medtech*,
https://doi.org/10.1007/978-981-16-7174-6_2

2 World Exports

Statistics from the United Nations make it possible to trace how the foreign trade of medical devices generally developed. Two sets of data are available for this perspective. First, there is the *International Trade Statistics Yearbook*, published since 1955. For the period until 1991, the data primarily covers trade in market-economy countries; statistics for China and USSR, for example, are either unavailable or only very general. Medtech goods are divided among four different categories: electromedical equipment (code no. 7741), X-ray apparatuses (7742), orthopedic aids (8996), and medical instruments (872). Details on export countries are available since 1976 for the three first categories and since 1980 for medical instruments (except for the figures on US exports, which date back to 1972, and German exports, which are available since 1977). In the first part of the 1970s, medtech was still an emerging business whose export volumes were too low to catch the attention of the United Nations. Figures 2.1, 2.2, 2.3, 2.4, 2.5 present and discuss the corresponding information.

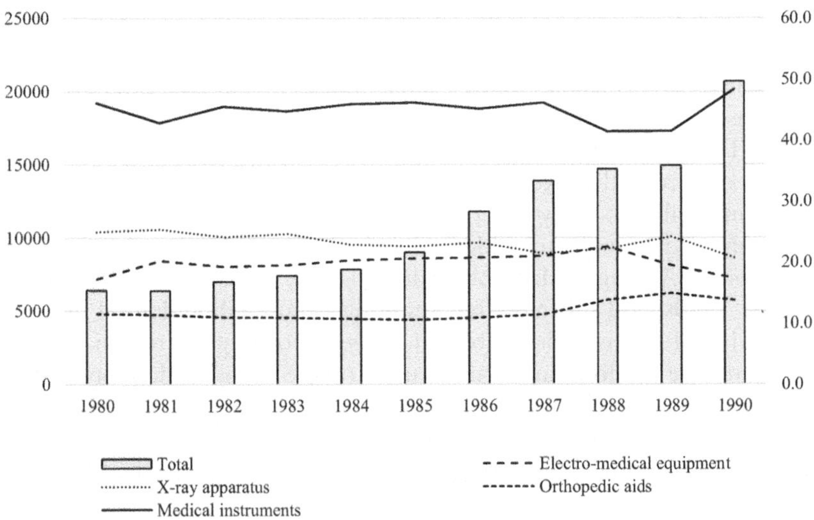

Fig. 2.1 Medtech exports by capitalist countries, in millions of dollars and by type as a %, 1980–1990. (Source: United Nations, *International Trade Statistics Yearbook*, 1980–1990)

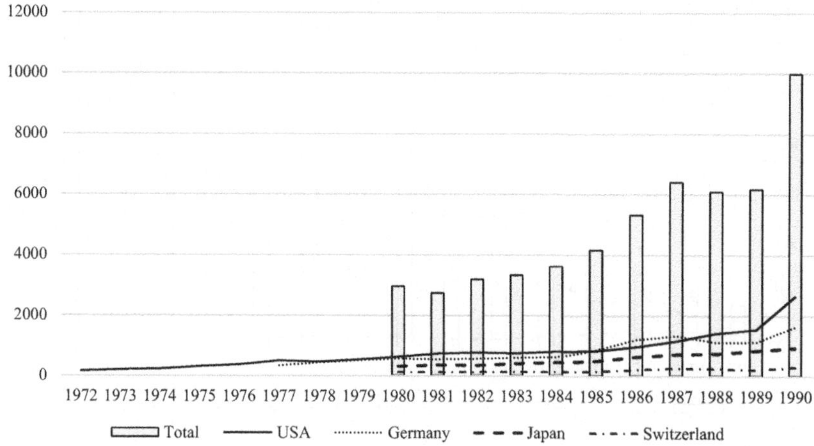

Fig. 2.2 Exports of medical instruments by capitalist countries, in millions of dollars, 1972–1990. (Source: United Nations, *International Trade Statistics Yearbook*, 1972–1990. Note: Data is for all countries available only since 1980 (1977 for Germany))

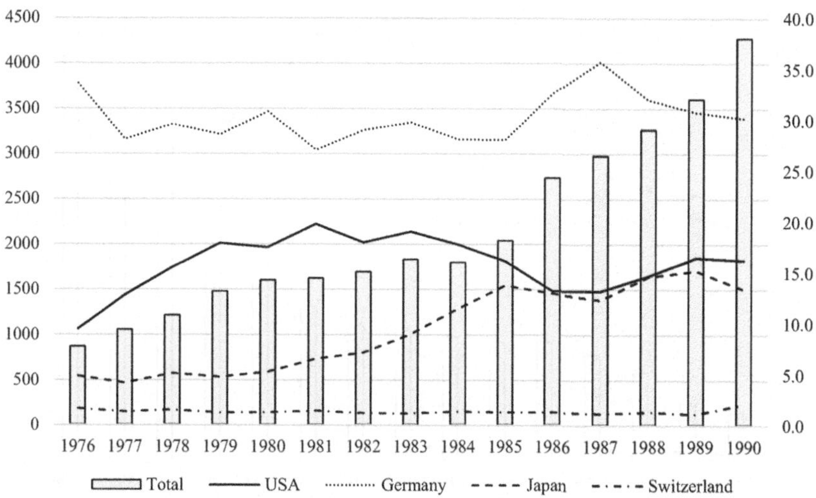

Fig. 2.3 Exports of X-ray apparatuses by capitalist countries, in millions of dollars and by country as a %, 1976–1990. (Source: United Nations, *International Trade Statistics Yearbook*, 1976–1990)

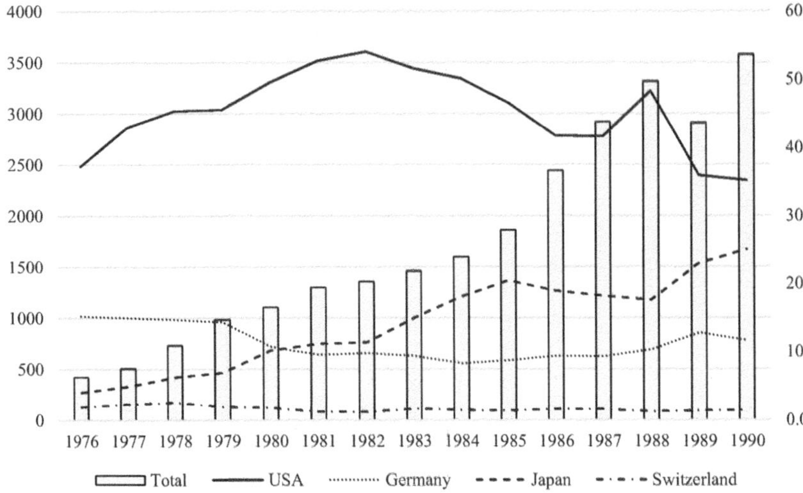

Fig. 2.4 Exports of electro-medical equipment by capitalist countries, in millions of dollars and by country as a %, 1976–1990. (Source: United Nations, *International Trade Statistics Yearbook*, 1976–1990)

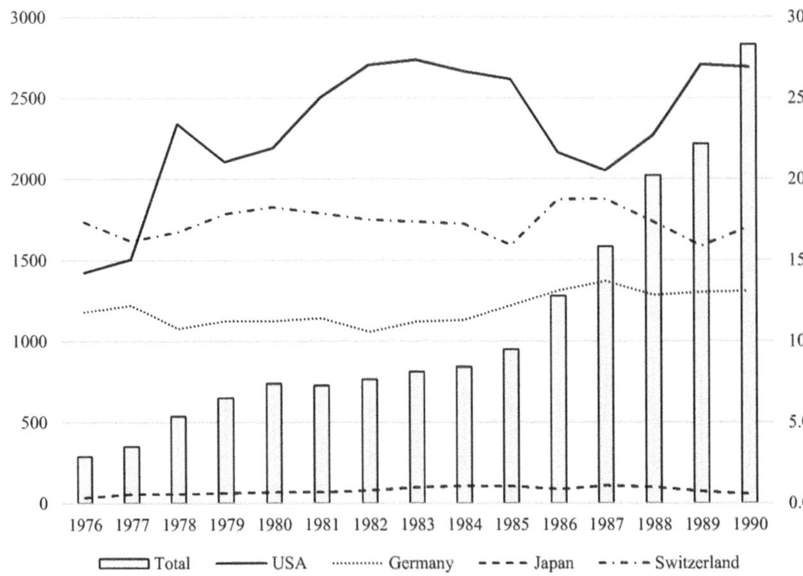

Fig. 2.5 Exports of orthopedic aids by capitalist countries, in millions of dollars and by country as a %, 1976–1990. (Source: United Nations, *International Trade Statistics Yearbook*, 1976–1990)

Figure 2.1 gives a general overview of medtech exports for the 1980s, including all four of the above categories. The general trends show a slight growth during the first part of the decade (from 6.4 billion dollars in 1980 to 9 billion in 1985), followed by an accelerating growth during the second part (20.7 billion in 1990). However, data available for the 1970s already demonstrates a period of fast development (see Figs. 2.2, 2.3, and 2.4); in that context, the years 1980–1985 appear as a period of relative stagnation. The breakdown by type of product highlights an important element of stability during the 1980s. On average, medical instruments had a 44.9% share of total exports, X-ray apparatuses 23.3%, other electromedical equipment 19.9%, and orthopedic aids 11.9%. This general data emphasizes that X-ray apparatuses (including CT scanners) represented only one-quarter of medtech exports. Even despite that relative size, the segment has attracted the attention of several scholars in economics and management who have emphasized that the multinational enterprises engaging in this industry since the early twentieth century were able to maintain their domination over the medtech industry through continual investment in research and development (Gelijns & Rosenberg, 1999). This is, however, only one minority aspect of the dynamics of the medtech industry. As for the breakdown by country, relative stability is evident across the 1980s. Exports were dominated by the United States (26.1% on average from 1980 to 1990), Germany (19%), and Japan (11.3%), while Switzerland lagged behind with 4.4%. The first countries represented more than half of the total exports by capitalist countries.

Next, the evolution of exports by type of goods shows some regional specificities. First, data for general medical instruments is available for the United States and Germany since 1972 and 1977, respectively. The figures for American exports capture the acceleration that occurred in the mid-1980s. One can observe first a steady growth, with exports going from 150 million dollars in 1972 to 621 million in 1980 and 828 million in 1985. Then, growth accelerated and reached 2.7 billion in 1990. Germany followed a similar trend from 1977 on, enabling the country to overcome the United States as the number-one nation in 1986–1987. Japan and Switzerland, too, exhibit a development similar to the general trend.

For the following three types of equipment, the available data makes it possible to calculate market shares for each country between 1976 and 1990. The development of CT scanners obviously had a major impact on exports of X-ray apparatuses (see Fig. 2.3). The British company EMI developed the first CT scanner for medical use in 1971. Soon after, American and German companies engaged in this new, promising technology (Blume, 1992). EMI, which had no previous experience in the healthcare market, withdrew in 1980 and sold most of its operations to the American multinational General Electric (GE), which already dominated the market for X-ray equipment in the United States. The American CT scanner market grew rapidly: the proportion of hospitals with scanners went from 0.5% in 1973 to 38.1% in 1980 and 57.3% in 1984 (Trajtenberg, 1990, p. 58). However, Germany—more specifically the multinational enterprise Siemens (see Chap. 6)—maintained its overall dominant position in the industry, with an average share of 30.6% of exports from 1976 to 1990. Major innovations stemming from the advent of the CT scanner led to the emergence of two newcomers. First, during the second part of the 1970s, the mass production of a first generation of scanners enabled American firms to strengthen their position in world markets, particularly GE and Picker. Consequently, the US share went from below 10% in 1976 to a peak of 19.8% in 1981. Second, US and German firms were challenged by a second generation of scanners developed by Japanese firms during the 1980s, in particular Toshiba. Japan's share of exports rose from 5.2% in 1980 to 15.2% in 1989. Switzerland, meanwhile, was an insignificant player in the industry during the period in question (averaging 1.4% of exports from 1976 to 1990).

Exports of other electro-medical equipment represent a value slightly lower than X-ray apparatuses but also demonstrate faster development, with an increase from 419 million dollars in 1976 to 3.6 billion in 1990 (see Fig. 2.4). This "other" category includes a broad range of devices, including diagnostic machines (ECG and endoscopes), patient-monitoring equipment, laser systems, audiological equipment, and pacemakers. Electronics played a major role in the development of this field, which contributed significantly to the formation of the medtech industry. Electro-medical equipment attracted companies from the pharmaceutical industry, like Abbott Laboratories, Bayer, and Johnson & Johnson, and led to the formation of conglomerates through M&As (see Chap. 3). This development occurred mostly between the mid-1970s and the mid-1990s. Unlike X-ray apparatuses, general electro-medical equipment was not dominated by Germany. The country had an average export share of merely 10.7% for the period from 1976 to 1990, with the ratio trending generally downward. Instead, the United States dominated the field (with an average share of 44.1%) but also confronted the growing presence of

Japanese firms in the 1980s. The US share jumped from 1976 (37.2%) to 1982 (54.1%), likely due to the important success of pacemakers—a market controlled by American firms, particularly Medtronic. In 1982, American hospitals spent nearly 500 million US dollars on purchases of pacemakers and cardiovascular products (Foote, 1992, p. 98). Then, the share started to decline and returned to about one-third in 1990. It was only a relative decline, however, as the rapid growth of the market enabled US exports to pursue further growth. Japan shows the most impressive change, with a constant development that transformed the country from relative obscurity (a market share of 4.1% in 1976) to the world's second-leading exporter (25% in 1990). This was clearly the result of the competitiveness of electronics giants such as Olympus, Toshiba, and Hitachi (see Chap. 5). Switzerland played only an insignificant role (with an average share of 1.5%) in this field, too.

Finally, exports of orthopedic aids represented the smallest medtech area but still presents a general trend similar to those in other segments, with an acceleration of growth in the mid-1980s; aging populations were a key factor behind the increase of demand in implants and protheses. Another specificity of orthopedic aids is that electronics had hardly any impact on the field, unlike their influence in shaping the markets for X-ray apparatuses and electro-medical equipment. Technological innovation in orthopedics tied into the development of new materials and micromechanics (Anderson et al., 2007). This characteristic explains the high competitiveness of Switzerland and the nearly complete absence of Japan. Switzerland was the world's largest exporter in 1976 (see Fig. 2.5). Although it lost that top rank to the United States, it stayed in second with a stable market share over time (averaging 17.3% from 1976 to 1990). Orthopedic equipment is a comparative advantage of Switzerland in the global medtech industry, and it attracted inward investments from many American firms (see Chap. 7). The United States experienced a general increase in its share during this period, going from 14.2% in 1976 to 26.9% in 1990, and established itself as the world's leading exporter in 1977. Germany also maintained a stable position (12.4%), while Japan's share was very low (0.8%).

Second, for the period after 1992, I use statistics from the online Comtrade (https://comtrade.un.org/data/) database. At the time of this study, full data was available through 2017. The database divides medtech into three different categories: instruments and appliances used in medical, surgical, dental, and veterinary sciences (HS code 9018), orthopedic appliances (9021) and X-ray, alpha, beta, and gamma radiation apparatuses (9022).[1] Figures 2.6, 2.7, 2.8, 2.9 and Tables 2.1, 2.2, 2.3 present the results.

Figure 2.6 offers a composite view of medtech exports, including all medical instruments, orthopedic appliances, and X-ray equipment. The trajectory from 1992 to 2017 has three basic phases: slow growth in 1992–2000 (following a period of intense development in the late 1980s; see Figs. 2.1, 2.2, 2.3, 2.4, 2.5), high growth in 2001–2012, and slow growth again in 2012–2017. One of the driving forces of this overall expansion was the orthopedic-appliance segment, whose share of the total general medtech exports grew from 14.7% in 1992 to 19.6% in 2000 and 28.4% in 2017. On the other hand, the relative importance of X-ray apparatuses declined from 19.9% in 1992 to 15.7% in 2000 and 11.2% in 2017. The share of general medical instruments held stable at an average of 62.1% over the period as a whole. This structural change largely explains the decline of Japan, a country that focused on X-ray equipment and electro-medical equipment. Between 1992 and 2017, Japan's share of global

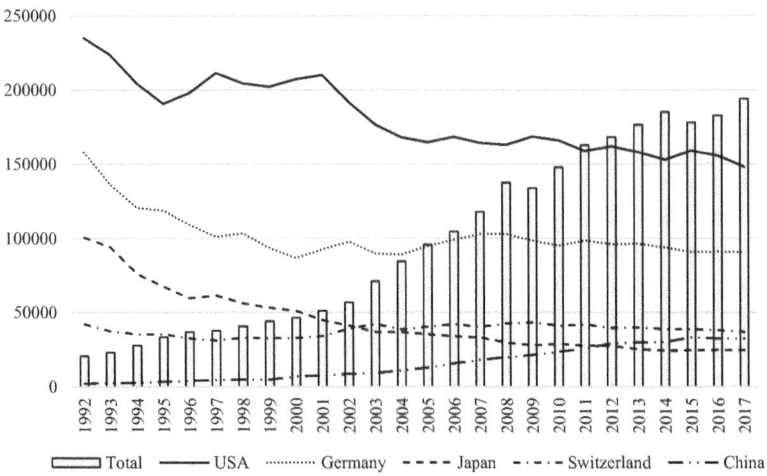

Fig. 2.6 Global exports of medtech, in millions of dollars and by country as a %, 1992–2017. (Source: Comtrade (HS codes 9018, 9021, and 9022))

[1] MRI equipment is classified under 9018.

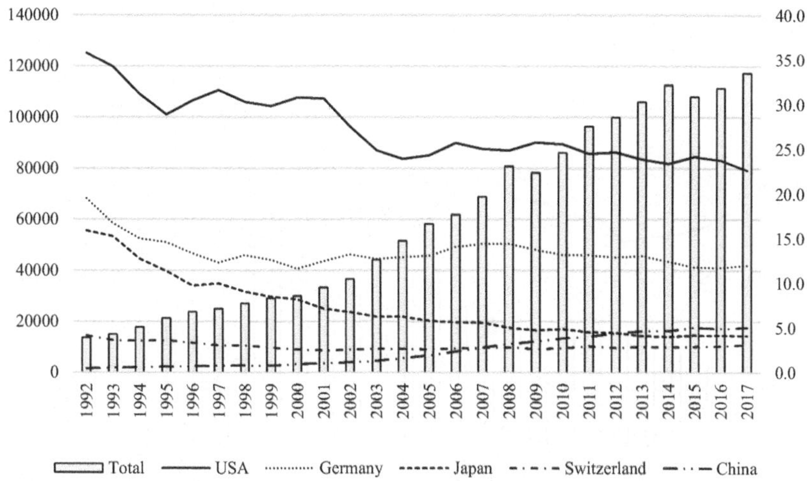

Fig. 2.7 Global export of medical instruments, in million dollars and by country as a %, 1992–2017. (Source: Comtrade (HS code 9018))

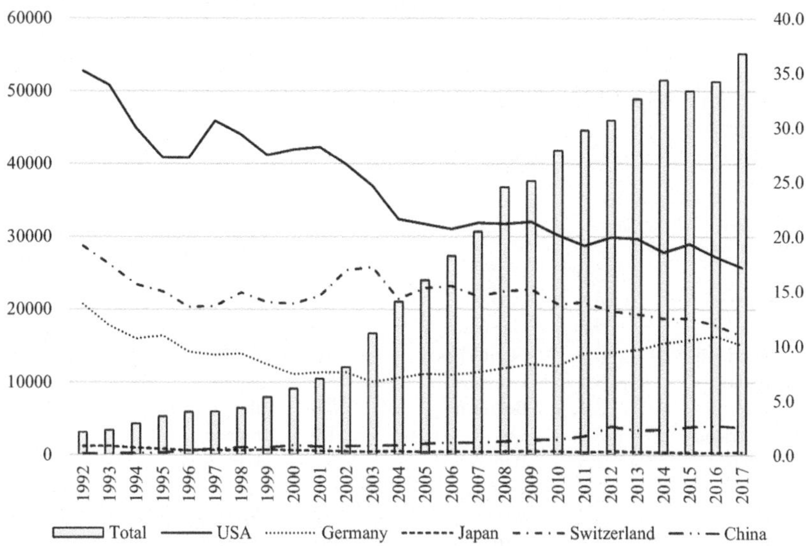

Fig. 2.8 Global exports of orthopedic appliances, in millions of dollars and by country as a %, 1992–2017. (Source: Comtrade (HS code 9021))

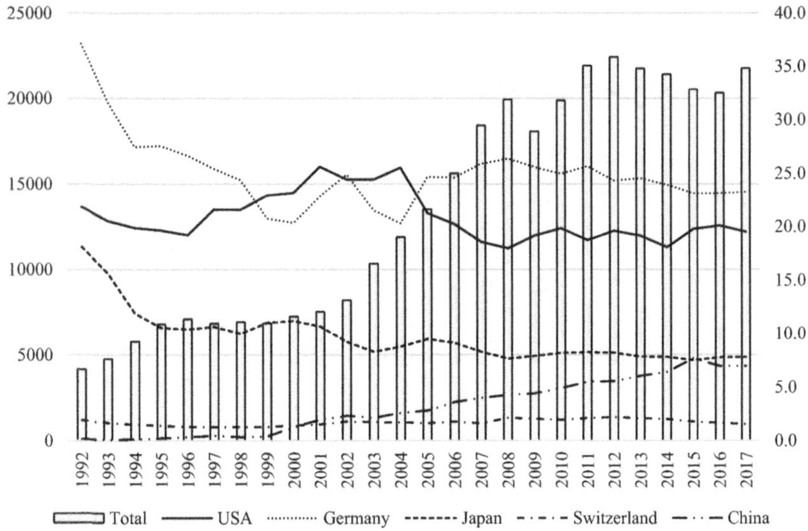

Fig. 2.9 Global exports of X-ray apparatuses, in millions of dollars and by country as a %, 1992–2017. (Source: Comtrade (HS code 9022))

Table 2.1 Top 10 largest importers of medical instruments in 1992, 2000, and 2017

1991		*2000*		*2017*	
Country	*Share (%)*	*Country*	*Share (%)*	*Country*	*Share (%)*
USA	23.0	USA	18.5	USA	19.8
Germany	16.8	Japan	9.2	Germany	7.7
Japan	9.8	Germany	8.0	Netherlands	7.0
Netherlands	6.2	Netherlands	5.1	China	6.4
Canada	5.1	France	5.0	Japan	4.9
Spain	5.1	Belgium	5.0	Belgium	4.9
Switzerland	3.0	UK	4.9	France	3.9
Sweden	2.5	Italy	4.3	UK	3.2
Australia	2.4	Canada	3.2	Italy	2.8
China	2.2	Spain	2.5	Mexico	2.4
Top 10	76.2	Top 10	65.7	Top 10	63.0

Source: COMTRADE (HS code 9018)

Table 2.2 Top 10 largest importers of orthopedic appliances in 1992, 2000, and 2017

1992		*2000*		*2017*	
Country	*Share (%)*	*Country*	*Share (%)*	*Country*	*Share (%)*
Germany	23.4	USA	12.8	USA	20.7
Japan	13.4	Germany	10.1	Germany	9.4
Netherlands	8.9	Japan	9.8	Netherlands	9.4
USA	7.6	Netherlands	7.1	France	6.1
Canada	7.2	France	6.6	China	5.6
Spain	6.5	UK	6.1	Japan	5.2
Switzerland	5.5	Italy	5.8	Belgium	5.1
Sweden	5.0	Switzerland	4.3	UK	3.8
Australia	3.8	Canada	3.5	Switzerland	3.2
Denmark	2.2	Belgium	3.2	Italy	3.0
Top 10	83.5	Top 10	69.3	Top 10	71.3

Source: COMTRADE (HS code 9021)

Table 2.3 Top 10 largest importers of X-ray apparatuses in 1992, 2000, and 2017

1991		*2000*		*2017*	
Country	*Share (%)*	*Country*	*Share (%)*	*Country*	*Share (%)*
USA	33.6	USA	22.7	USA	19.4
Germany	14.1	Japan	8.2	China	15.1
Netherlands	8.1	France	8.2	Japan	6.4
Japan	6.3	Germany	6.2	Germany	5.6
Canada	4.2	China	6.1	France	4.5
China	4.2	Netherlands	4.1	Netherlands	4.0
Spain	3.2	Italy	3.7	India	2.9
Brazil	3.1	UK	3.1	UK	2.9
Rep. of Korea	2.8	Canada	3.0	Rep. of Korea	2.3
Sweden	2.5	Spain	2.5	Singapore	2.1
Top 10	82.0	Top 10	67.7	Top 10	65.2

Source: COMTRADE (HS code 9022)

medtech exports decreased from 14.1% to 3.5%. It was surpassed in 2003 by Switzerland, a country specializing in orthopedic appliances, which maintained an average global share of 5.2%. As for the United States and Germany, their positions as the leading and second-leading exporters of medtech products, respectively, were never challenged, even if their dominance over the industry weakened over time. Emerging countries like China (0.3% of global exports in 1992 and 4.6% in 2017) occupied a growing weight in the market due to the development of its domestic industry. As was the case in other industries, medtech companies also started to make sizable transfers of their low-value-added operations to low-wage countries in the 1990s (Vlckova & Thakur-Weigold, 2019). In this context, Mexico became an important manufacturer after the enforcement of the North American Free Trade Agreement (NAFTA) in 1994. American medtech companies moved plants to their neighbor to the south, giving birth to an emerging Mexican industry. Mexico's share of global medtech exports was only 1.6% in 1992 but grew to 3.3% in 2000 and 4.3% in 2017.

The next three figures show the evolution for each of the main categories of medtech goods. Figure 2.7 presents the trajectory of general medical instruments, a broad and diverse category of goods that accounts for more than 60% of medtech exports. The trend is very similar to the general evolution of the industry, with the domination and later relative decrease of the American and German shares, an important decline in the Japanese share (close to Germany in the early 1990s but overcome by China in 2013), a stable and low Swiss position, and emerging markets. China, which had less than 1% of the global-export share in the early 1990s, achieved impressive development and reached 5% in 2017, establishing itself as one of the largest exporters. Notable among other nations is the importance of Mexico, which I mentioned above. In fact, as there were only a few factories specializing in orthopedic appliances and X-ray apparatuses that moved to Mexico, the country's share of global exports in medical instruments is higher than that for all medtech goods (6.1% of world exports in 2017). This points to the effects of the relocation of low-value-added activities to this country. All the American medtech giants like Medtronic, Johnson & Johnson, and General Electric have assembly plants in Mexico. Hence, the United States is the first—and almost only—destination market for Mexican medical-instrument exports (97.7% in 1995, 95.9% in 2000 and 93.5% in 2017).

Table 2.1 gives an overview of the largest importers of medical instruments. Western countries and Japan have clearly been the dominant importers. China has emerged as of late (6.4% in 2017), while exports to Mexico most likely include in-firm trade by American companies with subsidiaries in the country. Countries with high GDP and large healthcare markets, like the United States, Germany, and Japan, are also the largest importers. Finally, one can observe a slight decrease in the combined share of the top ten largest markets over time, which suggests a growing volume of exports to a broader range of countries.

Next, Fig. 2.8 illustrates exports of orthopedic appliances. Development in the area has been impressive, propelling the value of exports from 3.1 billion dollars in 1992 to 9.1 billion in 2000 and 55.2 billion in 2017. An obvious contributor to this growth was population aging. As of 2017, Western countries, Japan, and China are the largest markets (see Table 2.2). The dramatic expansion in exports naturally attracted newcomers in the orthopedic-appliance industry. The three dominant nations in 1992 (USA, Switzerland, and Germany) had a combined share of 68.1%, which dropped to 38.2% in 2017. The precipitous decline in US exports is an outcome of active M&A strategies that American multinationals pursued in the industry from the 1990s onward. While they were dependent on sales in their domestic market, American manufacturers of orthopedic protheses and implants took over numerous companies around the world, particularly in Switzerland, and established themselves as global leaders. Production at foreign subsidiaries thus affects the levels of direct exports from their home country. Germany was able to benefit from the growing demand. It showed an increasing share after 2003 and eventually reached the level of Switzerland, which experienced a relative decline together with a stagnation of export value from 2010 onward. Finally, Japan is nearly absent from this industry, although it is an important market. Chinese firms demonstrated slow development, reaching 1% of global exports in 2005 and 2.6% in 2017.

Finally, Fig. 2.9 presents global exports of X-ray apparatuses. The total export value expanded from 4.1 billion dollars in 1992 to 7.3 billion in 2000 and 21.8 billion in 2017. The growth was impressive but less dramatic than the general trend, especially relative to orthopedic appliances. The X-ray industry has traditionally been dominated by large multinational companies in electric appliances and electronics, mostly based in the United States, in Germany, and in Japan; one could also count Philips, a Dutch company, among the biggest players. Germany was the uncontested leader in 1992 with 37.1% of world exports, while the United States and Japan came in at 21.9% and 18.1%, respectively. The 1990s saw a decline in German exports, with Japanese producers (see Chap. 6) challenging Germany, while American companies developed their foreign sales and overcame Germany between 1999 and 2004. Japan experienced a slight decline but kept its position around 10% of the global export total. Since 2005, the United States, Germany, and Japan have maintained stable positions. A major trend in X-ray apparatus exports in the twenty-first century is the continuous growth of China, which has increased its share of exports from 1.3% in 2000 to 6.9% in 2017.

The main markets for X-ray devices are more diverse than those for other medtech products are. The largest importers include not only Western countries and Japan but also other countries that have invested in the development of their healthcare systems (see Table 2.3). Considering the industry's high concentration in large companies and its high-tech specificity, the development of a domestic industry based on small and medium-size enterprises would appear difficult. For these markets, is thus necessary to import the requisite equipment. This explains why Brazil was among the ten largest importers, along with several Asian countries like China, South Korea, and Singapore. The growth of the Chinese market is particularly notable, rising from 4.2% of world imports in 1992 to 6.1% in 2000 and 15.1% in 2017. The numbers suggest that the development of a local X-ray apparatus industry, as the development of exports shows, is not sufficient to meet the needs of the local healthcare system alone. It also suggests that local Chinese firms focus on low-tech equipment and that the country needs to import high-tech devices (see Chap. 9).

This general overview of the global medtech exports from the early 1970s on illustrates a general growth trajectory that began in the 1980s and accelerated after 2000. The first full data set for one country in the *International Trade Statistics Yearbook* appeared in 1972 for the United States, which exported 150 million dollars of medical instruments that year. That number represented only 6.1% of the national production for 1972, according to a census of manufacturers.[2] The world's largest medtech industry was evidently still largely focused on its domestic market in the early 1970s. Corresponding data for other countries is unavailable, as national production is usually unknown, but the American example suggests that there was nearly no integrated world market for medtech products at that time besides X-ray apparatuses, a specific type of product dominated by German multinationals. In 1980, the total medtech exports by capitalist countries amounted to 5 billion dollars, or 0.25% of total

[2] Census of Manufacturers, value of shipments for medical equipment and supplies (except ophthalmic goods), in million USD (seasonally adjusted), https://www.census.gov/manufacturing/m3/historical_data/index.html (accessed 12 July 2018).

world exports.[3] In 1992, global medtech exports had a value of 21 billion dollars (0.56% of total world exports). The American medtech industry was becoming more oriented toward foreign markets, but exports of medical instruments still came to just 12.3% of domestic production in 1990. The 1990s are when the real breakout occurred. Global medtech exports grew to 194 billion in 2017 (1.11% of world exports), a dramatic increase that outstripped the development rate of global trade at that time. The percentage of US-produced medical instruments heading to foreign markets reached 20.8% in 2000 and 32.9% in 2016. As for the American medtech business overall, including X-ray apparatuses and electro-medical equipment, the ratio of exports to total production was even slightly higher, reaching 22.3% in 2000 and 35.5% in 2016.[4] A fast-growing and more integrated global market emerged in the 1990s.

Finally, the general overview of world trade between the 1970s and 2017 illustrates the dominant position of the United States over time. The few exceptions are sectoral: X-ray apparatuses are dominated by Germany; Japan shows a strong competitive advantage in electro-medical and X-ray equipment; Switzerland once had a dominant position in orthopedic appliances and has kept a strong second rank since the late 1970s; and China has become an important exporter since 2000. These various dynamics are explored in Chaps. 5, 6, 7, 9.

3 Innovation

This section analyzes the dynamics of innovation in the global medtech industry since the 1960s via a database of medtech-related patent applications (IPC code A61B) using the worldwide PATSTAT database of the European Patent Office (EPO), which includes some 90 million patents. Information about assignees was added from the EPO worldwide bibliographic database DOCDB. This medtech database has been developed in cooperation with Centredoc SA, a Swiss intelligence company.

It includes a total of 521,365 patents and 647,399 assignees (a patent application sometimes mentions more than one assignee) for the period 1960–2014. Next, we identified the nationality of patents on the basis of

[3] Calculated based on World Bank, exports of goods, current US dollars, https://data.worldbank.org (accessed 10 August 2020).

[4] The data for the years prior to 2007 is unavailable in the Census of Manufacturers as electro-medical appliances were included as part of general electric machinery.

the place of residency of assignees (mostly enterprises and universities) through the address mentioned on each patent application. If a Japanese company applied for a patent through its German subsidiary, then, the assignee would be considered German. This method has been chosen to enable comparisons of the medtech industry across various countries. The place of earliest application may have been easier to identify, but that data point does not properly reflect the nationality of assignees; after all, many individuals and companies do not apply for patents in their home countries but often directly in the United States or, since the 1980s, to the EPO. In some cases, identifying the place of residency was problematic because the information about applicants, such as their place of residency, is not always available. According to the EPO, the countries of about half of the patents in PATSTAT are unknown. In order to overcome this problem, we used the Patent Standardized Name (PSN) and standardized names of applicants with the KUL algorithm and the Harmonized Applicants Names of the OCDE. Then, we could share the country code through PSN with the same ID. This reduced the rate of patents by applicants from unknown countries considerably; the overall rate comes to just 6.8% of all assignees for the period 1960–2014.

The next step involved focusing on five countries (United States, Japan, Germany, Switzerland, and China) and breaking the data down by decade. The five countries in question were selected because they hold dominant positions in the medtech industry (United States, Japan, Germany and China) or in a specific field of this industry (orthopedic appliances in the case of Switzerland). We manually classified assignees for the five countries into three groups (enterprises, universities and research centers, and individuals). We also added a fourth group (government agencies) for the United States and China.

The general evolution of patent applications in the medtech industry (IPC code A61B) between 1960 and 2014 is shown in Fig. 2.10. Table 2.4 gives data related to assignees, also by decade and country. The results are slightly different, as some patent applications mention several assignees. On this basis, five major periods can be identified, their specificities resulting from technological change, transformation of political environment, and limits of the data.

First, the 1960s appears as a decade slow growth. Although the number of patents nearly tripled, going from 438 in 1960 to 1103 in 1969, the overall level was still low in comparison to the following decades. This period was dominated by X-ray equipment and mechanical instruments; it

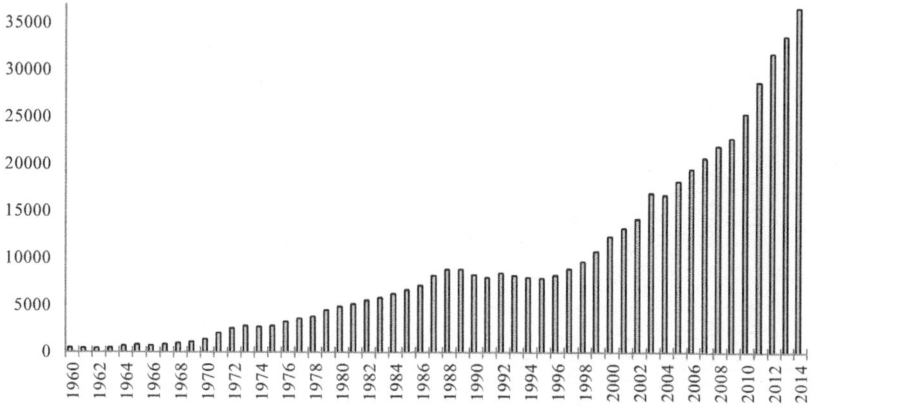

Fig. 2.10 Patent applications for medtech, 1960–2014. (Source: PATSTAT)

did not see major technological transformation except for the development of pacemakers. The United States occupied a dominant position during the decade, with 30.4% of assignees, while Germany was second with 13.8%. Companies from both countries had a strong competitive advantage in the core technologies for medical equipment. Moreover, one must note the quasi-absence of Japanese patents, despite companies in the country being innovative and carrying out research during the 1960s. The bias relates to the fact that Japan only adopted IPC in 1978 and did not apply IPC codes to numerous former patents, particularly during the 1960s (Kawashima & Shimizu, 1989).

Second, a first period of high growth is evident during the next two decades, with the number of patent applications peaking at 8814 in 1989. The most important technological change during the 1970s and 1980s was the advent of electronics, a paradigm shift in the medtech industry, because core technology shifted from mechanics and electricity to electronics. The most important equipment from these two decades was undoubtedly computed tomography (CT scanners). Moreover, one can observe a change of balance between the United States and Germany on the one side (relative declines to 13.4% and 5.5% in the 1980s, respectively) and the fast growth of Japan, which accounted for 37.7% of assignees in the 1980s. The rise of Japan as a leader was not the only effect of the country's adoption of the IPC—the competitiveness of Japanese

Table 2.4 Assignees of medtech patent applications by country and decade, 1960–2014

	1960–1969	*1970–1979*	*1980–1989*	*1990–1999*	*2000–2009*	*2010–2014*	*Total*
Total world	**5577**	**23,282**	**65,758**	**95,974**	**247,229**	**209,579**	**647,399**
USA	1698	5064	8825	22,120	75,821	50,933	164,461
%	30.4	21.8	13.4	23.0	30.7	24.3	25.4
Germany	772	2025	3611	7902	16,253	9202	39,765
%	13.8	8.7	5.5	8.2	6.6	4.4	6.1
Japan	107	4572	24,707	33,227	58,055	33,484	154,152
%	1.9	19.6	37.6	34.6	23.5	16.0	23.8
Switzerland	115	305	378	854	3261	1746	6659
%	2.1	1.3	0.6	0.9	1.3	0.8	1.0
China	0	0	763	4706	24,349	39,057	68,875
%	0.0	0.0	1.2	4.9	9.8	18.6	10.6
USSR/Russia	138	4166	17,061	7411	11,386	6634	46,796
%	2.5	17.9	25.9	7.7	4.6	3.2	7.2
Korea	2	13	131	729	7283	10,625	18,783
%	0.0	0.1	0.2	0.8	2.9	5.1	2.9
Spain	50	107	155	384	973	885	2554
%	0.9	0.5	0.2	0.4	0.4	0.4	0.4
India	0	4	20	41	40	41	146
%	0.0	0.0	0.0	0.0	0.0	0.0	0.0
Others	848	3349	7131	12,736	44,474	32,040	100,578
%	15.2	14.4	10.8	13.3	18.0	15.3	15.5
Unknown	1847	3677	2976	5864	5050	24,502	43,916
%	33.1	15.8	4.5	6.1	2.0	11.7	6.8
Difference	0	0	0	0	284	430	714
%	0.0	0.0	0.0	0.0	0.1	0.2	0.1

Source: PATSTAT

electronics companies was another. One question to keep in mind, however, is if these assignees were from large diversified giant companies or specialized medtech firms (see Chap. 5).

Third, the 1990s was a decade of stagnation and decline, with an average of 8586 applications per year and a low of 7875 in 1995. The major explanation for this stagnation was the collapse of the USSR, which was actively engaged in R&D in the medtech industry and even had a share of assignees of 25.7% in the 1980s—higher than the United States and second after Japan. The Russian share in the 1990s, however, dropped to 7.7%. At the exception of the Soviet case, then, one can see a continuing growth of patent applications by major countries, led by Japan in front of the United States and Germany. China also appeared during the decade, with 4.9% of assignees in the 1990s against 1.2% in the 1980s. Still, the absence of a major breakthrough innovation during the decade contributed to the sluggish growth of patent applications.

Fourth, the medtech industry experienced a new period of high growth between 1998 and 2009, with the patent application total going from 9616 to 22,566. A new technological change supported a renewal of R&D and the entry of numerous newcomers: information and communication technology (ICT). Knowledge developed outside the field of traditional medtech began to find applications in medical equipment and devices, such as items for diagnosis or assisted surgery. On this point, too, it will be necessary to examine whether the technological change was an opportunity for newcomers to enter the medtech industry or not. Regarding the location of assignees, a shift between the United States (30.7% from 2000 to 2009) and Japan (23.5%) was again realized. Both countries, however, accounted for more than half of all assignees. China established itself as number three (9.8%) before Germany (6.6%).

Finally, a fifth period—one of accelerated growth—has taken shape since 2009. The number of patent applications reached 36,613 in 2014, or 61% more than the number in 2009. The driver of this fast growth has not been a major technological innovation, but rather the rise of Chinese assignees. From 2010 to 2014, China became the second-leading company with 18.6% of the world's assignees, topping Japan (16%) and getting closer to the United States (24.3%). A look at the largest Chinese assignees during this period shows the domination of universities and public research organizations. Six of the top ten appliers were universities, including the first (Chinese Academy of Sciences, 849 applications) and the second (Shanghai Jiao Tong University, 360 applications). Interestingly, the four companies include neither any state-owned enterprise nor any firm with foreign capital. The first joint venture with a Western firm was Siemens Shanghai Medical Equipment (220 applications).

Table 2.5 shows the results of the breakdown of assignees into three categories (enterprises, individuals, and universities and research centers, with the third category including government agencies in the case of the United States, and hospitals for China), highlighting a different evolution between the four countries. The following section details the dynamics.

Firms are the most important assignees, regardless of country or period, except for the United States and Japan since 2000, when individuals became the largest assignees. A look at the largest individual assignees in

Table 2.5 Medtech patent applications by category, 1960–2014

	1960–1969	*1970–1979*	*1980–1989*	*1990–1999*	*2000–2009*	*2010–2014*
Applications total						
USA	1698	5062	8825	22,120	75,661	50,703
Japan	115	4572	24,707	33,220	58,050	33,470
Germany	772	2025	3610	7891	16,250	9202
Switzerland	115	305	378	854	3261	1744
China	n/a	n/a	763	4706	24,350	39,067
Firms, as a %						
USA	67.6	57	51.7	59.8	37.1	33.3
Japan	86.1	85.4	92.8	92.6	78	74.2
Germany	74.6	72.4	59.4	53.8	57.9	62.2
Switzerland	67	67.2	76.5	76.1	70.2	62.8
China	n/a	n/a	5.5	7	19.7	19.3
Firms, average						
USA	3.38	3.35	3.03	4.05	5.6	4.94
Japan	3.3	8.47	23	19.5	23	24.65
Germany	6.12	8.83	7.01	6.14	9.21	8.74
Switzerland	2.57	3.36	3.01	4.19	8.27	5.86
China	n/a	n/a	1.00	1.18	2.19	7.27
Top 10 firms, patents						
USA	289	658	1049	3031	10,112	6202
Japan	75	2331	15,660	18,808	28,456	17,963
Germany	394	972	1337	2259	5970	3651
Switzerland	53	129	138	355	1466	680
China	n/a	n/a	10	49	749	2192
Top 10 firms, % of total firms						
USA	25.2	22.8	23	22.9	36	36.8
Japan	75.8	59.7	68.3	61.1	62.9	53.7

(*continued*)

Table 2.5 (continued)

	1960–1969	*1970–1979*	*1980–1989*	*1990–1999*	*2000–2009*	*2010–2014*
Germany	70	66.3	62.3	53.2	63.4	63.8
Switzerland	68.8	62.9	47.8	54.6	64	62.1
China	n/a	n/a	23.8	14.9	15.6	29.2
Individuals, as a %						
USA	25.9	36.3	40.5	33.4	58.1	61
Japan	13.9	14.3	6.9	6.7	17.6	20.7
Germany	23.7	27.3	37	43.9	38.8	33.5
Switzerland	33	32.5	23.5	23.2	27.1	32.4
China	n/a	n/a	55.6	66.3	61.6	54.6
Individuals, average						
USA	1.37	1.24	1.21	1.29	1.59	1.62
Japan	1.23	1.4	1.68	1.42	1.75	1.94
Germany	1.38	1.35	1.38	1.36	1.58	1.49
Switzerland	1.12	1.3	1.33	1.29	1.43	1.42
China	n/a	n/a	1.12	1.25	1.66	1.89
Universities and R&D centers, as a %						
USA	6.5	6.7	7.8	6.8	4.8	5.7
Japan	0	0.3	0.3	0.7	4.4	5.1
Germany	3.4	0.3	3.6	2.3	3.3	4.2
Switzerland	0	0.3	0	0.7	2.6	4.8
China	n/a	n/a	38.9	26.7	18.7	26.2
Universities and R&D centers, average						
USA	5.33	4.24	4.57	6.05	14.6	11.6
Japan	0	1.43	1.06	2.16	9.06	7.32
Germany	3.71	1.4	4.06	4.07	4.39	4.53
Switzerland	0	1	0	1.2	4.1	7
China	n/a	n/a	1.26	1.28	3.41	14.7

Source: PATSTAT

Note: the number of patents for the last column is based only on a five-year period, against ten-year for the others. This difference impacts on the average number of patents. For China, Universities and R&D centers includes hospitals

the United States and Japan after 2000 also shows that most have been engineers in large corporations (see Chaps. 4 and 5). The reason why these companies increased the use of their engineers' names as (co-) assignees is unclear. It is not related to a change in regulation regarding patenting in the United States (the Leahy-Smith America Invents Act was modified in 2012) but obviously to a new practice by firms, probably in-firm rewards for innovative employees. Despite this bias, the domination of firms is remarkable; however, the trend is different between the United

States and Germany, where the share of companies declined between the 1960s and the 1990s, and Japan and Switzerland, where firms exhibited a growing presence during the period in question. A look at the positions of the most important companies in the medtech industry shows additional differences. The share of the top 10 largest firms sits at a lower level in the United States but presents an increasing concentration in the country. In Japan, Germany, and Switzerland, the position of the top 10 largest firms decreased until the 1990s and then increased again thereafter. Since 2000, then, the concentration of R&D has been a global trend. The next section discusses the changes expressing the dynamics at that time in Japan, Germany, and Switzerland. However, beyond these variations, firms in all the countries share a similarity: a growing average number of patents, which means that firms built organizational facilities for R&D and invested more in this activity.

Individual assignees are the second-largest actor in patent applications in the global medtech industry. They have a particular significant weight in the United States for the reasons explained above. From a perspective encompassing the four countries, including the United States, though, the average number of applications per assignee remains low—constantly below two—although a slight increase is noticeable.

Universities and R&D centers present a different evolutionary picture. They carved out a strong position in the United States in the 1960s, followed by Germany in the 1980s, but the growth of their presence is a relatively new phenomenon in Japan and Switzerland. The expansion started after 2000 in these two countries, which have both surpassed Germany. Moreover, the domination of US universities is evident in the high number of average patent applications per institution.

Finally, one must discuss the specific position of China in this context. Data is unavailable before the 1980s—a time when the medtech industry was obviously very basic. The impressive growth in the number of Chinese patent applications since the 1990s highlights a general feature that presents a stark contrast with the situations in other countries. First, the private sector has a very low share of applications despite its development over time. Moreover, the average number of patents by firm and the ratio of patents coming from the top 10 largest firms were dramatically low until the 2000s. Private Chinese medtech companies were mostly small firms with limited research capabilities. Data for the years 2010–2014, however, shows a drastic change, with the average number of patent applications by firm exceeding the same values in the United States and

Switzerland and roughly equivalent to the number in Germany. Moreover, the share of the top 10 firms doubled in comparison with the rates in the 1990s and 2000s. The proportion is still below those in Western countries, but the concentration of research at a handful of competitive firms is remarkable.

The second feature of innovation in the Chinese medtech industry from a comparative perspective is the decline of the public sector (universities, public research centers, government organizations, and hospitals). The public sector's share of all patent applications went from more than one-third of all applications in the 1980s, when none of the Western countries in this analysis had more than 10%, to less than 20% in the 2000s before making a slight comeback in 2010–2014. Amid that general decline, however, there has been a major shift in the primary source of applications: from hospitals to universities. The growth of university-based research also explains the uptick in public-sector applications since 2010. Over the same time frame, the average number of applications from universities rose quickly and amounted to 14.7 in 2010–2014, a level even higher than that in the United States. While research used to be very dispersed in the 1980s, it appears to have been converged on universities after 2010.

Lastly, the data for medtech patent applications in China shows a high but declining proportion of individual applicants since the 1990s, with the 1980s being a special decade when the number of applications was generally very low. The percentage of individual applicants in China is the highest rate in this study, but the lack of information about individual applicants and the methodological challenges of properly identifying them (as the PATSTAT database has only names spelled in Roman characters, which makes identification difficult) make it impossible to offer a precise explanation. A look at the individuals with the largest numbers of applications in 2010–2014 suggest that a high proportion of them work in universities. This would corroborate the argument that research has recently concentrated at these institutions.

4 Mergers and Acquisitions

The third quantitative source used to analyze the global dynamics of the medtech industry is the Thomson One database on mergers and acquisitions (M&A), which includes more than one million cases of M&A

realized around the world since the 1970s.[5] I culled a selection of all deals including a company characterized as medtech (SIC code 361) in April and May 2018. I have eliminated double entries, management buyouts, and self-purchases of shares from the set.

The process identified a total of 10,572 cases of companies or division of companies in the medtech industry being taken over by other firms. Figure 2.11 shows the breakdown of said cases by year. A general trend of growth is evident, with the number of cases going from 2 in 1980 to 318 in 2000 and 601 in 2017. Beyond this tendency, one can observe some short phases of stagnation, such as during the second part of the 1990s, after the burst of the IT bubble in 2000, and after the world financial crisis of 2007–2008. This shows that M&A in the medtech industry is not an activity driven purely by the specificities of the sector but also impacted directly by the conditions of the financial system. In terms of average annual growth rate, the M&A figures indicate that the highest growth occurred during the 1980s (with an average annual growth rate of

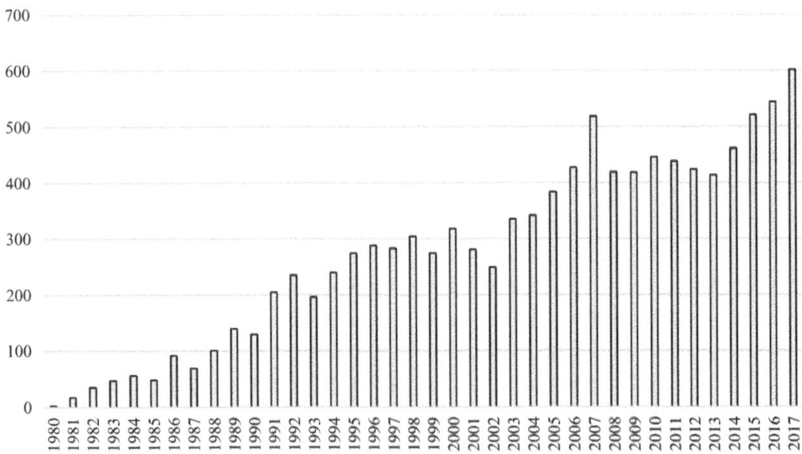

Fig. 2.11 M&A in the global medtech industry, number of cases by year, 1980–2017. (Source: Thomson One. Note: This data expresses the number of medtech firms, or medtech divisions of a firm, acquired by other companies)

[5] https://www.thomsonreuters.com/en/press-releases/2016/january/thomson-reuters-ma-database-surpasses-one-million-deals.html (accessed 14 July 2010).

36.9% from 1982 to 1989),[6] followed by the 1990s (8.8%), the 2000s (5.5%), and 2010–2017 (4.8%); growth has been stable for many years. This trend is important, as most of the medtech conglomerates formed in the 1980s and 1990s through a process of merging a broad range of other companies (see Chap. 3). M&A represented a fast-growing activity during this period.

Next, let us have a look at the breakdown by country. Data on the countries with the top 15 highest M&A case totals appears in Table 2.6. The most important feature in the data is the overwhelming domination of American companies, which represent more than 5300 cases of acquisitions—half the total. Previous data on foreign trade and patents also showed the importance of the United States, and Chap. 3 will detail the substantial share of American companies in the ranking of the top 100 largest medtech firms in 2014. The abundance of medtech acquisitions in the United States is a major specificity of both the industry itself and its dynamic growth. The Thomson One database does not make it possible to distinguish between acquisitions of small companies and startups on the

Table 2.6 Top 15 countries by number of M&A cases, 1980–2017

Country	*Number of cases*	*As a % of total*	*Acquisition by domestic firms, as a %*
USA	5312	50.2	81.7
UK	603	5.7	58.5
Germany	566	5.4	46.8
China	477	4.5	80.9
France	470	4.4	59.6
Canada	354	3.3	50.3
Japan	326	3.1	90.2
Sweden	265	2.5	54.3
South Korea	245	2.3	86.1
Australia	205	1.9	73.2
Italy	177	1.7	45.2
Netherlands	153	1.4	39.2
Israel	142	1.3	37.3
Switzerland	141	1.3	27.0
Denmark	102	1.0	27.5

Source: Thomson One

[6] The growth rate in 1980–1981 (+750%) was eliminated because it was too high, stemming from the sparsity of data in 1980.

one hand and acquisitions of divisions or subsidiaries of large companies on the other. However, as cases studies will explore in Chap. 4, takeovers have played a key role in the formation of medtech conglomerates in the United States and the constant reorganization of their business portfolios.

The second characteristic of this breakdown by country is an important concentration beyond the special case of the United States. The seven countries with the highest case totals, each with a share of more than 3%, account for more than 75% of the total of medtech firms acquired, and the combined share of the top fifteen, each with an individual share of at least 1%, slightly exceeds 90%. These countries are all in North America, Western Europe, or East Asia, with Australia and Israel rounding out the group. An analysis of the percentages of medtech firms in a given country acquired by another company in that same country (i.e. domestic M&A) makes it possible to identify various types.

First, not only does the United States account for half the total cases, but more than 80% of those cases are domestic acquisitions. This results from the presence of numerous large medtech companies that have acquired new businesses or strengthened their position in a field through the purchase of existing firms. However, one cannot consider American medtech firms as purely domestic-oriented; indeed, their M&A strategies stretch beyond national borders. As Table 2.7 shows, American companies are also large acquirers of companies in other countries, acting as the acquiring parties in 26.2% of the cases in Switzerland, 20.5% in Germany, 5.2% in China, 3.4% in Japan, and 18.7% in other countries. American companies have constantly been the most prominent foreign acquirer in all the countries, after domestic firms.

Table 2.7 Matrix of acquisitions by country, as a %, 1980–2017

	USA	*Germany*	*Japan*	*Switzerland*	*China*	*Others*
USA	4342	116	11	37	25	702
Germany	55	265	2	20	4	84
Japan	65	11	294	3	11	39
Switzerland	38	22	1	38	1	60
China	15	0	1	0	386	36
Others	797	152	17	43	50	2828

Source: Thomson One

Note: Targets in columns; acquirers in rows

Second, East Asian countries (China, Japan, and South Korea) exhibit a very high level of domestic M&As (between 80 and 90%). Strong government regulation of the medtech industry and market domination by powerful organizations (large private companies in Japan and South Korea and the central government in China) make these countries difficult to access for foreign companies. Moreover, these countries show no signs of any regional integration. Japanese firms took over only 11 Chinese companies (2.3% of the total) and 5 in South Korea (2.1%), while Chinese firms purchased only 1 Japanese company (0.3%) and none in South Korea. As for South Korean firms, they took over 3 firms in Japan (0.9%) and none in China. Companies from these three countries invested more in the United States than in any other East Asian nation. In effect, there is no "East Asian medtech industry," unlike the regional integration in sectors like electronics and machinery (Shioji & Tanaka, 2020).

Third, most of the European countries have a share of domestic M&As varying between 40 and 60%. The area thus appears relatively open to the presence of foreign firms, which benefits American companies—always the largest foreign acquirer of medtech companies. The US share is particularly high in the United Kingdom (23.5%), for example. Canada shows similarities to the European model (domestic M&As at 50.3% and M&As by American acquirers at 34.7%), but Australia appears much more isolated (73.2% domestic M&As; 13.7% by American firms).

Fourth, two small European countries, namely Denmark and Switzerland, present a high share of foreign takeovers, with domestic M&As at a low 30% of as the total. Although American companies are the acquirers in over 20% of the takeovers in both countries, Denmark and Switzerland present a highly balanced perspective where large numbers of acquiring companies from a broad variety of European countries are present.

Finally, the evolution of M&A cases in the global medtech industry by country over time shows the gradual emergence of new nations since the mid-1980s, as well as the decline of the share of American cases in the long run. While M&As in the United States represented basically all the identified cases in the early 1980s (although their number was very low), the share decreased to 66.7% in 1990, 54.1% in 2000 and 37.4% in 2017. This means that a growing number of companies outside the United States became capable of attracting investors. Among the countries selected for this book, Germany was the first to experience an important development, reaching a peak at 9.3% of all cases in 2003, before entering a phase of relative decline (4% in 2017). Next, Japanese cases appeared in the early 1990s and showed constant growth, reaching 5.7% in 2017. China started to rise later but demonstrated rapid growth: while it sat constantly below 2% until 2001, it went to 8.1% in 2010 and 12.5% in 2017, becoming the world's largest country for M&As after the United States. Meanwhile, Switzerland shows strong fluctuations without any clear general trend and occupies a relatively low level, generally (averaging 1.1%). Consequently, the general evolution of M&As cases in the global medtech industry shows a major shift from acquisitions centered on the United States toward a more polycentric model, where the United States accounts for about 40% of cases, China 12%, and the rest of the world about half (Fig. 2.12).

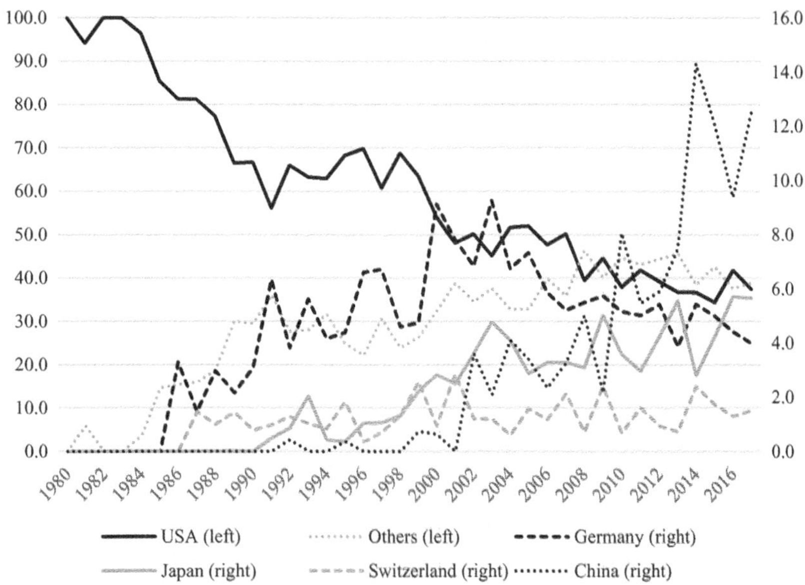

Fig. 2.12 M&A in the global medtech industry, shares of main countries by year, as a %, 1980–2017. (Source: Thomson One. Note: This data expresses the number of medtech firms, or medtech divisions of a firm, acquired by other companies)

5 Conclusion

The quantitative data analyzed in this chapter makes it possible to trace the formation and general evolution of the global medtech industry, a process that occurred in three distinctive phases.

First, before 1980, the industry was in a formative period. The low export levels and ratio of exports to domestic production in the case of the United States, slow growth in patent applications, and likely low numbers of mergers (which impossible to discuss on the basis of the Thomson One database) suggest the absence of a medtech industry per se. There were hundreds of companies, universities, and individuals that invented, developed, and manufactured medical instruments, devices, and equipment, but these activities were hardly integrated into a single industry. Companies were focused on special fields and sold most of their goods to local doctors and hospitals, some of them gaining international competitiveness along the way. Excellent examples of this trend include X-ray equipment and orthopedic appliances, where German and Swiss companies dominated. These firms were not, however, focused on the ***medtech industry*** but rather on their own special field.

Second, the 1980s and 1990s represent a period of intense change marked by a general growth, the integration of the world market, and the probable formation of diversified medtech companies—firms that include various fields of medical instruments and equipment. This period was largely dominated by American companies in terms of export, patent applications, and M&As, although German firms maintained their competitiveness and Japanese enterprises emerged as major innovators and acquirors. In addition to being major innovators and exporters, American companies also adopted an aggressive acquisition strategy during this period. The portions of this book focusing on the world's largest firms (Chap. 3) and case studies of American companies (Chap. 4) will demonstrate that the M&A growth of this period was driven by the diversification of American companies into other fields of medical technology. It was this process that led to the formation of a medtech industry proper. In other countries, M&As either occurred only in the domestic market (Japan) or focused on specific fields (Germany and Switzerland), which meant that the activities did not hence lead to the formation of diversified medtech firms. At the end of the twentieth century, the United States exerted total domination over the global medtech industry.

Third, since 2000, one can observe an acceleration in the growth of all the pertinent indexes, from world exports to patent applications and M&As. At the same time, the global domination of the United States has seen increasing challenges from Japan and China since 2010. The rapid growth of the Chinese medtech industry, characterized by a shift from universities and public research centers to private companies, is a major feature of this period. Unlike the automobile industry, for example, the development of the Chinese medtech industry was not the result of foreign companies investing in the country to produce for world markets; the number of acquisitions of Chinese firms by foreign companies is negligible. The driving force of this growth was domestic innovation, as the changes in patent applications show.

Another important trend in the twenty-first century is the growing importance of university-based research outside the Unites States. American universities played an important role as innovators from the 1960s onward, and the statistics on patent applications reflect universities' more intensive engagement in medtech research after 2000, a change particularly visible in China, Japan, and Switzerland. An important pending question, which I will discuss in the following chapters, is how academic research supported the development of startups and, indirectly, the growth of the medtech industry.

References

Books and Academic Articles

Anderson, J., Neary, F., & Pickstone, J. (2007). *Surgeons, Manufacturers and Patients: A Transatlantic History of Total Hip Replacement*. Palgrave Macmillan.

Blume, S. S. (1992). *Insight and Industry: On the Dynamics of Technological Change in Medicine*. MIT Press.

Foote, S. B. (1992). *Managing the Medical Arms Race: Public Policy and Medical Device Innovation*. University of California Press.

Gelijns, A. C., & Rosenberg, N. (1999). Diagnostic Devices: An Analysis of Comparative Advantages. In D. C. Mowery & R. R. Nelson (Eds.), *Sources of Industrial Leadership: Studies of Seven Industries* (pp. 312–358). Cambridge University Press.

Kawashima, J., & Shimizu, M. (1989). Kokusai tokkyo bunrui. *Joho to kagaku to gijutsu, 9*(11), 503–510.

Trajtenberg, M. (1990). *Economic Analysis of Product Innovation: The Case of CT Scanners*. Harvard University Press.
Shioji, H., & Tanaka, A. (Eds.). (2020). *Higashi ajia yui sangyo: tagenka suru kokusai seisan netowaku*. Tokyo: Chuo keizaisha.
Vlckova, J., & Thakur-Weigold, B. S. (2019). Global Value Chains in the MedTech Industry. *International Journal of Emerging Markets, 15*(1), 70–62.

CHAPTER 3

Formation of Medtech Big Business

1 Introduction

The rapid growth of the medtech industry outlined in Chap. 2 corresponds with the emergence of large companies. Until the 1980s, this industry predominantly consisted of two firm types: large multinational enterprises specialized in electric appliances and electronics, and small specialized companies. The former were focused on X-ray devices. They engaged in this business during the interwar years and maintained their competitive advantage over time through continuous investment in R&D (Gelijns & Rosenberg, 1999). This enabled them to develop CT scanners in the 1970s and 1980s, as well as MRI equipment from the 1990s (Trajtenberg, 1990; Blume, 1992). The latter firm type was developed locally to answer the needs of doctors and hospitals. These firms were usually specialized in one kind of equipment (e.g., surgical instruments, implants, monitoring devices, or pacemakers). Originally focused on their domestic market, they expanded internationally through export. Their growth, however, was limited compared with manufacturers of medical imaging equipment due to their strong specialization focus.

In 1989, the *Financial Times* published a list of the largest medtech companies (see Table 3.1), all with sales above 300 million USD. The list clearly shows the domination of electronics giants at that time. Medtronic, an American manufacturer of pacemakers that diversified through M&As (see Chap. 4), represented the only firm that did not produce X-ray devices

P.-Y. Donzé, *Medtech*,
https://doi.org/10.1007/978-981-16-7174-6_3

Table 3.1 Largest medtech companies in the world, 1987

Company	*Home country*	*Gross sales (billion USD)*
Siemens	Germany	2.61
General Electric	USA	1.76
Philips	Netherlands	1.19
Toshiba	Japan	0.82
GEC/Picker	UK	0.47
Medtronic	USA	0.43
Hitachi	Japan	0.32

Source: *Financial Times*, 4 May 1989

Table 3.2 Ten largest medtech companies in the world, 2010 and 2019

Company	*Home country*	*Market share % (2010)*	*Market share % (2019)*
Johnson & Johnson	USA	9.5	9.7
Medtronic	USA	6.2	9.7
Siemens	Germany	6.3	5.4
GE Healthcare	USA	6.5	4.7
Abbott Laboratories	USA	2.6	4.5
Stryker	USA	2.8	3.9
Cardinal Health	USA	3.5	3.7
Becton Dickinson	USA	2.9	3.0
Boston Scientific	USA	3.0	2.8
Philips	Netherlands	4.4	2.5

Source: Euromonitor, Passport database

and CT scanners. This data is incomplete, however, as the newspaper neglected to include some major medtech firms, notably Johnson & Johnson, which had medtech sales of 2 billion USD in 1987.[1] Companies that fell outside medical imaging were therefore more important than they appear in Table 3.1, even though they were clearly not dominant.

Two decades later, the medtech industry offered a very different structure. According to the consulting company Euromonitor, the ten largest manufacturers of medical and surgical equipment presented a much more diversified profile (see Table 3.2).[2] First, there were only three electronics

[1] Johnson & Johnson, Annual Report, 1987.
[2] https://go.euromonitor.com/passport.html (accessed 9 January 2021).

multinationals (Siemens, GE and Philips) and each lost market shares between 2010 and 2019. Together, these three companies had a cumulated share of 17.2% of the world's medtech market in 2010 and it declined to 12.6% in 2019. Therefore, medical imaging technology was no longer the main driver behind the development of the industry. Second, one must stress the domination of US firms in this new ranking. Except Siemens and Philips, which used to be dominant players in the medtech industry from the interwar years onwards, all of the largest firms were American. Moreover, none of these were specialized in a specific field of application. They were diversified medtech conglomerates that offered a broad range of goods and services. Medtronic, which was still a small firm in 1987 relative to giants like Siemens and GE, overcame its competitors and established itself in 2019 as number 1 in the world (together with Johnson & Johnson).

Although information in Tables 3.1 and 3.2 came from different sources, it suggests a major transformation of the global medtech industry between the 1980s and 2010s. The objective of this chapter is therefore to provide an analysis of this transformation and to shed light on the emergence and development of the largest companies that dominate medtech today.

2 Methodology

To discuss the formation of the largest companies currently dominating the global medtech industry, I selected firms on the basis of the ranking made by the US-based business news website Medical Design & Outsourcing (MDO; https://www.medicaldesignandoutsourcing.com/), which belongs to the WTWH Media company. This company regularly provides a ranking of the 100 largest medtech firms in the world. As a baseline, I used the ranking given in 2016 derived from figures for 2014. However, this list included several shortcomings, with some major non-US firms missing and an overestimation of US companies in the lower ranks. Therefore, I focused on companies above one billion USD sales in 2014, because this made it easier to identify the major companies that were missing. The MDO ranking included a total of 65 companies above this mark. I added three companies: Roche (Switzerland), the global leader in diagnostic devices; Mindray Medical (China), the largest medtech firm in China; and Toshiba Medical (Japan), one of the leading firms in the Japanese medtech industry.

The next step involved identifying the value of gross sales in 1960, 1980 and 2000; the dates for the founding of the firms; entry into the medtech business; and firms' initial public offering (IPO). This data was collected from annual reports when available, business directories (Moody's, Nikkei), news press sources such as the *New York Times* and *Financial Times*, as well as the publication series *International Directory of Company Histories*. All values were converted into USD on the basis of exchange rates given by the Measuring Growth Foundation (https://www.measuringworth.com/). The results for this database are presented in Table 3.3.

3 World's Largest Medtech Firms in 2014

Based on the information given in Table 3.3, a total of 68 companies had medtech sales over one billion USD in 2014. Before discussing the characteristics of these companies, one must evaluate their total share of the global medtech market. As MDO (2016) gave no estimate, I refer here to the report published by the consulting firm Evaluate (2014), which is used by several business news companies in the US, including Forbes. It valued global medtech sales at 380 billion USD in 2014. In comparison, the total sales of the top 68 largest medtech firms amounted that year to 365 billion USD—that is, 96% of the global market. Although there is a major methodological bias associated with comparing figures from two different sources, this illustrates the largest companies exert strong dominance over this industry. Moreover, if one looks at only the top 10 largest firms, which are all over 10 billion USD in medtech sales except Baxter International (9.968 billion), their collective share of the global market would amount to 43%. As for the top 20 largest firms, their collective share would be 64%.

What are the main characteristics of these 68 companies? First, in terms of nationality, the overwhelming presence of US companies is striking. It confirms the major weight of this country in terms of macroeconomic data, discussed in Chap. 2. More than half of the largest firms are headquartered in the US (35), among which are the two largest firms (Medtronic and Johnson & Johnson) and six in the top 10. Their cumulated share amounts to more than 205 billion sales, which equates to 56% of the total sales of the top 68 and 54% of the global market according to Evaluate (2014). On average, US firms had 5.8 billion sales. Next, the most important countries are Japan (9 companies, average of 3.7 billion), Germany (7 and 6.7 billion), Switzerland (3 and 7.9 billion) and UK (3 and 2.8 billion). Other nations have only one (Belgium, China, Italy, Netherlands and Spain) or two companies (Denmark, France and Sweden).

Table 3.3 Largest medtech companies in the world, 2014

Rank	*Company*	*Home country*	*Revenues 2014 (million USD)*	*Revenues 2000 (million USD)*	*Revenues 1980 (million USD)*	*Revenues 1960 (million USD)*	*Foundation*	*Medtech*	*IPO (first)*
1	Medtronic	USA	28,833	5551	270	0.2	1949	1949	1978
2	Johnson & Johnson	USA	25,137	10,281	1540	100*	1886	1947	1944
3	Philips Healthcare	Netherlands	19,817	2798	Unknown	Unknown	1891	1918	1912
4	GE Healthcare	USA	17,639	3000	600*	80*	1892	1920	1892
5	Fresenius Medical Care	Germany	16,739	5631	Unknown	–	1912	1966	1986
6	Roche	Switzerland	11,770	3699	149*	–	1896	1968	Unknown
7	Siemens Healthcare	Germany	11,652	3767	1232	25	1847	1888	1899
8	Cardinal Health	USA	11,395	6135	–	–	1971	1999	1983
9	Becton, Dickinson and Co	USA	10,282	3618	942	43	1897	1897	1962
10	Baxter International	USA	9968	2719	Unknown	Unknown	1931	1950s	1961
11	Stryker Corp	USA	9946	2289	36	Unknown	1941	1941	1979
12	Alcon	Switzerland	9812	2554	130	Unknown	1945	1945	2002
13	Owens & Minor	USA	9772	3503	Unknown	Unknown	1882	1882	1971

(*continued*)

Table 3.3 (continued)

Rank	*Company*	*Home country*	*Revenues 2014 (million USD)*	*Revenues 2000 (million USD)*	*Revenues 1980 (million USD)*	*Revenues 1960 (million USD)*	*Foundation*	*Medtech*	*IPO (first)*
14	Danaher	USA	8213	–	–	–	1969	2006	1979
15	Fujifilm Holdings	Japan	7895	Unknown	Unknown	Unknown	1934	1936	1949
16	Bayer	Germany	7792	1814	–	–	1863	1990s	Unknown
17	Boston Scientific	USA	7477	2664	5*	–	1979	1979	1992
18	Essilor International	France	7452	1823	Unknown	–	1849	1849	1975
19	B. Braun Melsungen	Germany	6801	2216*	Unknown	Unknown	1839	1839	unlisted
20	Zimmer-Biomet	USA	5997	1040	Unknown	4	1927	1927	2001
21	Hitachi (Hitachi Medical)	Japan	5625	1042	110*	12*	1910	1949	1949
22	St. Jude Medical	USA	5541	1178	12	–	1976	1976	1977
23	3M Co.	USA	5420	3135	499	Unknown	1902	Unknown	1946
24	Olympus Corp	Japan	5030	1814	113	Unknown	1919	1919	1949
25	Abbott Laboratories	USA	5000	2924	Unknown	–	1888	1972	1929

26	Smith and Nephew	UK	4634	1135	102	–	1856	1986	1937
27	Cerner	USA	4425	404	Unknown	–	1979	1979	1986
28	Grifols	Spain	4365	250	10	Unknown	1940	1940	2006
29	Terumo	Japan	4043	1284	183	1*	1921	1921	1982
30	Getinge Group	Sweden	3584	571	Unknown	Unknown	1904	1904	1993
31	C.R. Bard	USA	3416	1098	300*	9	1923	1923	1963
32	Toshiba	Japan	3300*	1160	367	7	1939	1939	1949
33	Varian Medical Systems	USA	3099	690	55	Unknown	1948	1960	1959
34	McKesson	USA	2885	2706	–	–	1833	Unknown	Unknown
35	Hologic	USA	2705	93	–	–	1985	1985	1990
36	Dentsply International	USA	2674	889	200	Unknown	1899	1899	1993
37	Hoya	Japan	2532	201	–	–	1941	1987	1961
38	Edwards Lifesciences	USA	2493	804	Unknown	Unknown	1958	1958	2000
39	Intuitive Surgical	USA	2384	26	–	–	1995	1995	2000
40	Steris	UK	2238	760	–	–	1985	1985	1992
41	BioMerieux	France	2180	587	Unknown	–	1963	1963	2004
42	Coloplast	Denmark	2067	503	16	Unknown	1957	1957	1983
43	Paul Hartmann Group	Germany	2067	Unknown	Unknown	Unknown	1818	Unknown	Unknown
44	Waters	USA	2042	795	20	Unknown	1958	Unknown	1973
45	Bio-Rad	USA	2019	725	46	Unknown	1957	1957	1966

(*continued*)

Table 3.3 (continued)

Rank	*Company*	*Home country*	*Revenues 2014 (million USD)*	*Revenues 2000 (million USD)*	*Revenues 1980 (million USD)*	*Revenues 1960 (million USD)*	*Foundation*	*Medtech*	*IPO (first)*
46	Sonova Holding	Switzerland	1994	272	12	Unknown	1947	1947	1994
47	Hill-Rom Holdings	USA	1988	1112	150*	Unknown	1929	1929	1978
48	Nipro	Japan	1964	747	Unknown	–	1954	1965	1987
49	Draegerwerk	Germany	1826	1137	Unknown	Unknown	1889	1902	1979
50	Teleflex	USA	1809	411	–	–	1943	1981	1967
51	The Cooper Cos.	USA	1797	197	Unknown	–	1958	1970	1983
52	Miraca Holdings	Japan	1749	–	–	–	2005	2005	2005
53	ResMed	USA	1678	115	–	–	1989	1989	1995
54	ConvaTec	UK	1650	–	–	–	2008	2008	2016
55	Bruker	USA	1623	74	Unknown	–	1960	1978	2000
56	IDEXX Labs	USA	1601	367	–	–	1983	1983	1991
57	William Demant Holding	Denmark	1585	366	Unknown	Unknown	1904	1904	1995
58	Halyard Health	USA	1574	–	–	–	2014	2014	2014
59	Nihon Kohden	Japan	1367	607	64	Unknown	1951	1951	1961
60	Elekta	Sweden	1330	235	Unknown	–	1972	1972	1994
61	Mindray Medical	China	1322	Unknown	–	–	1991	1991	Unknown
62	Smiths Medical	USA	1277	628	121	6.5	1851	1958	1914

63	Agfa-Gevaert	Belgium	1219	1400	Unknown	–	1964	1964	1999
64	Sirona Dental Systems	USA	1161	886	–	–	1997	1997	2006
65	Carl Zeiss Meditec	Germany	1154	185*	Unknown	Unknown	1846	1898	2002
66	Amplifon	Italy	1147	443*	Unknown	Unknown	1950	1950	2001
67	Invacare	USA	1142	1013	20*	–	1971	1971	1984
68	DJO Global	USA	1113	143	Unknown	–	1978	1978	2001

Sources: Own elaboration on the basis of MDO (2016), IDCH (1988–2014), *New York Times*, *Financial Times*, and companies' annual reports

Notes: Values with an * are estimates by the author based on extrapolations

Therefore, there is a strong geographical concentration in the US, Western Europe (Germany and Switzerland) and East Asia (Japan). The development of the medtech industry in these countries is investigated in detail in later chapters.

Second, the size of these companies has an average of 5.3 billion sales but presents a broad variety. There are five giant firms with more than 15 billion sales. They include both multinational companies of the electric appliance industry that used to dominate the medical imaging equipment market from the interwar years onwards (Donzé & Wubs, 2019), such as GE and Philips, and new conglomerates built through intense M&A activity, such as Medtronic, Johnson & Johnson, and Fresenius. All of these are diversified conglomerates. Next, there are 18 mid-range companies above the average, but these still diverge considerably from the giants. These companies are mostly based in the dominating nations (US, Germany, Japan and Switzerland) and nearly all have diversified, except Alcon (ophthalmic supplies), Roche (diagnostic equipment), St. Jude (cardiology), Stryker (implants), and Zimmer Biomet (implants). Finally, about two-thirds of these largest companies fall below the average. Most are specialized in a specific field of medtech business, where they have acquired a competitive advantage, such as Cerner (IT health services), DJO Global (orthopedic equipment), Grifols (blood products), IDEXX (diagnostic devices), Sonova (hearing aids), Steris (sterilization equipment), and Varian Medical (oncology treatment equipment). This breakout by size of the companies highlights that large companies are much more diversified than smaller ones. The latter therefore present as targets for the former, which built their diversification on the acquisition of independent companies.

Third, a look at the years of foundation and entry into the medtech business clearly underscores that most of these companies were created as medtech firms. 41 of them were medtech firms since their beginning (60.3%) and six others engaged in this field within 20 years following their foundation (8.8%). Moreover, although medtech itself is a new industry, the overwhelming majority of the largest firms are relatively old: 18 were founded in the nineteenth Century (26.5%), 18 others between 1900–1945 (26.5%), and 15 between 1946–1969 (22.1%). Hence, only a quarter were created during the last five decades, and most were US companies. Additionally, more than one-third of the companies that came from outside of the medtech industry were among the 15 largest firms in 2014. Except Medtronic and Becton, Dickinson & Co., all of the ten largest companies are newcomers. Companies that were originally outside of the medtech industry essentially came from electrical appliances and electronics (GE, Hitachi, Philips, Siemens, Toshiba), optical instruments (Hoya, Olympus, Zeiss), and pharmaceuticals (Abbott, Baxter, Bayer, Fresenius, Johnson & Johnson, Roche). They invested in medtech by applying their technology to medicine and via the takeover of other companies. This, however, does not mean that investing in medtech is a new trend. Thirteen of the 24 firms that were originally non-medtech, of which their date of entry into medtech is unknown, diversified into this new field before 1970.

This brief analysis of the age of medtech firms demonstrates that this industry is not dominated by startups but by companies that have been established for several decades. Hence, the process of their development is a major issue. How and when did the largest medtech firms grow? What was the role of M&A in their diversification as medtech firms? The following chapters tackle in detail several case studies, but it is necessary to address this question for the largest companies as a whole. The lack of available financial data regarding medtech sales before 2000 represents a major source of methodological bias in conducting such an analysis. Many companies did not disclose medtech sales because they were not listed or because this activity was too small to form a separate division within the company. Medtech sales are missing for three companies in 2000 (4.7% of medtech firms at that time), 24 in 1980 (46.2%), and 25 in 1960 (69.4%). On average, available data on medtech sales grew from 26 million USD in 1960 to 261 million in 1980, 1.6 billion in 2000 and 5.5 billion in 2014. This general trend shows that medtech was a small business until the 1980s, where it then entered into a phase of rapid development at the end of the twentieth century. The formation of large firms in this industry is consequently a new phenomenon. A brief comparison with a dominant high-tech company such as IBM highlights the rapid growth of medtech business. IBM was far bigger than the largest medtech companies over the last six decades but its growth was much slower: gross sales increased from 1.4 billion USD in 1960 (54 times larger than medtech firms) to 26.2 billion in 1980 (100), 88.4 billion in 2000 (55), and 92.8 billion in 2014 (17; IBM, 1960–2014).

The rapid growth of medtech firms since the 1980s notably resulted from capital provided by financial markets. Except B. Braun, all were listed in 2014. However, although most of the largest companies in 2014 are relatively old, they went public late. Only seven had their IPO before the end of World War II, among which were the electronics giants GE, Philips and Siemens, as well as pharmaceutical firms Abbott and Johnson & Johnson. Thus, they were large non-medtech companies with a medtech division. Thirteen other companies were listed in the period 1945–1970. The overwhelming majority (42 cases, or 66.7% of all known cases) obtained their IPO after 1970, particularly after 1990 (25 cases). This capital was particularly used to take over other companies towards strengthening a competitive advantage in a specific field or towards diversifying and establishing themselves as a general medtech group.

How did M&A support the growth of the largest medtech firms? To answer this question, one can look first at the relationship between the number of M&A cases in the period 2000–2014 and the growth of medtech sales during the same period. Figure 3.1 clearly shows that the relationship is negative. A high number of M&A cases does not mean the firm grew more rapidly. However, Fig. 3.2 simultaneously demonstrates a positive relationship between the number of M&A cases and the size of the company in 2014. Large companies took over many more firms than

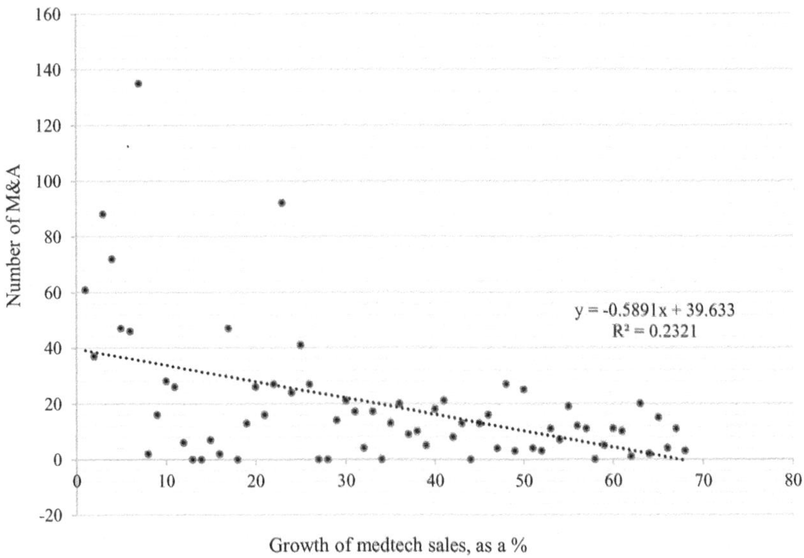

Fig. 3.1 Number of M&A cases and growth of medtech sales by the largest medtech companies, 2000–2014. (Source: Thomson One M&A database and Table 3.3)

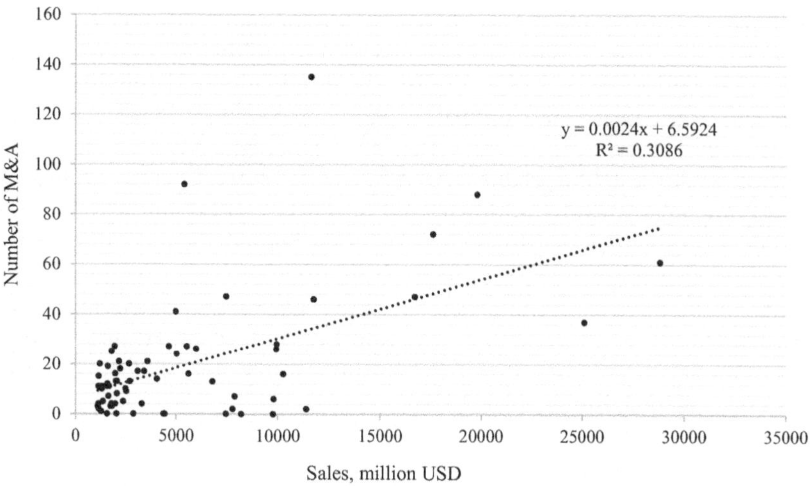

Fig. 3.2 Number of M&A cases (2000–2014) and medtech sales by the largest medtech companies, 2014. (Source: Thomson One M&A database and Table 3.3)

did small companies. They also grew slightly less than did smaller firms: in 2000–2014, the average annual growth of the top ten largest amounted to 8.8%, against 10.1% for others. Large companies took over more companies to access new markets and internalize new technology towards consolidating their competitive advantage. The cases of GE (Chap. 4) and Siemens (Chap. 6) are excellent illustrations of this trend. In contrast, smaller firms took over fewer companies, usually in the same field as their core competence, and grew more rapidly because they strengthened their domination in their field. This model is embodied by specialized firms such as Zimmer Biomet in the US (Chap. 4), Olympus and Terumo in Japan (Chap. 5), and Karl Storz in Germany (Chap. 6).

4 Conclusion

The macroeconomic indicators presented in Chap. 2 highlight that the global medtech industry followed development in various phases, from a formative period (1960s–1970s), to a change in industrial structure and growth (1980s–1990s), and, finally, to an acceleration of growth and globalization from 2000 onwards. The brief analysis conducted on the largest firms in the global medtech industry in 2014 emphasized that these companies represented the key drivers of development in this sector. There is a clear shift from an industry comprising few multinationals and numerous SMEs prior to the 1980s towards the domination of large firms since the end of the twentieth Century.

The global medtech industry therefore experienced a deep structural change after the 1980s, characterized by the rapid development of diversified companies, mostly headquartered in the US. IPOs and M&As were major tools for such development. The next chapters focus on the formation and development of the medtech industry in various national contexts, in the three most important countries (US, Japan and Germany), in Switzerland as an example of a successful European country, in France as an example of an unsuccessful European country, and in China as the fastest-growing country since 2010.

References

Other Published Sources

Evaluate. (2014). *Welcome to the Evaluate MedTech: World Preview 2014, Outlook to 2020*. Evaluate Ltd. Retrieved February 2, 2021, from http://info.evaluategroup.com/rs/evaluatepharmaltd/images/2014WPM.pdf

IDCH. (1988–2014). *International Directory of Company Histories* (150 vols.). St. James Press.

Medical Design. (2016). *Medtech's 100 Largest Players*. Retrieved May 18, 2019, from https://www.medicaldesignandoutsourcing.com/

Books and Academic Articles

Blume, S. S. (1992). *Insight and Industry: On the Dynamics of Technological Change in Medicine*. MIT Press.

Donzé, P. Y., & Wubs, B. (2019). Global Competition and Cooperation in the Electronics Industry: The Case of X-ray Equipment, 1900–1970. *Scandinavian Economic History Review, 67*(2), 210–225.

Gelijns, A. C., & Rosenberg, N. (1999). Diagnostic Devices: An Analysis of Comparative Advantages. In D. C. Mowery & R. R. Nelson (Eds.), *Sources of Industrial Leadership: Studies of Seven Industries* (pp. 312–358). Cambridge University Press.

Trajtenberg, M. (1990). *Economic Analysis of Product Innovation: The Case of CT Scanners*. Harvard University Press.

CHAPTER 4

The Lasting Competitive Advantage of US Firms

1 Introduction

Data on foreign trade, patent applications and M&As (Chap. 2), as well as the current ranking of the world's largest companies (Chap. 3) show a clear domination by American companies over the global medtech industry. Where does this competitive advantage come from and how was it possible to maintain it are the questions addressed in this chapter.

After World War II, the American medtech industry was basically divided into two different kinds of actors. First, there were few large corporations that produced X-ray apparatuses and electromedical devices. The most important was the multinational enterprise General Electric (GE). It had developed the Coolidge X-ray tube, an innovation patented in 1917 that dramatically improved the quality of X-ray pictures via a superior control of X-ray dosage (Janssen & Medford, 2009). This gave GE a competitive advantage in the American market and worldwide. Besides GE, there were only a handful of companies that produced X-ray and electromedical devices until the 1970s, the most important being Westinghouse Electric and Picker X-Ray. The first was a conglomerate that had been GE's most important rival in the electric appliance business since the late nineteenth century. It entered the X-ray device industry in 1930 when it merged two specialized firms (i.e., Wappler Electric Company and the American X-ray Corporation) to form Westinghouse X-Ray Co. (Radiology, 1930). It cooperated technically with Siemens in the 1960s but was still

P.-Y. Donzé, *Medtech*,
https://doi.org/10.1007/978-981-16-7174-6_4

lagging behind GE in America and unable to expand abroad. It withdrew from the X-ray business in 1971, selling its production facilities and sales network to the French group Compagnie Générale de Radiologie (CGR; Donzé & Wubs, 2019). As for Picker X-Ray, it was a family business founded in 1915 and specialized in radiological equipment. It experienced rapid growth supplying the United States (US) army during World War II and the Korean War, before expanding its production into Europe in the 1950s and moving to a CT scanner in the 1970s. It was purchased by the British group General Electric Company (GEC), a major company in electrical appliances that had a strong position in the medical imaging equipment business in the United Kingdom (UK; Palermo, 1995).

Second, there were hundreds of small- and medium-sized enterprises engaged in the development and production of specific surgical and medical devices. According to the Census of Manufacturers, in 1963, the American surgical and medical instruments industry (including dental equipment but excluding ophthalmic supplies) was a sector with 1314 companies (mostly small) and a total workforce of 51,420 persons.[1] Rodengen (2001) argued that, until the 1970s, most of these companies depended on medical doctors and surgeons with respect to innovation and product development. They were essentially created by mechanists and engineers that were able to answer some specific needs of medical practitioners. For example, this formed the beginnings of Medtronic, which began as a medical equipment repair shop that developed wearable pacemakers (IDCH, 2005) or Medi-Tech, a developer of catheters that became Boston Scientific (Rodengen, 2001). This industry developed steadily, reaching a total of 3377 companies and 208,100 employees in 1992.[2] Between 1963 and 1992, the number of companies therefore multiplied by four and the industry became more concentrated, with an average of workers by firm increasing from 39.1 to 61.6, and the total number of companies employing more than 100 persons increasing from 128 to 464.[3] The takeover of other companies active in the same medical technology field enabled the development of specialized medtech companies. For example, Bard & Co., a distributor of urological and surgical products, whose origins date back to 1907, was listed in 1963 and subsequently purchased several competitors, such as USCI (1966) and Davol Inc.

[1] Census of Manufactures, 1963.
[2] Census of Manufactures, 1992.
[3] Ibidem.

(1980), to consolidate its position (Bard, 1999). During the following decades, the growth became much lower, obviously due to relocation in Mexico and the globalization of companies. In 2016, the surgical and medical device sector employed 238,138 persons (without ophthalmic supplies).[4]

The fast development of the period 1960–1990 was characterized by a deep transformation of the institutional environment that supported the growth of this industry. The managers of some surgical devices gathered in 1965 and organized the Association for the Advancement of Medical Instrumentation (AAMI), whose goal it was to develop cooperation with medical doctors and health authorities to set up quality standards for their products (Rodengen, 2001, p. 35). This step was necessary toward building trust with the medical world and to consequently increase sales. It was strengthened during the next decade by state intervention. Following the Medical Device Regulation Act, adopted by Congress in 1976, the Food and Drug Administration (FDA) set up trials for medical devices before they could be marketed (Bartlett Foote, 1992). This regulation led to the institutionalization of research and development (R&D), as manufacturers had to follow specific rules, and to the end of their strong dependency on medical doctors. Medtech companies began to engage researchers from faculties of engineering to carry out their own research projects, sometimes in cooperation with doctors and hospitals, but no longer in the capacity of subcontractor. For example, Medi-Tech engaged its first full-time researcher, a graduate from Harvard and MIT, in 1976 (Rodengen, 2001, p. 45). Specialized medtech firms grew first on the basis of in-house research and then expanded through M&As.

The dynamics of the American medtech industry, its formation, growth and international expansion, are analyzed in the following sections. First, I focus on the evolution of production, as the United States is one of the few countries that offers precise statistics on this topic. Next, we move to a detailed analysis of foreign trade, patent applications and M&As in the American medtech industry. Finally, I discuss the evolution of the major types of actors in this industry: GE, the medtech giants, the presence of pharmaceutical firms, and startups.

[4] Annual Survey of Manufacturers, 2016.

2 National Production

The census and annual survey of manufacturers make it possible to gain a precise idea of the evolution of the medtech industry in the US. This data is important not only because this is one of very few countries for which we have such a statistic over the long-term, but also because the American medtech industry is the largest in the world—its dynamics shed a light on the general transformation of this industry.

Figure 4.1 shows the evolution of shipments between 1960 and 2016. The value has been deflated to better express the real changes, and the export of medtech as a percentage of shipments has been added. During the first part of the 1960s, the American medtech industry was a small sector with less than 1.5 billion dollars of shipments and a probable strong focus on the domestic market. It was approximately ten times smaller than

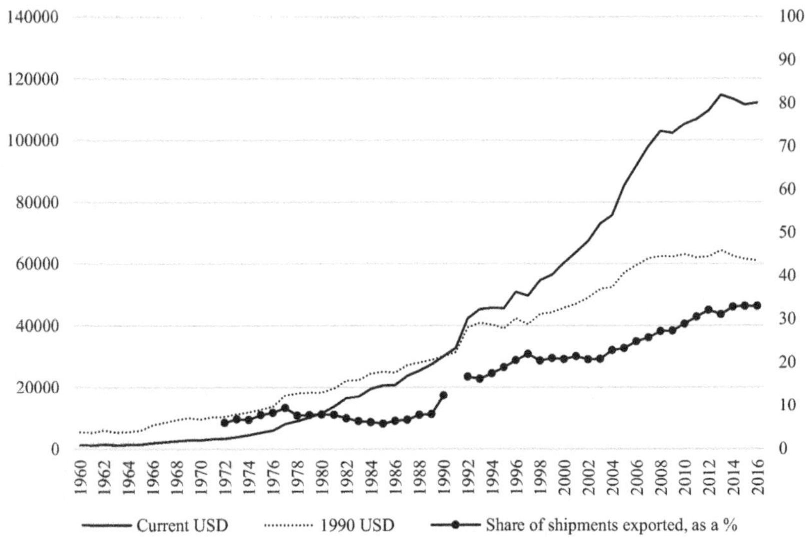

Fig. 4.1 Production of medical equipment and supplies in the US, value of shipments in million dollars, in nominal USD and in 1990 USD, and export as a % of shipments, 1960–2016. (Source: Census of Manufactures and Annual Survey of Manufactures; United Nations, *International Trade Statistics Yearbook*, 1972–1990 and COMTRADE. Note: This data includes dental, medical and surgical equipment, ophthalmic supplies, as well as X-ray and electromedical devices)

the automobile industry (USITC, 1981). This industry began to grow rapidly in the mid-1960s and experienced an important development based on the expansion of the domestic market until the end of the 1980s. In nominal terms, the total shipments increased from 1.9 billion dollars in 1965 to 2.9 billion in 1970 and to 30 billion in 1990. It was multiplied by approximately 10 during the 1970s and the 1980s (but only by three in real value). Moreover, the share of export to production was constantly low, with an average of 7.3% in 1972–1989. Therefore, these two decades offered formidable opportunities to American entrepreneurs and companies, but they scarcely went over national borders. They benefited from a growing domestic healthcare market, supported by various policies that subsidized research projects (e.g., the Artificial Heart Program, Artificial Kidney Program, War on Cancer) and supported demand through hospital construction (Medicare and Medicaid; Bartlett Foote, 1992). However, a major change can be observed in 1990—that is, for the first time, the share of export overcame the 10-% mark. It continued to expand, reaching 20.8% in 2000 and 28.9% in 2010, and supported the continuation of the rapid development of the medtech industry. Total shipments amounted to a nominal value of 60.3 billion in 2000 and 112.2 billion in 2016. A deflated value also shows a rapid expansion until 2006, followed by ten years of stagnation that can partially be explained by the end of the growth of export in 2012.

Next, the breakdown of shipments by type of products emphasizes the kinds of technology and equipment that supported the development of the American medtech industry (see Fig. 4.2). The period can be divided into three phases. First, during the 1960s, one can observe the domination of traditional goods. Surgical appliances and supplies (e.g., hospital furniture, implants, operating tables, orthopedic devices, sterilizers, and surgical implants) dominated with an average share of 41% of shipments, followed by surgical and medical instruments (e.g., blood-pressure apparatus, inhalators, knives, and thermometers) with 20%. These goods were usually developed by mechanists and artisans who answered the needs of medical doctors. Moreover, ophthalmic goods had a relatively high share, which was more important than X-ray and electromedical equipment that commonly express the advent of modern medicine based on high technology after World War II. The share of this category was similar to that of dental equipment. Second, the 1970s appear as a decade of deep mutation. Although surgical appliances and supplies and surgical and medical instruments maintained their lead, one can observe a fast increase of the

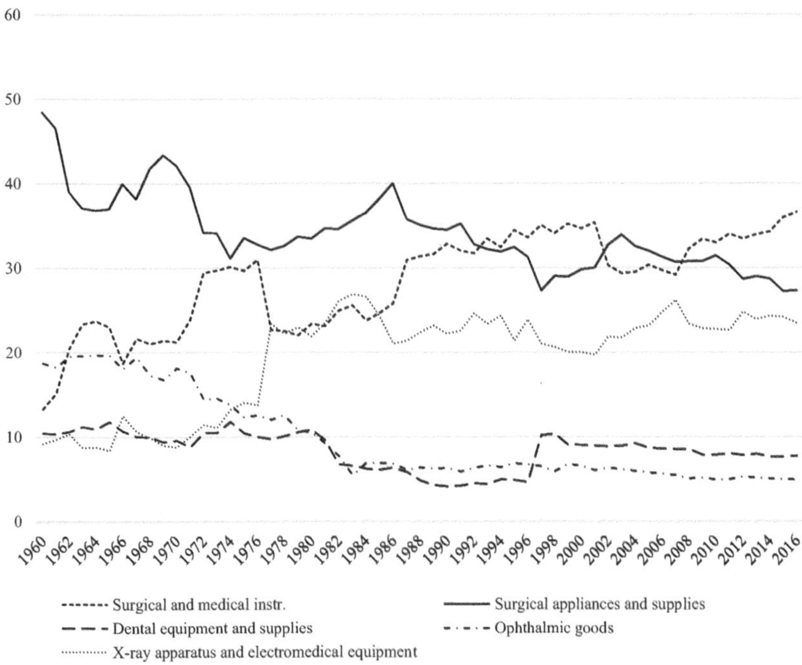

Fig. 4.2 Production of medical equipment and supplies in the US, with value of shipments per type of products as a %, 1960–2016. (Source: Census of Manufactures and Annual Survey of Manufactures)

share of X-ray apparatus and electromedical equipment, from 9% in 1970 to 22% in 1980. This clearly results from the advent of CT scanners and various patient monitoring devices based on electronics. In contrast, the share of low-tech products such as ophthalmic goods and dental equipment dropped during this decade. Third, since the 1980s, the structure of the American medtech industry has generally been stable, beyond small fluctuations. The gradual shift from surgical appliances and supplies (33% in 1980 and 27% in 2016) to surgical and medical instruments (23% to 37%) also resulted from a technological change, with the introduction of electronics and computer-assisted technology in medical instrumentation. X-ray apparatus and electromedical equipment are stable (23% on average in 1980–2016), like ophthalmic goods (6%) and dental equipment (7%).

Consequently, data on the national production of the medtech industry in the US clearly shows that it began as a small sector making traditional devices for American doctors in the 1960s. It entered a phase of growth at the end of this decade that was driven by the fast expansion of domestic demand. The launch of CT scanners and other new-generation equipment based on electronics caused a significant impact on this growth during the 1970s. In 1990, American medtech companies engaged more actively in export. Their technological advantage, as suggested by the growing share of medical and surgical instruments (which integrated new technology at that time), supported their expansion. At the beginning of the twenty-first century, the American medtech industry exported approximately one third of its production and continues to achieve an annual production of more than 100 billion dollars.

3 Foreign Trade

Export became significant in 1990 and has largely contributed to the growth of the American medtech industry ever since. This section analyses the development of medtech foreign trade using the COMTRADE database for the period 1991–2019. In the context of the growing US trade deficit during this period (from $67 billion to $851 billion),[5] the development of export and a general trend towards the increasing surplus of medtech products until 2013 is remarkable. However, since 2014, export has entered a phase of stagnation and the trade balance is declining, turning negative for the first time in 2019. Export experienced a general growth from 6.1 billion dollars in 1991 to 13.4 billion in 2000 and 44.5 billion in 2019, which represents a growing share of all export over the period, from 1.4% in 1991 to 2.7% in 2019. The American medtech industry is therefore a competitive sector in the general economy of the US. However, the formidable expansion of domestic demand and the global expansion of American companies through M&As led to a reduction of the trade surplus after 2000. While export was 1.8 times higher than import between the period 1991–1999, it declined dramatically to 1.1 higher in 2005 and has maintained an average of 1.2 higher during the period 2006–2017 (Fig. 4.3).

[5] United States Census, Foreign Trade, https://www.census.gov/foreign-trade/statistics/historical/goods.pdf (accessed 8 September 2020).

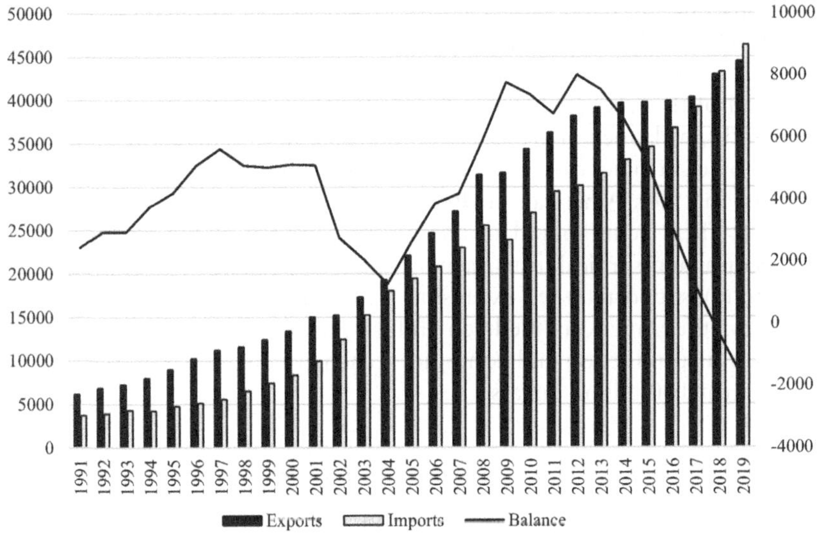

Fig. 4.3 US foreign trade of medtech goods (million USD), 1991–2019. (Source: Comtrade, HS codes 9018, 9021 and 9022)

A detailed analysis of the three main medtech product categories shows the coexistence of different dynamics, even though the impact of the globalization of US companies is visible everywhere. First, the trade evolution of general medical devices, the largest part of the medtech industry, expresses the competitiveness of a large variety of American companies (see Chap. 3). In nominal value, export increased from 4.3 billion dollars in 1991 to a peak at 29.7 billion in 2019. It was untouched by the global financial crisis (GFC)—specifically, while general export from the US declined 18% in 2009, the export of general medical devices stayed stable that year. These goods answer essential needs in healthcare systems and can hardly be manufactured by competing companies in other countries. The main export markets are Western Europe, Canada and Japan, that is, countries with highly developed healthcare systems. It is also important to note the growing importance of China in the twenty-first century. While this country represented only a market share of 0.8% in 1991 and 1.6% in 2000, it increased to 4.6% in 2010 and 9.2% in 2017, making China the fourth market for American medical devices that year, after the Netherlands, Belgium, and Japan.

As for import expansion, it is characterized by a shift from home countries of leading medtech companies to countries hosting subsidiaries of American multinationals. In 1991, the two most important suppliers were Japan and Germany. However, they gradually lost their importance against Mexico and Ireland. Following the NAFTA agreement, enforced in January 1994, many American medtech companies transferred assembly plants and the production of low-value activities over their Southern border. The share of Mexico in American import of general medical devices increased from 9.1% in 1991 to 15.7% in 2000 and 25.9% in 2017. The relocation of American medtech production facilities in this country largely explains the reduction of trade surplus after 2000. Ireland shows a similar trend but with a lower sweep. This country has also developed its medtech industry by attracting foreign multinationals with low wages and low corporate taxes (Fennelly & Cormican, 2006). In particular, American companies have established their manufacturing operations in this country for sales in the European Union (EU), but export to their home country as well. According to the *Irish Times* business ranking, the ten largest medtech companies in 2020 included eight American firms and one from Australia.[6] The share of import from Ireland grew from 1.8% in 1991 to 5.5% in 2000 and 8.4% in 2017.

Second, the foreign trade of orthopedic devices is another excellent illustration of the globalization of American medtech companies after 2000. In appearance, this industry lost its competitiveness over the years since 1991. During the 1990s, exports doubled, expanding from 908 million dollars in 1991 to 2.2 billion in 1999, and the balance of trade maintained its stability at approximately one billion. The US exported orthopedic devices to high-income and aging countries such as Canada, Japan and Germany. In the early twenty-first century, export entered a phase of rapid growth that peaked at 9.7 billion dollars in 2013, before stagnating. At the same time, import increased dramatically, leading to a decline of trade surplus and increasing deficit since 2014. However, this change in the foreign trade of orthopedic devices is not a reflection of the weakness of American companies but, instead, a reflection of their transformation into global enterprises.

The company Stryker offers a case in point (IDCH, 1999b; Stryker, 2002–2019). This company was founded in 1946 by an orthopedic surgeon from Michigan, Homer Stryker, who developed various devices to

[6] http://www.top1000.ie/industries/health (accessed 8 September 2020).

improve his professional practice. This small family business became public in 1979 and entered a period of development on the domestic market, developing and selling hospital beds, implants and endoscopic equipment. It commenced its acquisition of foreign companies with the takeover of a French company specialized in spinal implants, Dimso (1992), a majority stake in the Japanese distributor of medical devices Matsumoto Medical Instruments (1994), and the acquisition of the Swiss orthopedic device company Osteo (1996). Takeover was also pursued in the US, particularly with the orthopedic division of Pfizer in 1998. Between 2000 and 2017, Stryker made 41 acquisitions, 14 of which were outside the US (Thomson One database). It also opened a subsidiary in Ireland in 1998, where it employed in 2014 more than 2000 workers active in the development and manufacture of surgical and orthopedic devices.[7] Stryker was therefore transformed from a medium-sized company focused on the American market, with gross sales of 281 million dollars in 1990 to a multinational company with gross sales increasing from 2.3 billion dollars in 2000 to 9.9 billion in 2014.

The transformation of companies like Stryker had a significant impact on the structure of foreign trade. They shifted exporting from their American plants to globally organized enterprises that hold manufacturing capabilities throughout the world, from which they export to their end-markets, including the US. In particular, the rapid increase in importing after 1998 resulted from the opening of the Irish plant. The share of Ireland in imports increased from 5.3% of the total in 1995 to 44.1% in 2001 and remained above 40% until 2012. In 2017, the four largest partners of American imports of orthopedic aids where Ireland (34.6%), Switzerland (10.9%), China (8.6%) and Mexico (7.8%). They are all countries in which American firms have heavily invested.

Third, the trade of X-ray machines presents a trend similar to other medical devices, with a slow development in the 1990s, followed by rapid growth in the 2000s and a slow increase again since the GFC. The balance of trade also presents some fluctuations but is nearly balanced over the period (a total deficit of 682 million dollars for 1991–2017). Although GE is one the world's most competitive companies in this field, American export is not significantly overcoming import for two main reasons. First, unlike orthopedic devices, the globalization of GE's production system began in the 1980s. Rather than exporting from the US, GE had several

[7] *The Irish Times*, 23 September 2014.

plants abroad from which it exported to other countries—including probably to the US. In particular, like all major manufacturers, it had plants in China. The growing share of import from China includes not only cheap equipment made by Chinese companies but intracompany trade made by GE.[8] Second, import from Germany stayed high during the period, with an average of 32.7% of the total. X-ray equipment made in Germany by Siemens maintained competitiveness in the US. This also includes intracompany trade as this multinational also had an important subsidiary in America (see Chap. 6). Therefore, the foreign trade of X-ray machines since 1991 embodies the early globalization of this sector of the medtech industry.

4 Mergers and Acquisitions

Mergers and acquisitions (M&A) played a key role in the formation and growth of the medtech industry in the US. During the 1960s and 1970s, most companies in this business were specialized firms that developed on the basis of their core competences. However, they adopted a diversification strategy to related fields in the 1980s to enlarge the scope of their activities on the healthcare market, giving birth to diversified medtech groups (see Sect. 7 below). Figure 4.4 shows the turning point of the period 1980–1995. During these 15 years, the annual number of medtech companies or divisions of companies acquired (*target*) increased from 2 to 187 cases. The overwhelming majority of them were acquired by domestic companies (85.3%). Moreover, during the same period, American medtech firms (*buyers*) took over 1588 companies and divisions of companies, among which 1338 were in the US (84.3%). Hence, one can argue that the consolidation process of the American medtech industry began on the national market.

For example, the American Sterilizer Company was a small firm founded in 1894 to manufacture pressure sterilizers and to provide sterile processing services. It grew over the years in this business. Between 1983 and 1991, it realized eight acquisitions to strengthen its position on its core market (Medical Sterilization Inc.; Steel-Peel Packaging division of Bard Co.) and to diversify to hospital equipment (Bio-Design Inc.; Channel Industries Ltd.; Enterprise Systems Inc.; TRW Inc.; Basil Equipment Co.; Castle Cp.; medical product division of Vernitron Co.). It also sold its Hall

[8] *China Daily*, 14 July 2018.

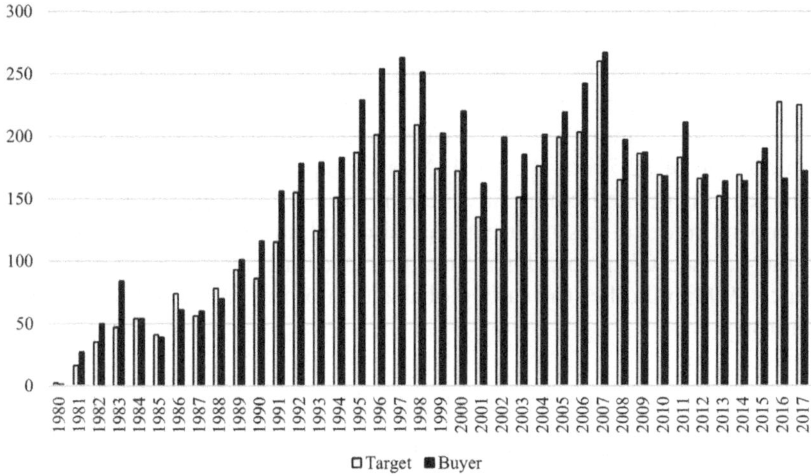

Fig. 4.4 M&A in the American medtech industry (number of cases), 1980–2017. (Source: Thomson-One database)

Surgical division to another American company in 1984, the pharmaceutical firm Bristol-Myers Co., which began a move to medtech (15 acquisitions in the period 1990–1995, among which 9 were in the US). Renamed AMSCO International, American Sterilizer was finally taken over by Steris Corporation in 1995, a former spin-off company from American Sterilizer founded ten years prior by a researcher who left the firm. It was also originally focused on sterilization equipment and funded by venture capital. It went public in 1992 and engaged in a process of growth and diversification through M&A. It acquired a total of 12 companies during the 1990s, all in the US, including American Sterilizer (IDCH, 1999a). In 2000, Steris had moved away from its original focus on sterilization technology and offered a broad range of healthcare equipment, from surgical tables to operating rooms, surgical lighting, video systems, and fluid waste management systems. Steris shifted from a small specialized company with 30 million dollars in sales in 1992 to a diversified company with more than 760 million sales in 2000.[9]

The rapid development of M&A was followed by a stabilization of cases over the long-term. Between 1995 and 2017, the average number of

[9] Steris Co., SEC Report, 2000.

medtech business acquired had an average of 182 cases per year. Although it is still largely domestic-focused, the share of takeovers by foreign firms had climbed slightly (to 19%). There are no dominant nations in these acquisitions, the largest being British firms (8% of all acquisitions by foreign companies), Canadian (6.3%) and German (3.6%). Companies from all over the world invested in the US, either to access the world's largest healthcare market or to acquire specific technology. The Japanese company Terumo, a manufacturer of medical thermometers that diversified to patient monitoring devices and other medical equipment, strengthened its position in the US with the acquisitions of Olson Medical Sales (1997), the cardiovascular business of 3M (1999), MicroVention Inc. (2006) and Caridian BCT (2011). As for Laser Industries Ltd., a company from Israel, it was obviously looking to internalize new knowledge when it purchased Advanced Surgical Technologies (1982) and Surgilase (1994). However, as embodied by the case of Siemens in Germany, there is no clear distinction between the expansion of the American market and the acquisition of specific technology (see Chap. 6). Taking over a company in the US often makes it possible to enlarge the scope of medtech knowledge and to reinforce a position in the world's largest healthcare system.

As for American medtech firms, they pursued their growth and diversification through M&As in the period 1995–2017. Purchasing other companies led to a consolidation of the industry and to the growing domination of the largest companies during this period (see Chap. 3). General Electric Healthcare (GE Medical Systems before 2004) took over 93 companies, among which 33 were abroad: Johnson & Johnson, with a total of 62 companies (15 abroad); Medtronic 79 companies (18 abroad); and Boston Scientific 71 companies (13 abroad). Of course, a large number of small- and medium-sized companies embraced the opportunity of M&A to consolidate and develop, but the general trend of this period is the consolidation of big business and a strong focus on the domestic market.

5 Innovation

The dynamics of innovation in the American medtech industry is analyzed here using data from patent applications between 1960 and 2014. Three major kinds of actors carried out R&D. First are private corporations. A focus on the top ten largest patent assignees per decade makes it possible to emphasize a turning point during the 1990s. Between the 1960s and 1980s, the dominant enterprises were specialized medtech firms, as well as companies from the electronics and electrical appliance industry (GE, Westinghouse and HP), pharmaceutical firms (Baxter, Parker, Davis & Co., Johnson & Johnson) and the conglomerate 3M. All had some divisions engaged in medical devices in relation to their other businesses. As for specialized medtech firms, they were mostly active in traditional fields like surgical instruments (Ethicon, Kendall), optical instruments (American Optical), X-ray machines (Picker), pacemakers and cardiac devices (Cordis, C. Bard), and diagnostic devices (American Cystoscope, Beckman Coulter). Diversified companies merely included Becton, Dickinson & Co. Most of these specialized companies have gradually disappeared from the ranking since the 1990s, giving their seat to a new generation of medtech companies characterized by a diversified portfolio of products, like Boston Scientific, Covidien and Medtronic. These new medtech giants grew from a process of M&As (see Sect. 7 below). A second kind of player is represented by the manufacturers of orthopedic devices and implants (Depuy, Warsaw and Zimmer). Finally, one must stress the arrival of foreign firms, particularly the German multinational Siemens, which invested significantly in the US in the 1990s (see Chap. 6) and the British firm Smith & Nephew, also specialized in orthopedic devices. GE and Ethicon represent rare companies that were able to maintain their position over time. The turning point of the 1990s is also characterized by the fast growth of the number of patent applications. GE became number one in the 1970s with only 119 patents but had a total of 3819 in the 2000s. Medtech became an innovation-intensive business over the last three decades. Moreover, R&D was not limited to American facilities but was organized over the borders. After 2000, Stryker was among the top 20 firm innovators in Germany and Switzerland, while six other US medtech companies were placed in the Swiss ranking (see Chap. 7).

Second, American universities and government research centers were the first in the world to significantly engage in patenting their research. The total number of applications increased from 112 in the 1960s to 3666 in the 2000s and to 2905 in the period 2010–2014. Until the 1970s, the NASA and military research centers were the largest assignees among research organizations, but the total number of patents was still low. Universities had few applications at that time but they were established as the main research centers in the 1980s and constitute the basis of the extremely rapid growth of applications by research centers since the 1990s. This change resulted from the adoption of the Bayh-Dole Act in 1980, which authorized universities and small businesses to retain patent and licensing rights to inventions resulting from research funded by the federal government (Mowery et al., 2001). Cooperation with private firms and licensing patents were already used by some universities in the 1970s, but the new legal framework encouraged rapid development. This was especially the case for the University of California (63 applications in the 1980s and 235 in the 2000s), Harvard University (27 and 255), Stanford University (32 and 127) and MIT (33 and 92). In the 2000s, 18 universities had more than 50 patent applications. What did these universities do with these patents? At first, they could sell the rights to use these patents through licensing contracts. At the University of California, for example, the total income from patents (medtech and other major fields like software and biotechnology) increased from 1.1 million dollars in 1970 to 2.1 million in 1980, 13.2 million in 1990 and 58.6 million in 1995 (Mowery et al., 2001, p. 107). The Bayh-Dole Act was also an important incentive for academic researchers to found startups (Aldridge & Audretsch, 2011). At the University of California, the number of startup foundations grew from 16 in the 1980s to 95 in the 1990s and 317 in the 2000s.[10]

The third type of innovators are individual assignees. In the US, individuals have a particularly high share of patent applications in comparison with other countries investigated in this book (see Chap. 2). A focus on the largest individual assignees sheds a light on the growing prominence of medical doctors until the 1990s, followed by a decline and the emergence of engineers as key innovators. University professors have had a minimal presence, but that does not mean that universities are not important places of innovation, as discussed hereabove with startups. Moreover, many of the medical doctors are persons working at university hospitals, like Michel Mirowski, a doctor born in Poland who migrated to Israel and then to the US, where he conducted research on the pacemaker. Though a medical doctor, he worked at Johns Hopkins University and applied for a total of 12 patents during the 1980s. The adoption of the Bayh-Dole Act resulted in a growing number of university professors applying for patents. Harrith M. Hasson, professor of medicine at the University of Chicago; Eric R. Cosman, professor of physics at the MIT; and Albert Macovski, professor of electrical engineering at Stanford University, were among the largest individual innovators in the 1980s. Entrepreneur surgeons are also worth mentioning, as they were quite numerous in the US relative to

[10] https://startups.universityofcalifornia.edu/#map (accessed 18 September 2020).

other countries. Peter J. Wilk, a surgeon in New York City and manager of an IP business (Wild Patent Management Corporation), individually applied for 79 patents during the 1990s. One remaining point of discussion is the way these medical entrepreneurs cooperated with medtech firms and were able to sell their innovations. A database of patents does not allow for the analysis of this issue, which should be undertaken as a qualitative analysis in further research. The extant literature suggests that some of them created their own companies to manufacture and distribute their innovations, while others sold their innovations to large companies (Chatterji & Fabrizio, 2007; Gelijns & Thier, 2002; Grossman, 2006). A general analysis of this phenomenon and its evolution over time is still to be performed. Finally, a constant decline is shown for engineers (including technicians and mechanics) followed by a rebirth in the 1990s. There was, however, a major change, as the first generation of engineers were mostly owners of small enterprises themselves, like Ernest C. Wood, a mechanist in Los Angeles who applied for eleven patents in the 1960s and 1970s for instruments codeveloped with the surgeon Peter B. Samuels. However, since the 1990s, engineers have tended to work for large corporations. For example, in the 2000s, the top 20 individual assignees included a total of at least 11 engineers working for Boston Scientific, Coridien, Ethicon, Siemens USA, St. Jude and Warsaw, and five other engineers working as independent inventors or heading their own startup.

6 The Competitive Advantage of General Electric

General Electric (GE) is currently one of the largest medtech companies in the world. The roots of its competitive advantage in healthcare business go back to the development of X-ray technology in the early twentieth century. GE developed the Coolidge X-ray tube in 1917, which became a benchmark for the use of radiological technology in medicine. Three years later it acquired an important stake in Victor X-Ray Corporation, a small manufacturer founded in Chicago in 1895 that became a GE partner on the American market. It was fully acquired in the following years and renamed GE X-Ray Corporation in 1930 (Janssen & Medford, 2009). Outside the US, GE expanded through licensing agreements and direct investments, such as in other fields of the electric appliance industry (Donzé & Wubs, 2019).

GE X-Ray Corporation was integrated into GE as one of approximately 120 departments of the conglomerate in 1951. The X-ray department encountered rapid growth driven by technological innovation, particularly in radiotherapy (e.g., cobalt therapy systems). However, it essentially depended on the domestic market. In 1961, export represented only 30% of X-ray equipment sales.[11] There were also some attempts to diversify to other fields of medical business through the application of GE's knowledge to healthcare. For example, GE Electronics Laboratory collaborated with the cardiac surgeon Dr. Adrian Kantrowitz to codevelop an implantable heart stimulator. The technology was then transferred to the GE X-ray department in 1961 for further development and marketing. The following year, this department launched the development electronic patient monitoring equipment. However, these new businesses did not grow as expected and GE withdraw from both, in 1976 and 1982, respectively (Janssen & Medford, 2009). The company did not publish detailed data about the X-Ray department at that time, and it is therefore difficult to correctly evaluate the failure of its diversification. The sales of GE Medical Systems (GEMS) amounted to approximately 250 million dollars in 1973, which represents approximately 2.1% of gross sales.[12] Therefore, this was not seen as an important business for GE.

The core competence GEMS relied in medical imaging and the company showed a keen interest for developing and manufacturing CT scanners and IRM, under the direction of Jack Welch who was entrusted with the management of this department in 1973 (Tichy & Sherman, 1993, p. 65). A CT scanner was first installed in 1976 at University of California, San Francisco School of Medicine (Tichy & Sherman, 1993, p. 315). Patent applications in medtech emphasize the technological leadership taken by GE in the 1970s (see Table 4.1). It became the largest American innovator in this industry. This dominant position as a producer of the CT scanner was strengthened by the development of IRM devices, the first one being marketed in 1982. Sales of GEMS reached one billion dollars in the early 1980s.[13]

The 1980s was a turning point in the globalization of GEMS. The company made several acquisitions that transformed it from an American to a global manufacturer. First, in 1980, it took over the offshore assets of the British company Thorn EMI's CT scanner business. It provided an extension of the sales network and a manufacturing plant out of the

[11] Taniguchi Collection, World Market Opportunities, 1961.

[12] Taniguchi Collection, Vol. 65, untitled business magazine, Winter 1981.

[13] Ibidem.

Table 4.1 Top 10 largest American firms by patent-application count in the medtech industry, 1960–2014

1960–1969	*1970–1979*	*1980–1989*	*1990–1999*	*2000–2009*	*2010–2014*
ETHICON (45)	GE (119)	GE (304)	GE (795)	GE (3819)	*COVIDIEN (1525)*
AMERICAN OPTICAL (41)	*AMERICAN OPTICAL (91)*	*ETHICON (130)*	*ETHICON (551)*	*ETHICON (1134)*	GE (1512)
GE (37)	*KENDALL (74)*	*PICKER (99)*	*UNITED STATES SURGICAL CO. (443)*	*COVIDIEN (1100)*	*BOSTON SCIENTIFIC (616)*
BECTON, DICKINSON & CO. (28)	*ETHICON (68)*	*UNITED STATES SURGICAL CO. (91)*	*MEDTRONIC (255)*	*MEDTRONIC (1074)*	*ETHICON (594)*
BECKMAN COULTER (27)	*BECTON, DICKINSON & CO. (67)*	3M (85)	HP (211)	SIEMENS (594)	*MEDTRONIC (509)*
WESTINGHOUSE (24)	*AMERICAN HOSPITAL SUPPLY CO. (62)*	*BECTON, DICKINSON & CO. (80)*	*SMITH & NEPHEW (177)*	*DEPUY (562)*	*COOK MEDICAL (374)*
PARKE, DAVIS & CO. (23)	JOHNSON & JOHNSON (52)	HP (76)	*BECTON, DICKINSON & CO. (165)*	*WARSAW ORTHOPEDIC (549)*	*WARSAW ORHTOPEDIC (325)*
AMERICAN CYSTOSCOPE (22)	3M (44)	BAXTER (71)	SIEMENS (152)	*BOSTON SCIENTIFIC (510)*	*DEPUY SYNTHES (294)*
BAUSCH & LOMB (21)	*PICKER (42)*	*C.R. BARD (58)*	3M (146)	*CARDIAC PACEMAKERS (418)*	*VOLCANO (238)*
JOHNSON & JOHNSON (21)	BAXTER (39)	*CORDIS (55)*	JOHNSON & JOHNSON (136)	*ZIMMER (352)*	SIEMENS (215)

Source: PATSTAT

Notes: (1) Numbers in parentheses correspond to numbers of patent applications. (2) Italic text represent specialized US medtech companies

US. Second, in 1982, GE founded a joint venture in Japan with the electric appliance manufacturer Yokogawa Electric, which had been the local importer of GE's CT scanners and X-ray devices since 1976. Japan was the second largest market in the world for medical imaging, but GE had to face intense local competition by companies such as Hitachi, Shimadzu and Toshiba, which had *"products that challenged the partnership [with Yokogawa]. Designed specifically for the Japanese market, those products were smaller, less expensive to operate and cheaper to buy."*[14] Hence, the role of Yokogawa changed from a distributor of GE goods to a codeveloper of new products (such as the CT Max System in 1986), which were then sold to other countries, including small American hospitals and clinics. Third, in 1987, GE acquired Compagnie Générale de Radiologie (CGR), a French company that had a strong position in Europe and Latin America (Tichy & Sherman, 1993, p. 220). GEMS was therefore reorganized around three poles: US (high-end CT scanners and MRI equipment), France (X-ray systems) and Japan (mid-priced CT scanners).

This globalization of production was accompanied by the expansion of the sales network. GE founded a joint venture with Samsung in South Korea (1984), acquired GEC's medical equipment sales and services in the UK (1989), set up another joint venture with Wipro in India (1989), opened GE Hangwei Medical Systems in China (1991), and took a majority stake in Vniiem, a company based in Moscow, to assemble and distribute CT scanners in Russia.[15] The share of GEMS foreign sales grew from less than 15% in 1985 to 50% in 1988 (Tichy & Sherman, 1993, p. 323).

In the mid-1990s, GEMS (renamed GE Healthcare in 2005) adopted a new strategy characterized by the diversification to other fields of medtech business, in particular to medical services (electronic medical record) and molecular diagnosis. This shift was realized through intense M&A activity to internalize new technology and access specific markets. GEMS took over 94 firms or a division of firms between 1995 and 2017, 32 of which were outside the US (Europe, Asia and Latin America). However, in-house R&D also supported the development of GE. In the 2000s, it maintained its position as the largest American patent assignee, with more than 3800 applications related to medtech during the decade, and was overcome only by Ethicon for few patents in the period 2010–2014 (see Table 6.1).

[14] Ibidem.

[15] General Electric, Annual Report, 1986–1991.

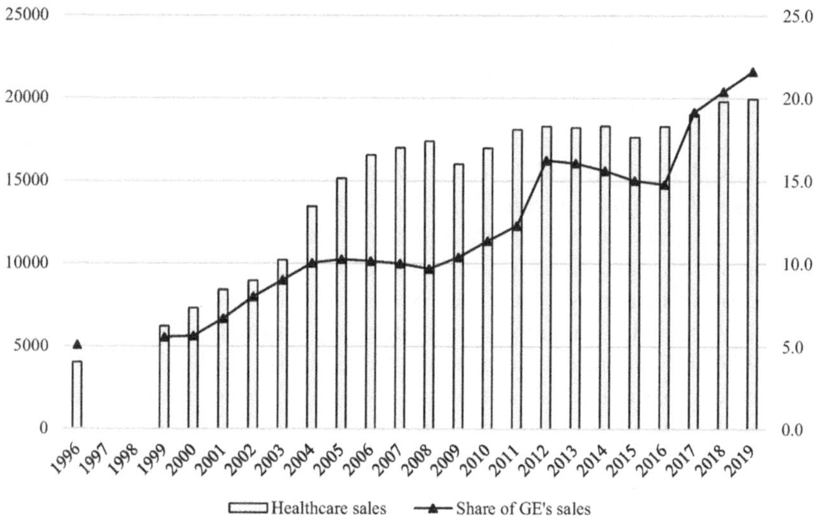

Fig. 4.5 General Electric, healthcare sales in millions and as a % of gross sales, 1996–2019. (Source: GE, annual reports, 1999–2019. Note: Sales of this division are not disclosed before 1999. The value for 1996 is taken from a mention in 2007 annual report)

The financial results of this strategic change are known in detail (see Fig. 4.5). Gross sales made an impressive development for ten years, increasing from 4 billion dollars in 1996 to 16.6 billion in 2006. This decade was followed by a phase of slower growth until a peak at 19.9 billion in 2019. Moreover, healthcare business maintained high profitability. Net earnings of this division represented an average of 17.4% of gross sales between 2000 and 2019 and have never been negative, even during the GFC. In comparison, the net earnings of GE as a whole only had an average of 6.5% during the same period, including four negative years (2015 and 2017–2019). Medtech has become one of GE's most important divisions over the last two decades.

7 The Formation of American Medtech Giants

Although GE maintained its dominant position in the American medical appliance industry throughout the twentieth century, it was challenged and overcome by companies with a different background. Three major types of newcomers were established as leading firms of the medtech industry in the early twenty-first century: specialized medtech firms that maintained a focus on their core competence, specialized medtech firms that diversified through M&As, and pharmaceutical companies that entered medtech business. The next section discusses the first and second types of newcomers, and the third type is analyzed in the section following.

7.1 Specialized Giants: Zimmer Biomet

Growth focused on the core competences of the company enabled the establishment of a handful of American firms among the world's largest medtech firms. This is particularly the case for Zimmer Biomet in orthopedic appliances and implants, and St. Jude Medical in cardiovascular surgery. This section addresses the example of Zimmer Biomet.

This company has its origins in a small company specialized in the manufacture of splints, which was founded in Warsaw, Indiana, in 1927 by a sales manager of the orthopedic appliance company DePuy (IDCH, 2002). Zimmer Manufacturing developed steadily, marketing the hip prothesis developed by Dr. Palmer Eicher in the 1950s, and launching various new orthopedic appliances. Sales amounted to 2 million dollars in 1951, 4 million in 1960 and 27.2 million in 1970. It was a successful and promising medium-size company, employing more than 500 people in 1970. It was taken over in 1972 by the American company Bristol-Myers, a large pharmaceutical and cosmetics group that started diversifying to medical devices, as did several other companies of this sector at that time (see Sect. 8).[16] Although integrated within a large firm with sales of approximately one billion dollars, Zimmer did not completely lose its autonomy, likely because its business was very specific within Bristol-Myers. It became a subsidiary of this group and benefited from resources provided by its new owner (particularly capital) to continue its development. It employed more than 2000 staff in the early 1990s and was a leader in the market for hip and knee prosthesis.[17] It therefore experienced rapid growth in the 1990s, driven by in-house innovations (the number of patent applications by the subsidiary Zimmer increased from 18 in the 1980s to 68 in the 1990s) and the acquisitions of several companies such as S&G Implants (1990) and Orthoplant (1991) in Germany, where it

[16] *New York Times*, 28 August 1971.
[17] *New York Times*, 18 September 1994.

reached 1 billion dollars in sales in 2000. The financial conditions of the company were very strong, with an 25.7% operating profit in 2000, and the potential for growth was excellent, particularly considering the aging population. However, Zimmer was overfocused on North America (63% of sales in 2000).[18]

Consequently, Zimmer was spun off and listed at New York Stock Exchange in 2001. The capital provided by such an operation made it possible to expand internationally by taking over numerous firms. It acquired a total of 30 companies between 2002 and 2016, 13 of which were outside the US. The most important were the Swiss company Centerpulse AG (former Sulzer Medica; 2003) and the American firm Biomet (2014), both of which were major producers of orthopedic appliances. Zimmer also purchased companies specialized in the distribution of medical devices in China (2010), Denmark (2011), and the Czech Republic (2015) to strengthen its expansion into foreign markets. While sales grew to 4.2 billion dollars in 2010 and 8 billion in 2019, North America's share declined steadily but remained high (61% in 2019). Therefore, the firm remains strongly dependent on its domestic market, which is also the largest in the world. Moreover, one must stress that M&A was not used to diversify to new fields and to establish the firm as a general medtech company. Still today, Zimmer Biomet remains focused on technologies and devices broadly related to orthopedics, claiming it is *"a global leader in musculoskeletal healthcare."*[19]

7.2 *The "world's most diversified health care company":[20] Johnson & Johnson*

Johnson & Johnson (J&J) was founded in 1886 as a firm specialized in the manufacture and distribution of healthcare supplies, notably band-aids and antiseptic materials. It soon became a global leader in these product types and opened subsidiaries in Canada (1919) and the UK (1924) to expand its markets. The core competences acquired in antiseptic supplies for surgeons led J&J to develop new technologies and devices for sutures (IDCH, 2001a). In 1947, the company acquired a small Scottish company specialized in the development of catgut and suture products, and

[18] Zimmer, Annual Report, 2002.

[19] Zimmer Biomet, Annual Report, 2019, p. 4.

[20] Slogan adopted by Johnson & Johnson in the early 1980s.

merged it with its own division specialized in this business, giving birth to a new subsidiary: Ethicon (IDCH, 1998).

The diversification of J&J towards medical devices began with this company. In the 1950s, it cooperated with High Voltage Engineering Co. to develop electronics devices for sutures and expanded in the following years toward related fields such as sterilization equipment and closing-surgical instruments. In the 1970s, it was the uncontested leader in this market in the US and contributed greatly to J&J's development. J&J had also diversified to pharmaceuticals in the 1950s through the acquisition of other firms and experienced rapid expansion worldwide (Foster, 1986). However, in the 1970s, medtech (including the subsidiary Ethicon) maintained a stable share of 31.9% of the gross sales of the group (see Fig. 4.6).

A second diversification phase to a broad range of activities (through M&As) occurred in the period 1975–1985. This represented an opportunity for J&J to strengthen its position in medtech business with various

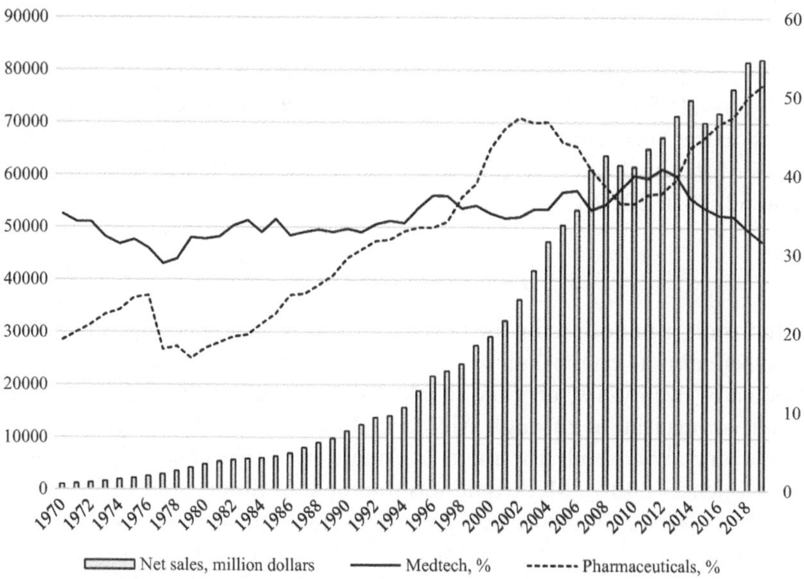

Fig. 4.6 Johnson & Johnson, net sales in millions, 1970–2019. (Source: Annual reports. Note: Lack of precise data for each division before 1970)

acquisitions in new fields, such as the manufacturer of surgical instruments Codman and Surgikos, the monitoring device-maker Critikon, the ophthalmic instrument producer Iolab, Ortho Diagnostic Systems, and the maker of products for laser surgery Xanar. The internalization of various capabilities also enabled J&J to launch during this period its own cardiovascular devices, orthopedic equipment and dental products. According to Christensen and Raynor (2013), this strategy to acquire disruptive companies, mostly small and specialized firms, enabled J&J to avoid the "innovator dilemma" faced by most large companies that focus predominantly on in-house incremental innovation.

In the 1990s, J&J entered a phase of rapid expansion, with gross sales increasing from 11.2 billion dollars in 1990 to 82 billion in 2019. Although the company operated a strategic shift toward pharmaceuticals during this period (29.4% of gross sales in 1990 and 51.4% in 2019), the share of medtech also grew steadily until a peak at 40% of its gross sales until 2012–2013, before declining to 31.1% in 2019—but maintaining a stable value at an average of 22.2 billion dollars in the period 2013–2019. The growth of medtech relied on three major elements: in-house R&D (with its subsidiary Ethicon, J&J was consistently the second largest applier of medtech patents after GE between the 1980s and 2000s, and after Covidien in the period 2010–2014, see Table 6.1); M&As (J&J realized a total of 80 acquisitions in the period 1990–2017, 20 of which were outside the US); and the expansion of overseas sales (the share of foreign sales of the medtech division grew from 37.5% in 1975 to 47% in 1990 and 52.3% in 2019).

7.3 *Diversified Giants: Medtronic*

Medtronic is undoubtedly the best example of a small specialized firm that succeeded in its establishment as the world's largest medtech company in the early twenty-first century thanks to a strategy of diversification and internationalization through M&As (IDCH, 1995). The beginnings of this company embody the myth of American entrepreneurship explored by Godelier (2007). Medtronic was founded in Minneapolis in 1949 as a repair workshop for medical equipment by a student in electrical engineering, Earl Bakken, and his brother-in-law. Bakken co-developed a broad range of instruments with medical doctors during the 1950s. One of them was a pacemaker, developed in 1957 for Dr. C. Walton Lillehei, a pioneer in heart surgery. Moreover, in 1960, Medtronic purchased the exclusive rights to produce and sell the first implantable pacemaker developed by Wilson Greatbatch and Dr. William Chardack.

Medtronic was established as the world leader in pacemaker manufacturing. However, the company was small. It focused on R&D, constantly improving its pacemakers and its sales in the US and Canada. It contracted Picker International, an American manufacturer of X-ray equipment, which had a worldwide distribution network, and in turn took charge of its foreign sales until 1969. Medtronic experienced rapid development, with its net sales increasing from 180,000 dollars in 1960 to 32.9 million in 1971. The growth continued during the 1970s largely due to the manufacturing of pacemakers. Medtronic entered the New York Stock Exchange in 1977. In 1980, sales amounted to 270 million dollars, 37% of which was realized abroad, mostly in Europe. Although it began to diversify with its opening of neurological (1976) and heart valve (1977) divisions, Medtronic's competitiveness was based on pacemakers—in 1980, they represented 86% of sales.[21]

During the following decades, the growth of the company occurred in two main phases (see Fig. 4.7). First, Medtronic adopted a strategy of related diversification during the 1980s and 1990s by moving from pacemakers to cardiovascular devices. Developing technology related to the heart was the core competence of the company. Although sales grew very quickly (to 865 million dollars in 1980 and 5 billion in 2000), pacemakers still represented two thirds of the business in the mid-1990s. The last figure published in annual reports was 65.6% of sales in 1997. As for the cardiac and vascular division (including pacemakers), it represented 87.5% of sales in 1992 and 75% in 2000. The division experienced a slight decline but remained core to the company. The development of Medtronic was particularly based on the acquisition of companies: 11 were taken over in the 1980s and 31 in the 1990s, 10 and 28 of which, respectively, were headquartered in the US. However, despite R&D being focused in the US, foreign sales amounted to more than 40% in the period 1992–1997, before decreasing to 34.6% in 2000.

Second, after 2000, Medtronic adopted an aggressive strategy of unrelated diversification within the medtech industry and established itself as a general medtech company. The shift from pacemaker development to a

[21] Medtronic, Annual Report, 1980.

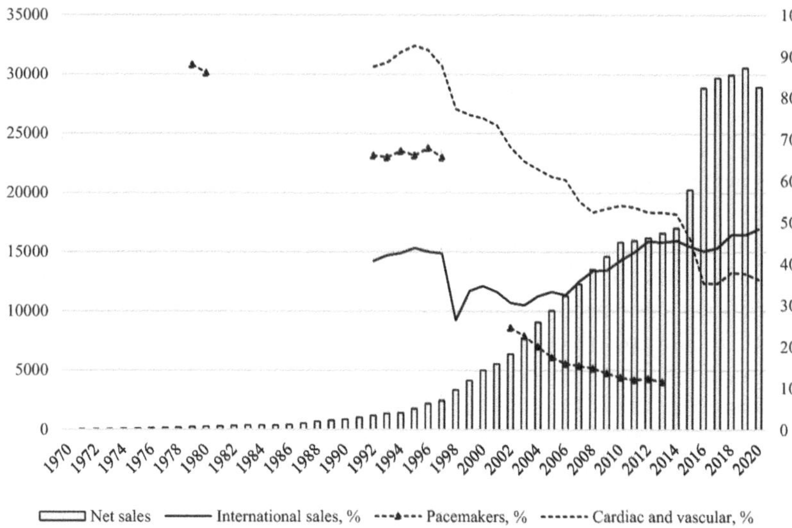

Fig. 4.7 Medtronic, net sales in millions, 1971–2020. (Source: Medtronic, annual reports, 1971–2020)

broad range of equipment necessary for cardiac surgery had enabled the company to acquire knowledge for the management of hospital services. This became a new source of growth. The other strategical objective was to gain a dominant position in merging countries. R&D and M&A were the tools used for this move. Medtronic became one of America's most innovative medtech companies in the 1990s (see Table 6.1). As explained in 2010 by Jean-Luc Butel, the head of international business of Medtronic, the development of new products is necessary; therefore, half of all gross sales came from products that did not exist two years prior.[22] Medtronic also established a capital-risk foundation, MD Start, with venture capital firms, toward financing the co-development of new devices together with medical doctors.[23] Moreover, Medtronic acquired a total of 76 firms in the period 2000–2016, 24 of which were outside the US. In particular, Medtronic purchased three companies in China, one in Turkey

[22] *L'Agefi*, 14 June 2010.

[23] https://www.mdstart.eu/ (accessed 28 October 2020).

and one in South Africa. The share of international sales grew to nearly half of all sales in 2020.

The result of these actions is impressive growth, with a peak of net sales at 30.6 billion dollars in 2019, before a slight decline in the 2020 fiscal year due to the COVID-19 crisis. Medtronic moved out of its initial core competence. The share of pacemakers dropped to 11.5% of sales in 2013 and is not mentioned separately in following annual reports. As for the cardiac and vascular division, it also declined to 54.1% in 2010 and 36.2% in 2020. The new divisions were also developed through the acquisition of other specialized companies, like the spinal care company Sofamor Danek Group (1999), the manufacturer of diabetes management systems MiniMed (2001), and especially Covidien, a general medtech company and one of the largest companies in this industry worldwide (2015).[24] The takeover of Covidien made Medtronic number one in the global medtech industry.

The development path followed by Medtronic, from an American startup to a global medtech firm, can also be observed in other large medtech firms in the US. This is particularly the case for Boston Scientific and Stryker. Other diversified medtech giants also emerged from small companies focused on distribution and sales rather than innovative start-ups, such as Becton, Dickinson & Co., or Cardinal Health. The process of growth, however, was similar, with development based on the takeover of small specialized firms to enable diversification and internationalization.

8 From Pharma to Medtech

Although drugs and medical devices belong to healthcare and share a similar market, most American pharmaceutical companies did not actively diversify to medtech. Among the 10 largest pharmaceutical firms based in the US in 2020, J&J was the only one to also be engaged in medtech.[25] Moreover, its presence in both fields results from a diversification process that occurred at the same time (see hereabove, pp. 84–86). Bristol Myers Squibb, Eli Lilly, Gilead Science, Merck, Pfizer and others maintained a focus on drugs and medicine. Several of these attempted some diversification but ultimately returned to their core competences.

[24] https://www.medtronic.com/us-en/about/history.html (accessed 28 October 2020).
[25] https://fortune.com/fortune500/2020 (accessed on 10 November 2020).

Abbott Laboratories is an excellent example of the diversification to medtech attempted by American pharmaceutical firms. The company's origins date back to the late 1880s, when a physician from Chicago, Dr. Wallace Cavin Abbott, began to manufacture and sell his own medication (IDCH, 2001a). He gathered capital from other doctors and founded Abbott Alkaloidal Company in 1900, renamed Abbott Laboratories in 1910. It developed as a successful American drug company over the years on the basis of in-house R&D and the takeover of several other laboratories beginning from the 1960s. It became a generalist pharmaceutical company, with sales growing from 120 million dollars in 1960 to 2 billion in 1980.[26] The first diversification to medical devices began with a launch into diagnosis and monitoring equipment developed in the 1970s. In 1970, Abbott founded a new subsidiary, Abbott Medical Electronics Co., a joint venture with SCI Systems, to develop electronic monitoring devices. It also acquired Sorenson Research Co., a small firm specialized in hemodynamic monitoring (1980), and developed a blood analyzer, an instrument that enabled Abbott to become the first company to market a diagnostic test for AIDS and hepatitis (1985). These devices soon became a hit for Abbott. The hospital group, which gathers various surgical supplies, testing devices and monitoring equipment, increased from 112 million dollars in 1970 (24.5% of total net sales) to 848 million in 1980 (41.6%) and 3 billion in 1990 (48.7%). After 2000, the medtech division diversified to a broad range of new fields, from pacemakers to brain simulation systems. Although the numerous changes concerning segment category outlined in annual reports make it difficult to gain a clear view of the recent development of the medtech division, sales outside pharmaceuticals and nutritionals expanded rapidly and recently became the largest segment of Abbott, increasing from 4 billion dollars in 2005 (17.9% of total net sales) to 7.4 billion in 2015 (36.5%) and 20 billion in 2019 (62.5%). This shift essentially resulted from the acquisition of numerous companies in the twenty-first century (21 acquisitions in the 1990s and 43 in the period 2000–2015) and from the spin-off of research-based pharmaceutical business in a new company, listed on the New York Stock Exchange, AbbVie Inc. (2011). Nowadays, it is one the largest pharmaceutical companies in the US. Since that year, Abbott has focused on medtech, nutrition and generic drugs.[27]

[26] Abbott Laboratories, Annual Report, 1960 and 1980.

[27] AbbVie, Annual Report, 2012.

A similar development path was followed by Bristol Myers (IDCH, 2001b). This pharmaceutical firm founded in 1887 diversified in the 1970s toward medical devices through the takeover of the orthopedic appliance manufacturer Zimmer (1972) and the dental equipment producer Unitek (1978). The share of medical devices was limited (13.9% of net sales in 1990), but the company announced its decision to refocus on pharmaceuticals in 2000.[28]

A rare example of a pharmaceutical company that engaged durably in medtech is Baxter; however, it lost its competitive advantage as a pharmaceutical firm and changed its core competence (Cody, 1990). Baxter was founded in 1931 as a pharmaceutical company specialized in the manufacturing and sales of intravenous therapy solutions. The interest for medical devices dates back to the mid-1950s, with the development of an artificial kidney and the launch in renal services for hospitals. It was therefore a related diversification from blood solutions. Baxter then expanded its expertise and developed various devices and supplies for transfusion. The acquisition of a handful of specialized medtech firms, such as American Instruments (1969) and Surgitool (1970), supported this diversification. Consequently, the medical specialties division, which gathers non-pharmaceutical goods, experienced rapid development—in 1975, it represented 45% of net sales.[29] It then strengthened its position in medtech with the takeover of American Hospital Company in 1985. Since then, Baxter has developed as a general healthcare company engaged in pharmaceuticals, hospital services (including monitoring and transfusion equipment) and medical devices. While the net sales of the company increased from 2.8 billion in 1991 to 11.1 billion in 2018, the share of non-pharmaceutical divisions grew from 74.2% to 81.2%.

The absence of American pharmaceutical companies in medtech business results from the specificities of the drug industry, particularly the large investments in R&D that have led to a deep consolidation of this sector since the 1990s (Chandler, 2009). All resources of pharmaceutical firms are focused on the development of new drugs and vaccines. Most of these have consequently divested from other businesses (Bristol Myers

[28] Bristol Myers Squibb, Annual Report, 1990 and 2000.

[29] Baxter Laboratories, Annual Report, 1975. Data for previous year does not separate medical devices and pharmaceuticals.

Squibb) or turned their pharmaceutical division into a spin-off (Abbott). The situation is similar in other countries, the Swiss company Roche being an exception, with its business in diagnostic equipment (see Chap. 7).

9 Conclusion

The objective of this chapter was to explore how American medtech companies have been able to build a competitive advantage since the 1960s, which in turn has supported their strong domination in the medtech industry globally. The analysis of production, trade, M&A and patent statistics, as well as case studies, made the emphasis of three main factors possible.

First, one must stress the importance of the domestic market. The US not only constitutes the world's largest healthcare market but is also characterized by rapid growth and development. Healthcare expenditure increased from 27.3 billion dollars in 1960 (5.2% of GDP) to 2486 billion in 2009 (17.6% of GDP; Folland et al., 2013). Although medical devices represent only a tiny share of this market (according to Donahoe, 2018, approximately 6% between the1980s and 1990s), the impressive development of healthcare expenditure represented an opportunity for most American medtech companies. They grew in their national market before expanding internationally, predominantly since the 1990s.

Second, medtech firms benefit from a favorable environment regarding innovation. The Bayh-Dole Act, adopted in 1980, was a major step in encouraging universities and companies to market the research results. Government funding, particularly through large-scale projects, developed rapidly in the 1980s. In 1985, federal support for health R&D amounted to nearly 7 billion dollars (Bartlett Foote, 1992, p. 59). For many firms, the development of new medical technology was an opportunity for them to diversify, shifting away from being specialized to becoming general medtech groups. Diversification occurred in a two-stage process (related diversification followed by unrelated diversification).

Third, the presence of a well-developed capital market is another important factor. As M&A was a major way to grow, many medtech firms went public and accumulated external capital to be able to acquire companies, not only in the US but also abroad. The formation of global medtech giants was directly supported by the capital market. This is particularly the case for startup companies, which undertook innovative projects and contributed to the diversification and renewal of the American medtech industry. The existence of a broadly developed venture capital market encouraged the creation of hundreds of startups. According to the National Venture Capital Association (2015), total venture-capital investment in the American medtech industry grew from 184 million dollars in 1985 to 2.4 billion in 2000, and then reached a peak at 3.6 billion in 2008, before declining after the GFC (2.6 billion in 2014). Between 1985 and 2014, a total of 273 medtech companies backed by venture capital went public and 407 were acquired.

Medtech giants were therefore formed in the US on the basis of these three factors. Since the 1980s, the acquisition of innovative startups and small companies led to the formation of diversified conglomerates. Their large domestic basis enabled them to become large companies, where they then reorganized themselves as global organizations through the takeover of firms and relocation to specific countries such as China, Ireland and Mexico. General Electric (GE) represents the first move into global reorganization, but this example has been followed by all major American medtech companies since the 1990s.

References

Other Published Sources

Donahoe, G. (2018). *Estimates of Medical Device Spending in the United States.* Advanced Medical Technology Association. Retrieved June 20, 2020, from https://www.advamed.org/sites/default/files/resource/estimates_of_medical_device_spending_in_the_united_states_november_2018.pdf

IDCH. (1998). Ethicon. *International Directory of Company Histories, 23.* St. James Press, 1998, pp. 188–190.

IDCH. (1999a). Steris Corporation. *International Directory of Company Histories, 29.* St. James Press, 1999, pp. 449–451.

IDCH. (1999b). Strkyer Corporation. *International Directory of Company Histories, 29.* St. James Press, pp. 453–455.

IDCH. (2001a). Johnson & Johnson. *International Directory of Company Histories, 36.* St. James Press, 2001, pp. 302–307.

IDCH. (2001b). Bristol Myers Squibb. *International Directory of Company Histories, 37.* St. James Press, 2001, pp. 41–43.

IDCH. (2002). Zimmer Holdings. *International Directory of Company Histories, 45.* St. James Press, pp. 455–457.

National Venture Capital Association. (2015). *Yearbook 2015.*

Radiology. (1930). Westinghouse Forms X-Ray Company. *Radiology, 15*(3), 402–403.

USITC. (1981). *Automative trade statistics, 1964–1980.* USITC. Retrieved September 2, 2020, from https://www.usitc.gov/publications/332/pub1203.pdf

Books and Academic Articles

Aldridge, T. T., & Audretsch, D. (2011). The Bayh-Dole Act and Scientist Entrepreneurship. *Research Policy, 40*, 1058–1067.

Chandler, A. D. (2009). *Shaping the Industrial Century: The Remarkable Story of the Evolution of the Modern Chemical and Pharmaceutical Industries.* Harvard University Press.

Chatterji, A. K., & Fabrizio, K. (2007). *Professional Users as a Source of Innovation: The Role of Physician Innovation in the Medical Device Industry.* Working Paper, Duke University, https://faculty.fuqua.duke.edu/~ronnie/bio/Chatterji Fabrizio_July2nd.pdf

Christensen, C., & Raynor, M. (2013). *The innovator's solution: Creating and sustaining successful growth.* Harvard Business Review Press.

Cody, T. G. (1990). *Strategy of a Megamerger: An Insider's Account of the Baxter Travenol-American Hospital Supply Combination.* Quorum Books.

Donzé, P. Y., & Wubs, B. (2019). Global Competition and Cooperation in the Electronics Industry: The Case of X-ray Equipment, 1900–1970. *Scandinavian Economic History Review, 67*(2), 210–225.

Fennelly, D., & Cormican, K. (2006). Value Chain Migration from Production to Product Centred Operations: An Analysis of the Irish Medical Device Industry. *Technovation, 26*(1), 86–94.

Folland, S., Goodman, A., & Stano, M. (2013). *The Economics of Health and Health Care.* Pearson.

Foote, S. B. (1992). *Managing the Medical Arms Race: Public Policy and Medical Device Innovation.* University of California Press.

Foster, L. G. (1986). *A Company That Cares: One Hundred Years Illustrated History of Johnson & Johnson.* Johnson & Johnson.

Gelijns, A. C., & Thier, S. O. (2002). Medical Innovation and Institutional Interdependence: Rethinking University-Industry Connections. *Jama, 287*(1), 72–77.

Godelier, E. (2007). "Do You Have a Garage?" Discussion of Some Myths about Entrepreneurship. *Business and Economic History On-line*, vol. 5, https://thebhc.org/sites/default/files/godelier_0.pdf

Grossman, J. S. (2006). *Innovative Doctoring: Solutions Lie Within Us.* Innovative Doctoring.

IDCH. (2005). *Medtronic. International Directory of Company Histories*, 67. St. James Press, 2005, pp. 252–254.

Janssen, L., & Medford, G. (2009). *Envision: A History of the GE Healthcare Business*. Meadow Brook Farm.

Mowery, D. C., Nelson, R. R., Sampat, B. N., & Ziedonis, A. A. (2001). The Growth of Patenting and Licensing by US Universities: An Assessment of the Effects of the Bayh–Dole Act of 1980. *Research Policy*, *30*(1), 99–119.

Palermo, A. (1995). A Legacy of Caring-the History of Picker International. *GEC Review*, *10*(2), 103–119.

Rodengen, J. L. (2001). *The Ship in the Balloon: The Story of Boston Scientific and the Development of Less-Invasive Medicine*. Write Stuff Enterprises.

Tichy, N. M., & Sherman, S. (1993). *Control Your Destiny or Someone Else Will: Lessons in Mastering Change – The Principles Jack Welch Is Using to Revolutionize General Electric*. Doubleday.

CHAPTER 5

Japan: From Electronics to Medical Technology

1 Introduction

Japan represents one of the world's largest healthcare markets and is currently the home of some of the most important medtech companies. Unlike the US, however, which experienced the emergence and rapid growth of numerous medtech companies (e.g., Medtronic and Boston Scientific) during the final decades of the twentieth century, the Japanese medtech industry is structurally very stable. Several large multinational enterprises in the electronics industry (e.g., Hitachi, Panasonic and Toshiba) and specialized medical companies (e.g., Olympus and Terumo) have maintained their dominance in the market over time. Another important feature of the Japanese medtech industry is the minimal presence of foreign companies, which access the Japanese market through export but rarely invest directly in research and production—unlike in Western Europe. This restraint is a consequence of the specificities of the Japanese hospital system, which has a large number of small, private hospitals. Indeed, this is a major characteristic of the Japanese healthcare market compared with others worldwide. The Western hospital system, for example, comprises a lower number of large (often public) hospitals. Unlike in Western countries, the Japanese Government has not intervened to organize the hospital system, nor has it concentrated high-tech equipment in only a few establishments (Donzé, 2018b). In 2000, there were 73 hospitals per one million persons in Japan. This was far more than in Germany

P.-Y. Donzé, *Medtech*,
https://doi.org/10.1007/978-981-16-7174-6_5

(44.2), in the US (20.6) and in the Netherlands (13.1; OECD, 2018a). Moreover, due to competition between hospitals to attract patients, the hospitals usually attempt to acquire the latest technology (Ikegami, 2014). Independent doctors who work in private surgeries do the same. This competitiveness and the level of fragmentation within the Japanese hospital system represent driving forces for the diffusion of technology. In 2014, Japan had the highest density of magnetic resonance imaging (MRI) equipment. It was first, with 51.7 MRI machine per one million persons against 38.1 for the US, 30.5 for Germany and 12.9 for the Netherlands (OECD, 2018c). Simultaneously, however, the hospitals have less capital to invest in equipment compared with Western hospitals due to their smaller size. Therefore, it appears necessary to develop different equipment for the Japanese and Western markets. This difference represents a major obstacle to the development of foreign companies in the country. In the pre-war period, the ability for the co-development of medical equipment to occur with doctors increased the competitiveness of Japanese SMEs. Shimadzu, for example, was able to dominate the market for X-ray devices against the multinational Siemens during the interwar years (Donzé, 2018b). More generally, the manufacturers of medical instruments did not only import and copy products from Germany and the US but also adapted them to the needs of Japanese doctors and to the specificities inherent in the Japanese medical market (Donzé, 2016). After WWII, as I discuss in more detail below, General Electric (GE) was one exceptional case. In the mid-1980s, it co-developed a computed tomography (CT) scanner with Yokogawa Electrics to address a specific local demand. This knowledge enabled the US multinational to develop new markets going forward.

A second major characteristic of the Japanese medtech industry is the competitiveness of electronics companies in the field of diagnostic imaging devices (X-ray, CT scanners, and MRI), as emphasized by the foreign trade statistics for the global market (see Chap. 2). Japanese giants of the electronics industry, such as Toshiba and Hitachi, dominate the domestic market, together with several foreign companies such as GE and Siemens (Nishimura, 2010; Onuma, 2010). Electronics also represents the technology that enabled a convergence between an original business model outside of the medtech industry and the participation to this industry. Fujifilm, Omron, Panasonic, and Seiko Epson (among others) all diversified to medtech from another industry, and then established themselves as important players of the national medtech industry. The competitiveness of the electronics industry represented a benefit to the medtech. Similarly, another field of technological convergence was the optical industry, in which many companies like Hoya, Minolta and Olympus diversified to medtech in a process similar to that of some German firms such as Carl Zeiss. Finally, technological convergence explains the development of numerous specialized medtech SMEs, which was based on the exploitation of traditional know-how. For example, this is the case of the surgical needles producer Mani, a former metalworking workshop that became a world leader in syringes (Sakai, 2018).

The specificity of the national healthcare market, along with the technological convergence that acted as a major basis for development, enabled the formation and growth of the Japanese medtech industry in an environment that is highly protected. In such a context, however, the question arises regarding the capacity to innovate, particularly in terms of new technologies that are not directly related to existing ones (so-called disruptive innovations). Oshita and Ikeno (2016) argued that a major problem for medtech SMEs in Japan is that they are often neither the target of a merger by large companies, nor do they go public. In the US and in Western Europe, mergers and acquisitions (M&A) and initial public offerings (IPOs) represent important means to support the growth of medtech SMEs on the global market. In Japan, however, SME owners prefer to follow the traditional model of the gradual development of small and independent companies. Consequently, this chapter examines how the large, dominant medtech firms have been able to maintain their competitive advantage and expand internationally. More specifically, this chapter addresses the following questions:

1. Which firms embraced the opportunity to launch breakthrough innovations?
2. How have Japanese companies interacted with foreign firms?
3. How have Japanese universities supported the development of the medtech industry?

2 National Production and Foreign Trade

Along with the US, Japan is the second country to provide data on the national production of medical devices from a long-term perspective. As the various types of instruments and equipment used for medical purposes are included in different categories of the census of manufacturers and are not always available, the survey on pharmaceutical goods and medical devices published annually by the Ministry of Health, Labor and Welfare

(MHLW; *Yakuji kogyo seisan jotai tokei nenpo*) is used here. Moreover, this document provides data from 1984 on the foreign trade of medical devices that also includes the values between the various foreign trade statistical categories. It is therefore possible to illustrate the general development of Japan's medtech production and foreign trade over a longer period than is possible with the COMTRADE database, which is used in the other chapters (see Fig. 5.1).

First, Fig. 5.1 shows that the Japanese medical device industry experienced rapid growth during the 1970s and 1980s, which followed a decade of slow development. Specifically, total national production increased from 118.9 billion yen in 1970 to 1274.2 billion in 1990. These two decades constitute the heyday for X-ray machines, CT scanners and other medico-electric devices—that is, the fields in which Japanese firms were particularly competitive (see Chap. 2). For example, the share of X-ray devices increased from an average of 15.7% in the 1960s and 14.1% in the 1970s to a peak at 22.5% between 1989–1991. However, data for 1984 highlights that export represented only a small share of national

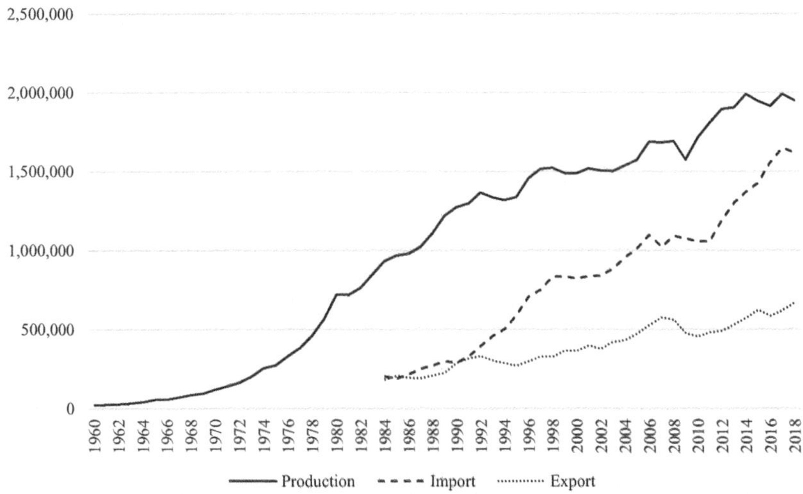

Fig. 5.1 Japanese production, import and export of medical devices in million yens, 1960–2018. (Source: MHLW, *Yakuji kogyo seisan jotai tokei nenpo*, 1960–2020. Note: Data for foreign trade prior to 1984 is not published in this document)

production (19.4%). The rapid growth of the Japanese hospital system during this period formed the main basis for the growth of the domestic medtech industry. The number of hospitals grew from 6094 in 1960 to 7974 in 1970, 9055 in 1980, before reaching an historical peak at 10,096 in 1990 (Japanese Historical Statistics, 24–28). This growth represents an excellent opportunity to sell a large number of medical devices. Japan therefore represents the country with the highest density of medical devices. For example, in 1999–2000, the number of CT scanners per million persons was 84.4 in Japan, 28.4 in South Korea, 25.1 in the US, 24.6 in Germany, 21 in Italy, 7 in France, and 5.4 in the UK (OECD, 2020).[1] Similarly, import was rather limited during the 1980s, where it represented an average of 22% of the domestic market between 1984–1989.[2]

The situation began to shift after 1990. The necessity to slow increasing health expenses together with the stagnation in population growth following 2000 led to a transformation of the hospital system characterized by a drop in the number of establishments (9266 in 2000 and 8372 in 2018; OECD, 2020). This meant a reduction in the number of customers for large equipment of approximately 20% between 1990 and 2018. Japanese companies had no choice but to expand into markets abroad. In the 1990s, however, export did not expand significantly, maintaining a mark of below 25% until 2000. Consequently, national medtech production entered a period of slower growth, with 1486.3 billion yen in 2000.

After 2000, Japanese medtech companies reoriented their businesses to foreign markets and experienced a new phase of development, reaching nearly 2000 billion yen in the period 2014–2018. Export played an increasingly important role, with 34.1% in 2007, and then declined during the global financial crisis (GFC) and Great Tohoku Earthquake (2011), before reaching beyond the 30% mark from 2015 onwards. Diagnostic imaging systems (22.8% of export in 2018), medical laboratory equipment (22.8%) and various types of treatment equipment (17.5%) represent the most important goods. The most important markets are the United States and China (MHLW, 2020).

The most striking feature of the Japanese medtech industry since 1990 has been the rapid growth in imports. The share of imports on the national medical device market has developed dramatically, from 22.7% in 1990 to

[1] Data is missing for many countries prior to 2000.

[2] The size of the domestic market is evaluated as production—export + import.

42.2% in 2000 and 55.8% in 2018. Since 2015, foreign goods have consistently represented more than half of the market. This growing dependence is not the result of the globalization of Japanese firms, unlike the case of American companies importing to the US from their subsidiaries in Mexico or Ireland (see Chap. 4). In particular, import comes from the US and represents the new competitiveness achieved by US firms in the fields of the application of information technology to medical devices and the new generations of medical imaging equipment. Bio-related robotic equipment (27.3% in 2018), various medical treatments (26.3%) and ophthalmic supplies (13.5%) constitute the most important goods.

The consequence of this strong dependence on the import of foreign (mostly American) devices led to the establishment in Japan of many foreign firm sales subsidiaries. The annual survey for the Japanese medical industry, which has been conducted by the service company R&D Co. since 1988, makes it possible to highlight the presence of foreign companies in specific areas of the medtech industry (R&D, 2014). In 2013, for example, foreign multinational enterprises dominated the market in terms of MRI equipment, which is representative of high-tech in this industry. In the same year, with 28.5% of sales, GE was first, followed by Siemens (27.9%) and Philips (17.2%). Another field dominated by foreign-owned companies is artificial implants, where the largest players in 2013 were Stryker (19.6%), Johnson & Johnson (17.3%), Zimmer (14.2%), Medtronic (8.7%) and Biomet (7.6%). However, in the general medtech industry, foreign companies were only secondary, with the notable exception of GE. Table 5.1 shows that the US multinational was the only company to fall within the top-10 largest manufacturers in 2012, where it was ranked fifth. In contrast, all major importers of medical devices were foreign companies established in Japan, mostly from the US. This clear divide expresses two different ways to carry out innovation and organize firms. Japanese companies focus on R&D in their country and, thus, do not import devices manufactured in their foreign plants. In terms of foreign companies, they are generally not engaged in R&D within Japan (see Sect. 4 below) but import their high-tech products to Japan.

Moreover, this feature of the contemporary medtech industry in Japan is not a new one. During the 1970s, with the exception of Hewlett Packard Yokogawa, no foreign company or joint venture with foreign capital applied for more than 5 patents. Similarly, in the 2000s, there were almost no foreign firms within the 385 companies that applied for at least 5

Table 5.1 Top 10 largest manufacturers and importers of medical devices in Japan in billion yen, 2012

Manufacturers	*Value*	*Importers*	*Value*
Toshiba Medical System	227.5	*Johnson & Johnson*	*200*
Terumo	246.2	*Philips Electronics Japan*	*83.2*
Olympus Medical System	192.4	*Siemens Japan*	*78.3*
Nipro	145	*Boston Scientific Japan*	*74.2*
GE Healthcare	*98.1*	*Nihon Alcon*	*61.7*
Panasonic Healthcare	98.1	*Nihon Medtronic*	*59.4*
Hitachi Medical	87.2	*Covidien Japan*	*58*
Sysmex	87.1	*Nihon Stryker*	*53.9*
Nihon Kohden	87.1	*St Jude Medical*	*45*
Nikkiso	72.1	*Nihon Becton Dickinson*	*33.4*

Source: R&D (2014)

Note: Foreign companies are shown in italic

patents, with the exception of GE Yokogawa, which was ranked 41st with 97 patents (PATSTAT).

The lack of engagement from Japanese companies can be explained by general factors regarding foreign direct investments (FDIs) in Japan and particular factors linked with the medtech industry—both being related. First, one must keep in mind that Japan is one of the most closed countries in the world for inward FDI (Mason, 1995; Hoshi, 2018). Regulation, the distinctiveness of the Japanese market and high costs have prevented many foreign firms from investing in Japan. Therefore, in 2017, Japan had the lowest level of inward FDI stock among OECD countries, where it amounted to only 4.1% of GDP, against 24.1% for China, 40.5% for the US and 57.4% for the EU (OECD, 2018b). Second, in the field of medical devices, Altenstetter (2014) demonstrated that particularly regulation—for example, the lack of recognition of foreign standards and trials by Japanese authorities—was a major obstacle for foreign company investment within Japan. Moreover, the characteristics of the Japanese medical market (e.g., strong competition between numerous small private hospitals) require companies to develop specific devices or to adapt their equipment. In the field of X-ray machines and MRI equipment, Japanese hospitals tend to purchase smaller, simpler, and cheaper products. For example, most acquire head unit CT scanners, while US hospitals purchase whole-body machines (Foote, 1992). However, light instruments and implants do not represent an investment in equipment for medical doctors and hospitals but, rather, consumer goods. Therefore, the structure of the Japanese medical market has a lower impact on their sales. This is undoubtedly the reason why the medical implant field is dominated by foreign firms.

3 Mergers and Acquisitions

The domination of innovation in the Japanese medtech industry by large companies since the 1960s and the relative absence of newcomers can be explained as the result of either in-house research and development (R&D) or M&A. To further discuss this issue, an examination of M&A in the Japanese medtech industry between 1985 and 2017 is provided in this section. This examination is based on the Thomson One database, which was accessed in April 2018. Notably, data related to M&A prior to 1985 is unavailable for Japanese firms.

Figure 5.2 shows the general evolution of M&A between 1985 and 2017, approached both through Japanese companies that acquired another company or company's division (in Japan or abroad) and, therefore, extended their scope of activity (buyers), and Japanese companies that were taken over by another company (Japanese or foreign) and, therefore, disappeared (targets). For the entire period, a total of 978 cases were identified: 652 buyers and 326 targets. Hence, Japanese medtech companies purchased nearly twice the amount of companies that they acquired. Although a slight imbalance in favor of buyers could be observed globally (11,289 buyers against 10,572 targets in 1980–2017), the trend was very marked in Japan. It showed that existing companies have a high propensity not to exit the medtech industry but, rather, to consolidate and develop via M&A. As is discussed below, this difference also relies on the fact that Japanese companies acquire many more companies abroad than foreign companies acquire firms within Japan.

Both proxies present a similar general trend, with a low number of cases until the end of the 1990s, then an important development. There were only 108 cases in the period 1985–1999 (11% of the total). This trend is not specific to the medtech industry and can be observed for the Japanese economy overall. Changes in corporate governance and the liberalization of finance made M&As easier from the late 1990s onwards (Miyajima, 2007).

A detailed examination of the buyers demonstrated that these Japanese firms took over mainly other Japanese companies (in 64.4% of cases).

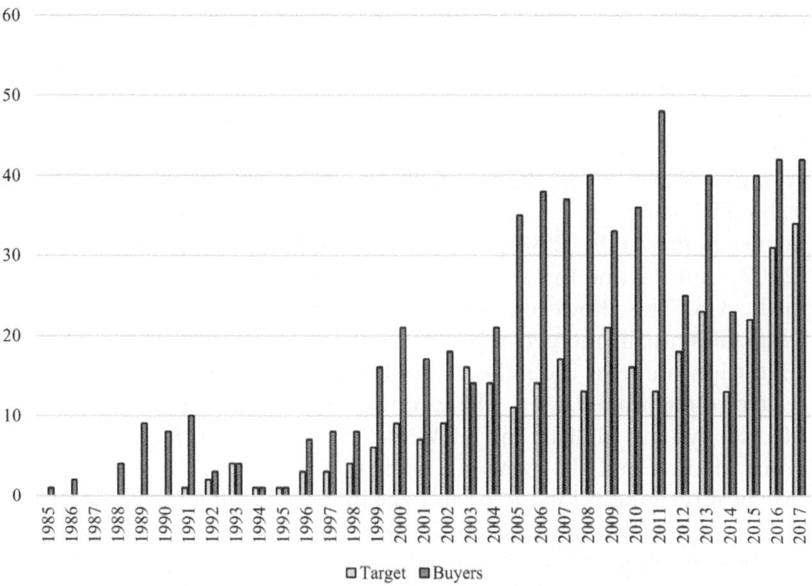

Fig. 5.2 M&As in the Japanese medtech industry by number of cases, 1986–2017. (Source: Thomson One database)

M&A is therefore a way of consolidating a national industry. When they acquired foreign firms, it was especially companies based in the US (15%) and in Europe (10.6%), rather than in neighboring East Asian countries. They took over only 14 companies in China (2.1%), 14 in South Korea (2.1%) and 2 in Taiwan (0.3%). Japanese medtech companies aimed to develop their technology and knowledge, as well as to access major markets, through their takeover of specialized small firms. Moreover, the acquisition of foreign firms occurred early. Among the 82 companies purchased up until 1999, only 24 were Japanese companies and more than half of all foreign M&As were realized before 2004. Since the mid-2000s, the acquisition of other Japanese companies became more important. For example, the general medical device manufacturer Terumo acquired a total of 14 foreign firms between 1997 and 2017, including 9 based in the US. Among these were Olson Medical Sales (1997), Micro Vention (2006), Caridian BCT (2011), Emergent Med Partners (2013), Kalila Medical (2016), as well as some divisions of 3M (1999), St Jude Medical

(2016) and Bolton Medical (2017). Terumo also made six acquisitions in Japan, as follows: Ikiken in 2001, the medtech division of Sumitomo Bakelite in 2001, the heart and lung division of Edwards Life Science in 2005, some property rights from Hisamitsu Pharma in 2005, Clinical Supply Co. in 2008, and Fuji Pharma in 2009. Olympus, one of the largest innovators in the medtech industry, made 10 acquisitions in Japan and 9 abroad, including Flemming in Germany (1990); PamGene International in the Netherlands (2000); and Cytori Therapeutics (2006), Asthmax (2007), Small Bone Innovations (2010) and a division of Stryker (2010) in the US. This, however, was rather exceptional, as Japanese medtech companies usually merged a smaller number of foreign firms. Toshiba, the largest innovator in the industry, took over only 6 firms, all abroad and related to medical imaging. These comprised two in South Korea (Comed Medical Systems in 2012 and TI Medical Systems in 2013), one in France (Olea Medical in 2015), one in Turkey (TMST in 2013), one in the UK (Medical Imaging NI in 2016) and one in the US (Vital Images in 2011). Although Toshiba internalized knowledge related to its core business (medical imaging) through M&A, this was obviously not the main way to maintain an innovative and competitive edge. Accordingly, in-house R&D played a major role for growth (see Sect. 4).

Next, the Japanese targets were mostly acquired by other Japanese companies (90.2%) and foreign firms held less than 10% of the acquisitions—this represents a high level in terms of international comparison. During the same period, the rate of acquisition of medtech companies by foreign firms amounted to 53.2% in Germany and 73% in Switzerland. Even in the US, where the merger of domestic firms is exceptionally high due to the large number of startups, the rate of foreign takeovers is higher than in Japan: 18.3%. As for China, which is also seen as a relatively closed country, the rate of foreign takeovers amounts to 19.1%. It is therefore not an exaggeration to emphasize the deep closure of the Japanese medtech industry to foreign companies.

Only 32 firms were taken over by foreign firms, mostly American (11 cases) and European (8 cases). One can conclude that Japan is not a major source of knowledge for global medtech companies—or, that these firms have difficulties accessing Japan through M&A, but the result is the same. It is remarkable that global leaders in medtech realized only very few acquisitions in Japan. GE (US), which has had a joint venture in Japan since 1982, purchased only Tanaka X-Ray Manufacturing in 1993 and a division of NEC Medical Systems in 1999. As for Siemens and Medtronic, they did not take a stake in any existing Japanese medtech company.

A second important finding is that the majority of these Japanese companies were taken over by relatively small firms. The 10 largest innovators in the period 2010–2014 based on patent applications (Table 5.2) had only a tiny share of these acquisitions (19 cases, or 8.1%). The purchase of Japanese companies was therefore not a way to strengthen the domination of large enterprises through diversification. Their organizational capabilities for in-house R&D, as well as the merging of foreign companies, provided the basis for their long-standing domination in the market. On the other hand, small specialized companies used domestic M&A to expand the scope of their activities and to internalize new knowledge. For example, this was the case for Nipro Co., a company based in Osaka and founded in 1954, which specialized during the 1960s as a manufacturer of small glass products, in particular for medical use (Nipro, 2017). It became listed on the Tokyo Stock Exchange in 1996 and realized several acquisitions that supported its diversification. These were the mechanical hearts division of Toyobo (2009), the cardiology products company Goodman Co. (2013), the medical division of the synthetic rubber maker Unitika (2015), the producers of surgical appliances and supplies NexMed (2017) and, more recently, Machida Endoscopes, a producer of a broad range of medical instruments (2018). These various takeovers allowed Nipro to establish itself as a general medtech company. Consequently, the sales of the Nipro medical division grew from 64.7 billion yen in the 2000 fiscal year to 132.8 billion in 2010 and 300 billion in 2017 (Nippro 2000–2017).

4 Innovation

The examination of patents for medtech technology applied by organizations and individuals based in Japan between 1960 and 2014 makes it possible to highlight a major feature of the Japanese medtech industry: the domination by a handful of large enterprises that have maintained their position over time. Enterprises in general, including small specialized firms, hold a total of 82.9% of the applications, far before individuals (14.2%), universities (2.2%) and government agencies (0.7%). Moreover, the concentration of research in a few large firms is striking. The 10 largest firms have a share of more than half of all applications (54%) and nearly two-thirds of applications made by companies (65.2%). Of course, this data does not provide any information regarding the size of the firms, but

Table 5.2 Top 10 largest Japanese firms for patent application in the medtech industry, 1960–2014

1960–1969	*1970–1979*	*1980–1989*	*1990–1999*	*2000–2009*	*2010–2014*
OLYMPUS (34)	TOSHIBA (797)	TOSHIBA (4156)	OLYMPUS (4666)	TOSHIBA (6749)	TOSHIBA (5284)
TOSHIBA (10)	OLYMPUS (467)	OLYMPUS (4253)	TOSHIBA (3846)	OLYMPUS (6418)	OLYMPUS (3275)
HITACHI (6)	HITACHI (293)	HITACHI (2165)	HITACHI (2893)	HITACHI (3469)	FUJIFILM (2433)
NIKON (6)	CANON (195)	PANASONIC (1120)	SHIMADZU (1610)	FUJIFILM (3445)	CANON (1715)
PANASONIC (5)	PANASONIC (184)	SHIMADZU (1021)	FUJIFILM (1505)	PENTAX (2294)	HITACHI (1652)
NEC (4)	SHIMADZU (140)	YOKOGAWA ELECTRIC (877)	*GE YOKOGAWA (1158)*	PANASONIC (1917)	*TERUMO (976)*
KOWA (3)	NIPPON ELECTRON (79)	CANON (716)	PANASONIC (1116)	KONICA MINOLTA (1612)	SEIKO EPSON (694)
OMRON (3)	FUJIFILM (64)	FUJITSU (598)	CANON (1071)	CANON (1475)	KONICA MINOLTA (690)
FEATHER (2)	FUJITSU (61)	FUJIFILM (591)	PENTAX (1059)	SHIMADZU (1077)	HOYA (664)
TERUMO (2)	OMRON (58)	MITSUBISHI ELECTRIC (469)	TOPCON (720)	*TERUMO (910)*	PANASONIC (580)

Source: PATSTAT

Notes: (1) Numbers in parentheses correspond to number of patent applications. (2) Italic represent specialized medtech companies. (3) Data for the 1960s is incomplete because Japanese companies at that time were not using the International Patent Classification system a look at the average number of patents applied by firms suggests these are large organizations. Specifically, the ten largest firms had, on average, more than 8300 applications for the entire period. Therefore, they needed specific research facilities to conduct such large-scale activity. For all firms, the average number of applications was 21.2, where this amounts to 1.7 for individuals and 7.4 for universities.

In comparison, in the US, patent applications by the ten largest firms represented only 13% of the total, and 32% of applications by companies. The relative importance of the largest medtech firms was therefore far less important in America. Even in Germany, where the industry is also dominated by large companies, applications by the top ten firms represented a similar share of applications by companies (61.9%), but the share was much lower with regard to total applications (36.7%). As for China, the top 10 firms had a share of 84.5% of the applications by companies in the period 1980–2014, but only 4.4% for the total. The industry has a focus on a handful of private companies but other actors conduct most of the R&D (see Chap. 8). Consequently, Japan is a country where the largest corporations dominate R&D not only among companies, but also within the overall medtech industry, including universities and individuals. Toshiba, the largest medtech firm in Japan, holds 13.4% of all applications by Japanese assignees, against only 3.7% for GE and 0.6% for Guangzhou Baodan Medical Equipment, which are the largest applicants in the US and China, respectively. Toshiba is only exceeded by Siemens, which holds a special position in the German medtech industry (see Chap. 6) and holds 19.4% of all patents applied by German assignees.

Despite the domination of the Japanese medtech industry by large companies, a more qualitative analysis of the largest innovators makes it possible to highlight major changes over time. Table 5.2 shows the 10 largest firms from the 1960s to the years 2010–2014. It illustrates the lasting domination of large companies from the electronics (e.g., Toshiba, Hitachi, and Panasonic) and optical instrument industries (e.g., Olympus, Canon, and Nikon). The competitive advantage of these firms relies on their continuous investments in R&D in the medtech industry. It strengthens their position and contributes to making it difficult for newcomers to enter the medtech industry with similar devices and equipment, as emphasized by Gelijns and Rosenberg (1999). However, it is necessary to discuss how the giants of the electronics industry were able to maintain their domination for over half a century. In the next section, I examine in detail the cases of Toshiba, Hitachi, Yokogawa Electric and Olympus.

The second feature of the Japanese medtech industry is the long-lasting presence of specialized medtech companies (i.e., companies whose core business is related to medtech or who commenced with this industry before diversifying). Most of these firms were founded before WWII and developed in the medtech industry by improving their core technology and diversifying gradually to related products. For example, the company Terumo was founded in 1921 by a group of scientists, including the famous bacteriologist Shibasaburo Kitasato (who won the Nobel Prize for medicine in 1901), to manufacture and distribute thermometers. It focused on measuring instruments and expanded in the 1970s toward disposable goods (e.g., plastic syringes and catheter), drugs and heart-lung machines. Therefore, R&D and diversification enabled the company to gradually reposition itself in terms of technology-intensive products while keeping its core competence on the development of devices for bed-side patient care (Terumo, 1982). The diversification process was mostly realized on the basis of in-house R&D. Terumo did not engage actively in M&A before the 1990s (see Sect. 7). A similar pathway for development can be observed in other specialized companies, such as the general instrument and equipment maker Shimadzu, which specializes in medical imaging. It was one of the largest patent applicants but took over only eight companies in Japan and abroad between 1989 and 2017.

Finally, the third characteristic of this industry is the very low presence of foreign companies. There is only one firm ranked in the top ten that has some foreign capital, GE Yokogawa Medical Systems, which is a joint venture founded in 1982 by GE and Yokogawa Electric and specializes in X-ray and MRI equipment. It was ranked the fifth largest patent applicant in the 1990s but disappeared from the top ten after 2000 (41st in the period 2000–2009 and was not ranked in the period 2010–2014). Siemens had only a total of four applications in the 1980s to 1990s through its joint venture with Asahi Chemical for the production of magnetic resonance systems. However, this company basically produced in Japan medical imaging equipment developed in Germany without carrying out much R&D.[3]

Besides private companies, there were a large number of individuals (14.1% of all applications), but most only applied for one or two patents and, therefore, there is no possibility of obtaining a statistical overview of

[3] Siemens Archives, Berlin, 16091, A History of Siemens Medical Equipment Business in Japan, 2000 (unpublished manuscript).

their profile on the basis of patent applications. A qualitative survey of the largest innovators makes it possible to highlight the variety of innovators and the general change over time from medical doctors to private companies.[4] In the 1970s, only eight individuals applied for more than five patents. Four of these were independent medical doctors, two were engineers at Toshiba and Hitachi, one was unknown but applied patents for endoscopes for Olympus and Pentax, and the last was completely unknown. During the following decades, applicants working in academia (engineering or medicine) accounted for 50% (1980s) and 60% (1990s) of the ten largest individual innovators. However, after 2000, engineers from the largest firms represented the largest share of individuals (100% from Fujifilm in the period 2010–2014).

Universities, on the other hand, scarcely applied for medtech patents before 2000 (2.2% of all applications). None had more than 10 before this date. In the period 2010–2014, the three largest applicants were the University of Tokyo (78), Osaka University (66) and Tohoku University (63). However, on the basis of patent applications, it is difficult to estimate joint research or technology transfers between academics and firms.

Viewed from patent applications, individuals and universities have not been a major source of innovation in the Japanese medtech industry, where large corporations and specialized SMEs have instead dominated R&D. As in other high-tech industries, medtech is characterized by a very low level of startups due to the strategy of large corporations (which prefer in-house R&D to taking over small companies), the scarcity of venture capital, and a career path for scientists and engineers that privileged working in large organizations (universities or companies; Shimizu, 2019). Various private and public initiatives have more recently taken to supporting the development of medtech startups (Oshita & Ikeno, 2016). Several private venture-capital companies specializing in supporting medtech startups have been founded, such as the Japanese Organization for Medical Device Development Inc. (2012) and MedVenture Partners (2013), which manages two funds with a combined value of approximately 150 million dollars.[5] In 2015, for example, Stanford University extended its Biodesign Program to Japan and cooperates with the University of

[4] The sources for this analysis are patent applications and online databases for research papers CiNii (https://ci.nii.ac.jp/ja) and research funding KAKEN (https://kaken.nii.ac.jp/ja/).

[5] https://jomdd.com/en/ and http://www.medvp.co.jp/english/index.html.

Tokyo, Osaka University and Tohoku University, as well as private partners such as the Japan Federation of Medical Devices Association.[6] In 2018, the Ministry of Health, Labor and Welfare (MHLW) opened the Medical Innovation Support Office to offer a shared platform for scientists, entrepreneurs and investors.[7] These organizations express a willingness to contribute to strengthening the competitiveness of the Japanese medtech industry through nurturing new actors. The impacts of this, however, are not yet visible.

5 Electronics Giants Diversifying to Medtech

Data on patent applications clearly illustrates that two types of companies dominate the Japanese medtech industry: conglomerates from electric appliances and electronics on the one hand, and firms from the optical industry on the other. This section discusses the formation and maintenance of a competitive advantage by electronics groups with a focus on three major players: Toshiba, Hitachi and GE Yokogawa. Of course, many other electronics companies developed businesses in the medical device industry, which mostly related to diagnostic equipment. Casio, Mitsubishi Electric, NEC, Panasonic, Sanyo, Seiko Epson, Sharp, and Sony, to mention only a few, have all had more than 100 patent applications in the field of medical technology since the 1980s. However, the three largest aforementioned firms (i.e., Toshiba, Hitachi and GE Yokogawa) have maintained their dominance in the industry. Table 5.3 gives an overview of the evolution of their gross sales between 1960 and 2000. Despite the lack of

Table 5.3 Gross sales for Toshiba Medical, Hitachi Medical and GE Yokogawa in million yen, 1960–2000

	1960	*1970*	*1980*	*1990*	*2000*
Toshiba	2400	15,943	83,200	118,000	125,000
Hitachi	unknown	9187	unknown	96,497	92,123
GE Yokogawa	–	–	–	62,449	117,800

Source: ***Kaisha soran***, Nikkei, 1962–2000; estimates of the author for Toshiba in 1960 and 1980–2000 on the basis of Toshiba Medical (1998)

[6] http://www.jamti.or.jp/en/.
[7] https://mediso.mhlw.go.jp/.

data regarding Hitachi, whose medtech business is too small to regularly disclose figures regarding gross sales, the general evolution is clear. Toshiba enjoyed a dominant position from the interwar years and maintained it at least until 2000. Hitachi grew as its main challenger but was never able to establish itself as number one. As for GE Yokogawa, a joint venture founded in 1982, it experienced rapid growth and reached the level of Toshiba in 2000. All three companies created for themselves a competitive advantage in the medtech industry from electronics and a focus on medical imaging equipment (e.g., X-ray devices, CT scanners and MRI).

5.1 Toshiba

Toshiba was founded in 1939 as a merger between two electric appliance companies, with capital from GE: Tokyo Electric and Shibaura Works. It is a general electric equipment manufacturer and one of the largest companies in Japan. The cooperation with GE enabled Tokyo Electric to become one of the largest manufacturers of X-ray devices in Japan during the interwar years. It adapted American equipment to the structure of the Japanese hospital market (i.e., smaller, simpler and cheaper devices) through cooperation with medical doctors, in particular Koichi Fujinami, a promoter of radiology in Japan (Donzé, 2018b). After 1945, Toshiba's competitive advantage in the field of medical technology relied predominantly on diagnostic devices. The company continued to work collaboratively with medical professors from the country's most renowned universities (Toshiba Medical, 1998). Toshiba's growth strategy in the medtech industry is characterized by a low level of internationalization, minimal diversification, and a strong focus on in-house R&D. Toshiba's major takeovers were aimed at strengthening its position in the field of medical imaging diagnostic systems (CT scanners and MRI). Notably, it merged the foreign firms Diasonics Magnetic Resonance (MRI systems, USA, 1989), Applied Superconectics (MRI systems, USA, 1990), Barco-NV Advanced (imaging solutions, UK, 2008) and Comed Medical Systems (radiation devices, South Korea, 2012). All of these companies are related to MRI technology. Moreover, patent application statistics also show that Toshiba did not keenly engage in R&D abroad. In the period 2010–2014, it had only nine patent applications in the US and none in Germany.

Based on these findings, the core competitive advantage of Toshiba remained medical imaging diagnostic systems. It established itself as the most important producer of CT scanners in Japan, but lagged behind in terms of MRI. In 2007, it had a 50-% share in the Japanese market for CT scanners and was only in the fourth position for MRI at 15% (Nishimura, 2010). This competitiveness relied on the development of numerous small and cheap CT scanners for specific segments of the market rather than on the multipurpose equipment developed by Western companies. The adaptation of foreign equipment to the specificities of the Japanese hospital market was necessary. Therefore, Toshiba focused its R&D on this technology and also set up a particular financial organization to support the acquisition of large equipment by medical doctors and hospitals. The subsidiary Toshiba Medical Finance was founded in Tokyo in 1970. As this field is the largest and most profitable in the medtech industry, the company could maintain number one in Japan. And it experienced an important development: the number of employees increased from 309 in 1960 to 1281 in 1995. Sales were less than 10 billion yen until 1967, and then extended beyond 90 billion in 1986 and 120 billion in 1988 (Toshiba Medical, 1998). Toshiba Medical Systems was acquired in 2016 by Canon in the context of heavy financial losses experienced by the Toshiba group. The total value of healthcare-related businesses within Toshiba (including Toshiba Medical Systems) was evaluated at 400 billion yen in 2014.[8] In 2018, Canon announced sales for medical equipment at 437 billion yen.[9]

5.2 Hitachi

Founded in 1910, Hitachi is also a general electric appliances company that diversified to electronics following WWII. Unlike Toshiba, it held no foreign capital during its formative years. Its engagement in medical devices dates back to the post-war years when, in 1951, it took over Shibuya Roentgen, a small assembly maker of X-ray devices founded in Tokyo in 1928. In 1962, Hitachi merged a second small maker of X-ray devices, Osaka Roentgen. The various manufacturing and marketing facilities owned in the field of radiography equipment were then gathered in 1969 into a new subsidiary, Hitachi Roentgen, which was renamed 'Hitachi Medical' in 1973 (Donzé, 2018b).

[8] *Nikkei Shimbun*, 23 March 2014.
[9] Canon, Annual report, 2019.

Like Toshiba, Hitachi based its growth during the last third of the twentieth century on in-house R&D and exhibited minimal interest in expanding its operations abroad. It remained focused on medical imaging technology. Between 1995 and 2010, it took over only three companies, of which two were based in Japan (Oki Medical Systems in 1999 and Aloka in 2010) and one in the US (Atlantis Diagnostics International, in 1995). In the second half of the 1990s, it opened sales subsidiaries in Singapore and Switzerland, followed by others in the US, China and the Middle East after 2000. This late expansion to foreign markets helped Hitachi identify a new development pathway. Gross sales grew to 141,075 million yen in 2004 and 166,237 million in 2011, with a share of foreign sales that amounted to 28.8% and 39.5%, respectively.[10] A reorganization of the Hitachi Group put an end to the autonomy of the medtech business in the period 2013–2014. It was reintegrated into the group as part of the electronic systems and equipment division, and details regarding medtech have not been disclosed since that time.

5.3 *Yokogawa Electric and GE*

Lastly, GE succeeded in establishing itself as a leading company in medical imaging equipment in Japan. This company has been a promoter of X-ray devices since the early twentieth century and is one of the largest US medtech companies (see Chap. 4). In Japan, it transferred production to its subsidiary Tokyo Electric (Toshiba since 1939) during the interwar years and established itself as a major competitor of Shimadzu, the main producer of X-ray devices until the war (Donzé, 2013). Following 1945, despite GE restarting technical cooperation with Toshiba in the early 1950s, medical devices were not included in the new agreements. Between 1945 and 1980, GE focused its healthcare business on the US market and accessed overseas markets via export. For the US multinational, the internalization of knowledge relating to CT scanners represented an opportunity to expand its healthcare business in the global market. In Japan, GE signed an agreement in 1976 with Yokogawa Electric for CT scanner sales (Nishimura, 2010). Japan constituted the second largest market for this equipment globally, with strong growth potential, and GE wanted to establish itself as a leader in Japan. Therefore, GE co-founded a joint venture with Yokogawa for the production and sales of MRI, CT scanners and

[10] Hitachi Medical, Annual Report, 2004 and 2011.

related devices in 1982: Yokogawa Medical Systems (YMS; renamed 'GE Yokogawa Medical Systems' in 1994, and 'GE Healthcare Japan' in 2009). The role of Yokogawa changed from a distributor of GE goods to a co-developer of new products (e.g., the CT Max System), which then began to be sold to other countries, including the US (small hospitals and clinics). GE's annual report for 1986 states that *"the price and performance of this new CT scanner [CT Max System] make GE the first supplier to place advanced CT capabilities within the reach of smaller hospitals and clinics."*[11] The partnership with Yokogawa made it possible for GE to acquire knowledge regarding the development of smaller and simpler devices for the middle- and entry-level market (Nishimura, 2010). This strategy enabled the US corporation to strengthen its presence in global markets. In Japan, GE Yokogawa experienced rapid growth, with sales growing from 8608 million yen in 1982 to 62,449 million in 1990. It then doubled until 2000 and amounted to 139,100 million yen in 2017.[12] In 2007, this company held the largest share of the market for MRI (25%), before Philips (24%), Siemens (23%) and Toshiba (15%; Nishimura, 2010).

6 Optical Companies in Medtech: Olympus

The second major type of Japanese medtech firm is represented by companies from the optical industry that engaged in the production and sales of medical devices. This diversification process essentially relies on the application of their core technology in optics to develop diagnostic instruments such as endoscopes. Data from patent applications shows that all of the major camera and optical instrument makers, including Canon, Hoya, Konica, Nikon, Olympus, and Pentax, have conducted R&D in the medical device field. Fujifilm presents as a special case among these firms. This company began as a manufacturer of films for cameras and expanded to X-ray films as early as 1936. The disruption to the camera market resulting from the advent of digital cameras led Fujifilm to refocus on digital imaging in the late 1990s and to apply this knowledge to the development of medical imaging equipment and solutions—a field in which it acquired a global competitive advantage.[13]

[11] Taniguchi Collection, General Electric, annual report, 1986.

[12] *Kaisha soran*, Nikkei, 1982–2000 and https://www.jetro.go.jp/en/invest/success_stories/gehealthcare.html (accessed 22 December 2020).

[13] *Toyo keizai*, 19 April 2014.

The uncontested leader among these was Olympus, before Canon took over the medical business of Toshiba in 2016.[14] Olympus' origins date back to 1919, with the creation of a small firm that specialized in the development of instruments and optical products (Olympus, 1969). It became famous during the 1930s with the production of cameras, and launched itself in the field of endoscopy following WWII. Olympus' growth relied on its core competence in optical technology applied to the medical field. It designed and improved endoscopes through collaboration with medical doctors and engineers from public research institutions. For example, the world's first gastro-camera was presented by Olympus in 1951 but required five more years of joint research with the Department of Internal Medicine at the University of Tokyo before being launched in the market. Following this, in the 1960s, Olympus moved to optical fiber technology through joint research with Osaka Institute for Industrial Technology (Yamaguchi & Shimizu, 2015). These relations between industry, medicine and public research facilities demonstrate that joint research was conducted in the medtech industry as it was in other sectors of the Japanese manufacturing industry at that time (Sawai, 2012). This type of collaboration continues today. Since 2000, Olympus has used their collaboration with renowned medical doctors in particular to advertise its innovation in its annual reports to investors.[15]

Olympus continued to pursue its growth in this core competence. In 1991, it held over 75% of the world market for flexible endoscopes (Gelijns & Rosenberg, 1999) and gradually diversified on this technical basis. Endoscopy itself was improved with the adoption of ultrasound and video technology in the 1980s. Moreover, Olympus applied its knowledge outside of diagnostics, notably through the development of cameras and video systems for surgery. The company was reorganized in 2004 with the separation of the main division into autonomous subsidiaries. The medtech division became Olympus Medical Systems. It reached gross sales of 266.3 billion yen in 2005.[16] The growth of Olympus relied on in-house R&D and on the internalization of knowledge from other organizations. Both of these sources of innovation were interrelated. Olympus invests large amounts of capital in R&D. In 2014, it was the world's sixth biggest

[14] *Nikkei*, 9 March 2016.

[15] See, for example, the 2017 Annual Report, https://www.olympus.co.jp/ir/data/pdf/ir_medical_2017_04.pdf (accessed 25 June 2019).

[16] Olympus, Annual Report, 2005.

R&D spender, with a total of 425 million USD, and the first non-US firm. This sum represented 8.4% of gross sales (Medical Design, 2016). Research, however, was not only occurring at the headquarters in Japan. The global organization created by Olympus has an important impact on R&D. For example, in the 2010–2014 period, Olympus Surgical Technologies America (OSTA), a subsidiary that gathers research facilities in the US, applied for 96 patents, the German subsidiary Olympus Winter IBE applied for 184 patents in the same period, and the headquarters in Japan applied for more than 3000. Therefore, Olympus benefits from local knowledge developed by its subsidiaries around the world.

External knowledge comes both from the cooperation and the takeover of companies. In Japan, Olympus notably took over the bone substitute business of Sumitomo Osaka Cement (2005) and the company Telos (medical equipment for surgery, 2007). Besides this, Olympus signed a contract with Terumo in 2001 for technical cooperation, and in 2013, it collaborated with Sony. The electronics giant received 11% of the capital of Olympus and became its largest shareholder (5% and third shareholder in December 2018). Both companies created a joint venture that year (i.e., Sony Olympus Medical Solutions, SOMED). The aim of this joint venture to date has been to use high-tech knowledge regarding digital imaging by Sony and medical technology for surgery by Olympus (Nikkei, 2017). Outside of Japan, Olympus acquired, for example, Human Group (automated blood-analysis instruments, Germany, 1990), Flemming (diagnostic equipment, Germany, 1990), Celon (medical instruments, Germany, 2004), Gyrus Group (surgical devices, UK, 2007), Spiration (respiration equipment, USA, 2010), Innov-X Systems (portable X-ray devices, USA, 2010), Spirus Medical (endoscope insertion assistance devices, USA, 2010) and Image Stream Medical (surgical image management solutions, USA, 2017). These different partnerships have enabled Olympus to consolidate its position in endoscopy and to diversify to other fields in the medtech industry. Medtech sales grew to 355 billion yen in 2010 and to 634 billion in 2019, impressive growth resulting from a huge increase in sales of endoscope devices in China.[17]

[17] Olympus, Annual Report, 2010 and 2019.

7 Specialized Firms: Terumo

Despite the overwhelming domination of firms from the electronics and optical instrument industries, the Japanese medtech industry also includes a broad range of smaller companies specializing in medical devices. Their growth and international expansion are typically based on the use of specific knowledge and are largely focused on their core technology, like specialized German medtech firms (see Chap. 6). This, for example, is the case for the manufacturer of cardiac monitoring instruments Fukuda Denshi (founded in 1939), the maker of syringes Mani (1956), the blood products and transfusion device company JMS (1965), and the producer and distributor of cardiovascular devices Kawanishi Holdings (1967). These firms have engaged in a diversification process within medtech since the 1990s. However, unlike US companies, in-house R&D (as opposed to M&A) occurring at headquarters represented the most important basis for this development.

The case of Terumo is a good example of a small specialized medtech company that was able to diversify and achieve global leadership in its field (Terumo, 1982; IDCH, 2003). The origins of this firm date back to 1921, when a group of medical doctors and scientists founded a company to develop clinical thermometers under the leadership of Shibasaburo Kitasato, a promoter of bacteriology in Japan and a professor at Keio University at that time. It dominated the market for thermometers in Japan and focused on this single product until the early 1960s. The first phase of diversification occurred with the launch of various supplies related to blood and the circulatory system, such as hypodermic needles (1963), vacuum blood tubes (1963) and blood bags (1969). In 1971, thermometers represented only 22% of sales, while syringes had become the main product (60%), and devices for blood circulation (8%) and other equipment (10%) followed with lower shares (Terumo, 1982, p. 284). The 1970s then represented a decade of first internationalization, with the opening of two subsidiaries in the US and in Belgium in 1971. Terumo distributed its products and began to manufacture some of them abroad. In 1980, the company employed nearly 4000 people, of whom 28.4% were working in foreign subsidiaries (Terumo, 1982, p. 285).

In 1982, Terumo went public and became listed on the Tokyo Stock Exchange. The supply of capital enabled the company to actively engage in R&D. The company became one of the largest applicants of patents among specialized firms, with 320 applications in the 1980s and 487 in the 1990s. Innovation focused on hollow fiber technology in particular and made the development of dialyzers, oxygenators, and artificial organs possible. It also continued to develop new equipment related to the monitoring of the circulatory system. Sales followed impressive growth, from 41.5 million yen in 1980 to 121.3 million in 1995 (see Fig. 5.3). The domestic market represented the main basis of this development, as foreign sales only amounted to 30% in 1993. During these 15 years, Terumo's sales increased from approximately half of Toshiba's medtech business to the same size.

A second phase of internationalization began in the mid-1990s with a focus on Asian markets. Terumo opened subsidiaries in China (1995 and 1996), the Philippines (1998), India (1999), Vietnam (2006), and Singapore (2011), as well as Chile (2007) and Russia (2013). Moreover, the presence on the US market was strengthened by the takeover of various companies. In the 1997–2017 period, Terumo acquired nine

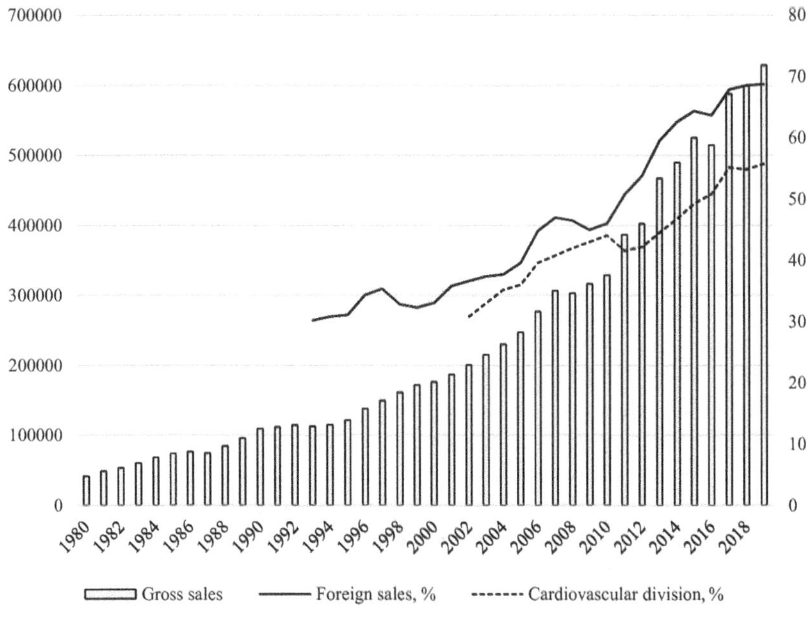

Fig. 5.3 Gross sales for Terumo in million yen, 1980–2019. (Source: Nikkei, *Kaisha yoran*, Tokyo: Nikkei, 1980–2005; and Terumo, annual reports, 2005–2019. Note: The share of foreign sales before 1993 is unavailable)

businesses in the US, and one company in each of the following countries: China, France, India, the Netherlands and the UK. All of these firms were essentially active in medical services. One of the US acquisitions was also the cardiovascular division of the American conglomerate 3M (1999). However, despite this acquisition, the R&D focus was maintained in Japan, where Terumo purchased the therapy business Sumitomo Bakelite (2001) and the heart-lung business Edwards Lifesciences (2005). It also acquired medtech companies in China, France, India, the Netherlands and the UK. Terumo's M&A strategy has been pursued and developed since 2016, with the takeover of several companies in the US and in China to strengthen the company's diversification operations. These recent acquisitions may contribute to the transformation of a company with a strong research and manufacturing basis in Japan into a more transnational organization.

During the second half of the 1990s, Terumo adopted a new strategy characterized by a refocus on cardiovascular business—related diversification from its knowledge in blood circulation monitoring and artificial organs—to strengthen its internationalization of sales. M&A played a major role in the company's access to new markets, but was less important for technological development. In the 1990–2014 period, Terumo applied for only 32 patents to its US subsidiary, against more than 2300 to its Japanese headquarters. The success of this strategy is impressive. Specifically, gross sales increased from 176 billion yen in 2000 to 629 billion in 2019. Terumo had become larger than the medical imaging giants like Canon (former Toshiba Medical), Hitachi and GE, and had reached the level of Olympus. This growth relied on cardiovascular business (30.8% of sales in 2002 and 55.7% in 2019) and foreign markets (33% in 2000 and 68.8% in 2019).

8 Conclusion

Two distinct phases of the evolution of the Japanese medtech industry since the 1960s can be observed. First, during the 1970s and 1980s, the rapid expansion of the domestic hospital system offered a strong basis for growth to electronics and large optical companies, which dominated the national market. There was a focus in these companies on in-house R&D and cooperation with medical doctors to offer equipment that was suitable for local hospitals. This type of business model established Toshiba,

Hitachi, GE Yokogawa and Olympus as large players in the medtech industry, despite them being only minimally oriented to foreign markets.

A deep change occurred in the 1990s with the shrinking of the domestic market (a decrease in the number of hospitals and in the population) and technological innovation in the global medtech industry (MRI, artificial implants and digitalization). Japanese electronics companies were late to engage in these new areas of medtech and gradually lost their competitive advantage in the domestic market. Their sales were exceeded by Olympus after 2000, whose global orientation via M&A was more advanced. Foreign firms (particularly those in the US) began to export massively to Japan during this decade. Nowadays, they hold a market share of more than 50% of the domestic medtech market. However, specialized medtech companies represented the firms that were the most capable of understanding the change in the industry. They adopted an M&A strategy toward internalizing new knowledge and diversifying, as well as toward expanding to foreign markets, as observed in the case of Terumo, whose sales exceeded those of the electronics giants after 2010.

Finally, from an international comparative perspective, the two main features of the Japanese medtech industry are represented in the high stability of its structure and the low number of foreign firms. Despite the change experienced in the 1990s, the new actors are not so much startups or a new generation of firms that use innovation to grow, as we can be observed in the US or in China, but specialized medtech firms that have been established for at least several decades. Although the Japanese Government adopted a new legal framework in 1999 to encourage technology licensing by Universities (Takenaka, 2005), the source of innovation remains within private companies. Moreover, like in other sectors of the economy, the presence of foreign companies remains low, although their export to Japan continues to increase (Russell, 2017).

References

Other Published Sources

IDCH. (2003). Terumo. *International Directory of Company Histories, 48*. St. James Press, 2003, pp. 393–395.

Nikkei. (2017, February 10). Geka shujutsu ni idomu Sony. *Nikkei bijinesu*, p. 17.

Nipro. (2017). *Sano minoru to nipuro no 70 nen*. Nipro.

OECD. (2018a). Hospitals (Indicator). Retrieved December 12, 2018, from https://stats.oecd.org/BrandedView.aspx?oecd_bv_id=health-data-en&doi=data-00541-en

OECD. (2018b). FDI stocks (Indicator). Retrieved December 12, 2018, from https://doi.org/10.1787/80eca1f9-en

OECD. (2018c). Computed Tomography (CT) Scanners (Indicator). Retrieved December 12, 2018, from https://doi.org/10.1787/bedece12-en

OECD. (2020). *Health Care Resources: Medical Technology*. Retrieved December 10, 2020, from https://stats.oecd.org/#

Olympus. (1969). *50 nen no ayumi*. Olympus.

Terumo. (1982). *Iryo to tomoni: terumo 60 nen no ayumi*. Terumo.

Toshiba Medical. (1998). *21 seiki he no kakehashi: Okyakusama totomoni ayunda Toshiba iyo kikai kaihatsu no rekishi*. Toshiba Medical.

Books and Academic Articles

Altenstetter, C. (2014). *Medical Technology in Japan: The Politics of Regulation*. Transaction Publishers.

Donzé, P. Y. (2016). The Beginnings of the Japanese Medical Instruments Industry and the Adaptation of Western Medicine to Japan, 1880–1937. *Australian Economic History Review, 56*(3), 272–291.

Donzé, P.-Y. (2013). Siemens and the Business of Medicine in Japan, 1900–1945. *Business History Review, 87*(2), 203–228.

Donzé, P.-Y. (2018b). *Making Medicine a Business: X-ray Technology and the Transformation of the Japanese Medical System (1895–1945)*. Basingstoke: Palgrave Macmillan.

Foote, S. B. (1992). *Managing the Medical Arms Race: Public Policy and Medical Device Innovation*. University of California Press.

Gelijns, A. C., & Rosenberg, N. (1999). Diagnostic Devices: An Analysis of Comparative Advantages. In D. C. Mowery & R. R. Nelson (Eds.), *Sources of Industrial Leadership: Studies of Seven Industries* (pp. 312–358). Cambridge University Press.

Hoshi, T. (2018). Has Abenomics Succeeded in Raising Japan's Inward Foreign Direct Investment? *Asian Economic Policy Review, 13*(1), 149–168.

Ikegami, N. (Ed.). (2014). *Universal Health Coverage for Inclusive and Sustainable Development: Lessons from Japan*. The World Bank.

Mason, M. (1995). Japan's Low Levels of Inward Direct Investment: Causes, Consequences and Remedies. In *Corporate Links and Foreign Direct Investment in Asia and the Pacific* (pp. 129–152). Westview Press.

Medical Design. (2016). *Medtech's 100 Largest Players*. Retrieved May 18, 2019, from https://www.medicaldesignandoutsourcing.com/

Miyajima, H. (Ed.). (2007). *Nihon no M&A: kigyo touji, soshiki kouritsu, kigyo kachi heno inpakuto*. Toyo keiyai hosha.

MHLW. (2020). *Yakuji kogyo seisan jotai tokei nenpo*. Tokyo: Ministry of Health, Labour and Welfare.

Nishimura, S. (2010). Gurobaru keiei to chiteki zaisan manejimento. In U. Okura, K. Suyama, & K. Ito (Eds.), *Gurobaru keizai ni okeru keiei to kaikaei no kenkyu* (pp. 95–134). Kansai University Press.

Onuma, M. (2010). Shinkyu sumiwake wo jikken suru seihin tenkai: shuyo kakusha ni yoru X-sen CT to MRI he no shigen haifu to seihin tenkai. In Hitotsubashi University (Ed.), *Nihon kigyo kenkyu no furonteiya, vol. 6* (pp. 47–63). Yuhikaku.

Oshita, H., & Ikeno, F. (2016). *Iryo kikai kaihatsu to bencha kapitaru*. Gentosha Media Consulting.

R&D Co. (2014). *Iryo kiki youhin nenkan*. R&D Co.

Russell, L. (2017). The Current State of Japanese Inbound FDI: Deterrents and Initiatives. *Hannan Ronshu, 52*(2), 13–35.

Sakai, K. (2018). Thriving in the Shadow of Giants: The Success of the Japanese Surgical Needle Producer MANI, 1956–2016. *Business History, 61*(3), 1–27.

Sawai, M. (2012). *Kindai nihon no kenkyu kaihatsu taisei*. Nagoya University Press.

Shimizu, H. (2019). Patterns of Spin-Outs and Innovation. In *General Purpose Technology, Spin-Out, and Innovation* (pp. 221–245). Springer.

Takenaka, T. (2005). Technology Licensing and University Research in Japan. *International Journal of Intellectual Property-Law, Economy and Management, 1*(1), 27–36.

Yamaguchi, S., & Shimizu, H. (2015). Orinpasu: ikamera to faiba sukopu no kaihatsu. *Hitotsubashi Business Review, 3*, 100–112.

CHAPTER 6

Germany: Between Siemens and Specialized Medtech Firms

1 Introduction

Germany holds a major position in the global medtech industry. In 2014, it had the third-most companies, after the United States and Japan, in the ranking of the top 100 largest medtech firms (Medical Design, 2016). Moreover, for the entire period from 1960 to 2014, Germany was the fourth-largest applier for medtech patents (accounting for 6.29% of the total), behind Japan, the United States, and China. Above all, however, the strength of the German medtech industry relies on the competitiveness of its firms, as the country's position near the top in rankings of total exports suggests (see below).

The specificity of the organization of the German medtech industry is the coexistence of a large multinational enterprise that has dominated the global medical-imaging market since the interwar years, Siemens, and numerous specialized medtech firms. One of the main objectives of this chapter is thus to discuss the nature of the relations between Siemens and other firms. Although some authors have argued that the German medtech industry formed a cluster and that the integrated organization was the basis for the industry's competitiveness (Steinle et al., 2007), they have not discussed the nature of the relations between Siemens and specialized firms. Literature on industrial districts has identified a specific form in existence since the 1990s, which Markusen (1996, p. 296) describes as a "hub-and-spoke district, where regional structure revolves around one or

P.-Y. Donzé, *Medtech*,
https://doi.org/10.1007/978-981-16-7174-6_6

several major corporations in one or few industries." The main distinguishing features of these districts are the presence of a network of small firms and big enterprises with strong connections to companies both inside and outside the district. These large enterprises play a key role in the dynamics of the district, especially as export drivers. Other works have emphasized the influence of leading firms on knowledge diffusion within the district (Ciapetti, 2011) and access to global supply chains (Campagnolo & Camuffo, 2011; Catalan & Ramon-Muñoz, 2013). From this perspective, one can discuss the relation of Siemens with specialized medtech firms to determine if this giant multinational is the driving force of the growth of the overall German medtech industry.

2 Foreign Trade

The lack of official statistics on the national production of medtech goods in Germany makes it necessary to focus on foreign trade data to get a general idea of the development of the German medtech industry over the last three decades. Foreign-trade statistics highlight some major characteristics of the German medtech industry between 1991 and 2019.[1] The Comtrade database shows that the sector not only experienced rapid development but also maintained its competitiveness in the global market. German exports of general medical devices (HS code 9018), orthopedic devices (9021), and X-ray machines (9022) went from a cumulative total of 4 billion USD in 1991 to 5.6 billion in 2000, 19.5 billion in 2010 and 27.6 billion in 2019; the growth was thus particularly fast after the turn of the century. Over that same period, the balance of trade for medtech products was always positive and increased dramatically (1.5 billion USD in 1991; 1.8 billion in 2000; 10.2 billion in 2019). This data shows that German medtech companies were able to keep and strengthen their competitiveness on global market over those years. Indeed, Comtrade statistics show that Germany was the world's foremost exporter of X-ray machines, second-leading exporter of general medical appliances, and in third place in exports of orthopedic devices in 1991—and it occupied essentially the same positions in 2017: first in X-ray machines and second for general medical devices, while falling slightly to fifth in orthopedic devices. Finally, one can observe an important change within the structure of German medtech exports since 1991. While general medical devices represent the

[1] Comtrade statistics are unavailable for East Germany until 1990. This section thus covers the period starting after the reunification of Germany.

largest category with a stable share (58.5% of the total on average from 1991 to 2019), a shift occurred between X-ray machines (33.6% in 1991 and 20.4% in 2019) and orthopedic devices (9.8% and 20.4%). This results from a technological change in medical-imaging equipment, with the advent of MRI, and general growth in orthopedic devices due largely to aging populations in developed countries (Fig. 6.1).

The evolution of Germany's foreign trade of general medical devices reflects the growing competitiveness of German medtech firms since 2000. Despite an increase in imports to meet the needs of German hospitals and doctors, the data indicates that the growth in exports has surpassed that rise. What this points to is the presence in Germany of many specialized medtech companies, particularly in the traditional field of endoscopy (see below). Their specific knowledge enables them to develop competitive products. Moreover, the opening of important countries like China (the second-leading export market in 2019, behind the US) and Russia (the eighth-leading export market in 2019) has supported export expansion.

Next, the export of orthopedic devices has grown impressively, from less than 500 million USD in 1991 to more than 5 billion since 2014. The major trends in the sector are a gradual reduction of the trade deficit and

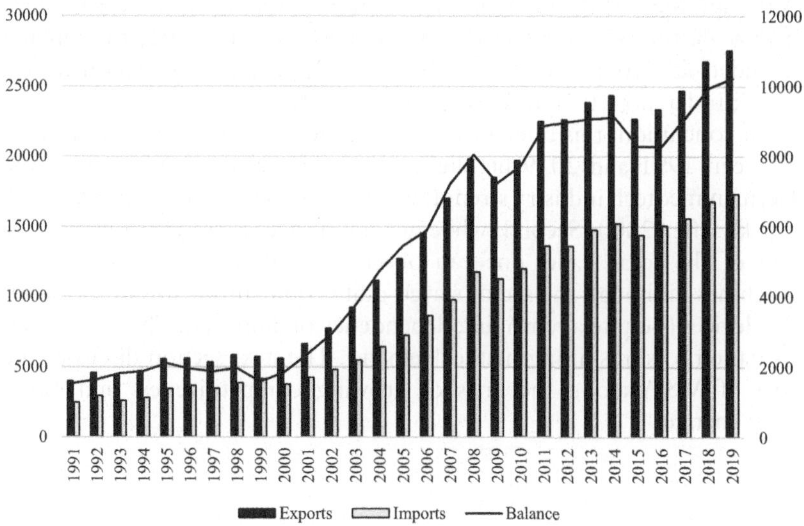

Fig. 6.1 German foreign trade of medtech goods (million USD), 1991–2019. (Source: Comtrade, HS codes 9018, 9021 and 9022)

then a shift toward a slightly positive balance since 2011. Despite the difference between exports and imports remaining very low throughout the period, one can observe that exports grew more than imports did in a context of expansion. This results both from the expansion of German firms active in spinal surgery and orthopedics, like Biedermann Technologies, and from the investments of foreign multinationals specializing in this field, like the US company Stryker, in Germany. The second case, American firms in Germany, has a particular impact on the balance of trade: Moving production to Germany both reduces imports and boosts exports to neighboring countries. However, imports from the United States and Switzerland, the two leaders in orthopedic devices, remain dominant throughout the period.

Finally, data on the trade of X-ray machines shows that, despite accounting for a declining share of overall medtech exports, the sector has sustained its high-level competitiveness over time. Exports of X-ray machines were 3.1 times larger than imports in 1991 and 4.1 times larger in 2019. The figures demonstrate the dominant position of Siemens in Germany and the ability of this multinational to export its equipment (see below). The structure of the ten largest export outlets also shows how German X-ray machines have grown more and more competitive around the world. Although the USSR (no. 4) and Japan (no. 6) were the only non-Western export destinations for German X-ray machinery in 1991, the ranking included four Asian countries (China, no. 2; Japan, no. 4; South Korea, no. 7; India, no. 10) and Russia (no. 8) in 2019.

In conclusion, this brief analysis of the German medtech foreign trade between 1991 and 2019 highlights two major characteristics. First, the German medtech industry strengthened its competitiveness and expanded quickly after 2000. Second, while general devices represented more than half of the total trade, one can observe a shift in export from X-ray machines (although the sector stayed quite competitive) toward orthopedic devices (despite a remaining dependency on imports). This change has its basic roots in shifting market demand. The next section discusses the role of M&A along the lines of growing competitiveness and structural change.

3 Mergers and Acquisitions

The statistics on M&A in the German medtech industry between 1986 and 2017 include a total of 462 cases where German firms took over other companies ("buyer" cases) and 587 cases where German companies (or divisions of companies) were the objects of the mergers ("target" cases) (see Fig. 6.2). The general dynamics during this period saw an increase in M&A projects during the first fifteen years, followed by a stabilization after 2000. A breakdown of the cases by firm nationality underscores the openness of the German medtech industry. Fewer than half of all cases involved German companies merging with other German companies (48.9%).

The companies taken over by German medtech firms were mostly based in Europe (26.8%), with North America accounting for only 17.1% of the total and Asia just 4.8% (other areas totalled 2.4%). In the United States, most German medtech firms were looking to internalize specific technologies: usually, they took over only one or two firms. Five companies acquired more than three US companies and became multinationals with deep

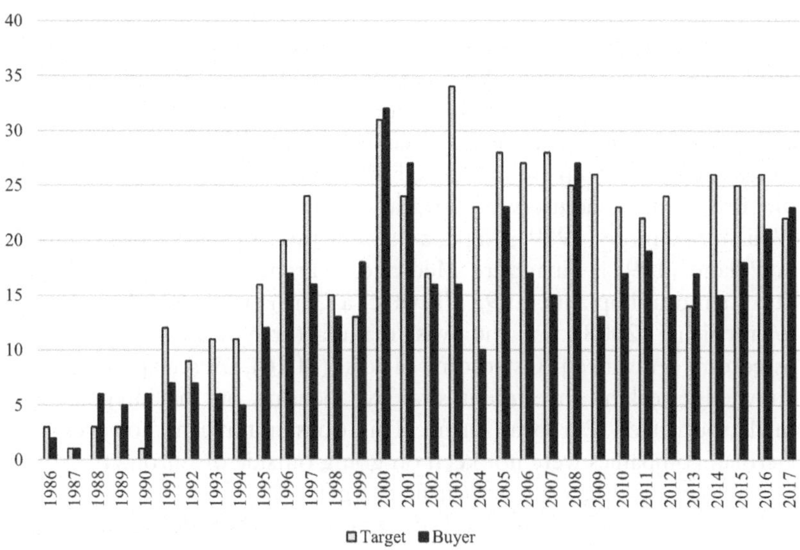

Fig. 6.2 M&A in the German medtech industry, number of cases, 1986–2017. (Source: Thomson-One database)

engagement stateside: BSN Medical, Fresenius Medical Care, Heraeus Holdings, Sartorius, and Schering. None are general-equipment companies: every one is a specialized firm that focuses on its core competencies to expand globally. In this context, US firms are, of course, essential for internalizing knowledge in certain fields. Above all, however, they serve to strengthen their German acquirers' presence in the US market. Fresenius Medical Care is a case in point. The company, specializing in dialysis devices, took over several firms active in medical services, such as St. John Dialysis Network (merged in 1999), Total Renal Care Holdings (2000), Franconia Acquisition (2000), Edwards Lifesciences (2001), Davita-Dialysis (2003), American Access Care (2011), Liberty Dialysis (2011), and Advanced Renal Care (2017). It also merged with manufacturing companies developing haemodialysis systems (Renal Solution in 2007, National Quality Care in 2009, and NxStage Medical in 2017) and biotech products (Nabi Biopharm in 2006), but the focus was clearly on the extension of service companies. Fresenius developed the same strategy, merging with dialysis service companies outside of the United States.

European companies merged by German medtech firms have mostly been based in neighboring countries (21 in France, 19 in the Netherlands, and 12 in Switzerland). German medtech firms thus tend to expand over their borders to build transnational European organizations for R&D and production. For example, Aesculap, a manufacturer of surgical instruments and devices, took over a total of eight firms, three based in Germany and five in Europe, all active in the same field: Meditec Reinhardt Thyzel, a German small company specialized in medical laser technology (1988); the British manufacturers of surgical instruments Downs Surgical and William Skidmore (1989); Chifa, a manufacturer of various devices based in Poland (1992); Financière Médicale, a French company which produces surgical implants (1993); Invitec, a German developer of software for medicine (2008); and the Swiss manufacturer of medical devices for osteotomy Advanced Osteotomy Tools (2016). Aesculap adopted a knowledge-seeking investment strategy, focusing on the integration of small specialized European firms. This does not mean, however, that German companies were not keen on going outside of Europe to acquire technology, but Europe was their first target.

Finally, the relatively low level of acquisition in Asia, despite the region representing an important outlet, suggests that access to the Asian market has relied on an export strategy rather than direct investment. German companies acquired just 22 companies in Asia, of which there were only five in China and two in Japan—two countries home to some of the world's most developed medtech industries. In comparison, US firms took over a total of 13 Japanese companies.

As for German medtech firms that were merged during this period by non-German companies, most of the acquiring companies were European firms, but at a slightly lower rate (23%, as opposed to the nearly 27% of the "buyer" cases involving European companies). The United Kingdom (39 cases), Switzerland (23) and Sweden (18) accounted for the bulk of these European cases. Companies from these countries generally sought specific knowledge anchored in Germany and took over firms to internalize that knowledge, rather than accessing the German medical market. For example, among the 39 companies purchased by British firms, all were active in the manufacturing of medical devices except two: healthcare service companies GHD GesundHeits and Zyto Service Deutschland, taken over by IK Investment Partners in 2010 and 2016, respectively. Swiss and Swedish companies, too, present a similar profile. Moreover, the sizable proportion of North American firms (21.6%) is a reflection of a strong desire to do exactly what these European countries were aiming for: internalizing specific knowledge and technology. The 119 acquisitions by American companies include all the major medtech multinationals from the United States, like Boston Scientific (four acquisitions), Bristol-Myers (two), Dentsply (four), General Electric (two), Medtronic (two), Pfizer (two) and Zimmer (two). Finally, Asian companies invested very little in Germany (3.2%; with all others also accounting for another 3.2%). Most of the Asian activity came from Japan (11 cases) and included large electronic multinationals with medtech divisions, like Panasonic, which purchased Bayer's diabetes-care business in 2015, as well as specialized medtech firms, like syringe manufacturer Mani (which took over Schuetz Dental in 2015) and the dialysis-equipment manufacturer Nikkiso (which merged with MeSys in 2006). In this context, Olympus offers a valuable case for study. An optical instrument company with a specialty in endoscope devices and endo-surgery instruments, Olympus is one the leading medtech firms in Japan (see Chap. 5). This firm established a European sales subsidiary in Hamburg in 1964 and acquired the rigid endoscope manufacturer Winter & Ibe in 1979.[2] On the basis of these two firms, Olympus started consolidating its position in Germany in the 1990s through the takeover of

[2] https://www.olympus-global.com/ir/data/integratedreport/pdf/integrated_report_2018e_03.pdf (accessed 15 May 2019).

various companies: the manufacturer of automated blood-analysis instruments Human Group (1990), the diagnostic equipment company Fleming (1990), the medical software company Soft-Imaging Systems (2004), and the manufacturer of medical devices Celon AG (2004). Finally, only one Chinese company, Tian Ying Medical Instruments, invested in Germany: in 2016, it took a 55% stake in Elexxion AG, a manufacturer of irradiation apparatuses.

Lastly, Siemens presents a particular case, one that illustrates the limits of a nation-based M&A database breakdown. As discussed in detail below, the German multinational developed quickly in the medtech business from 2000 onward through intensive takeovers, particularly in the United States. However, the projects almost always took place through the company's US subsidiary, which the Thomson One database considers an American company. On the surface, therefore, Siemens appears to be a small player in terms of the data on Germany used for this chapter; the company appears as an acquiror of just eight firms.

4 Innovation

The medtech patent database makes it possible to outline some features of the German medtech industry that support the results of the above M&A analysis. The growing ratio of foreign-owned enterprises among the top 20 largest companies applying for patents (4.8% in the 1960s and 33.3% in 2010–2014) signifies the strong interest abroad in acquiring German technology and pursuing R&D in Germany. Moreover, although numerous specialized German medtech firms were taken over by other German companies, they occupy a significant portion of the top 20 (66% over the entire period from 1960 to 2014) as newcomers continue to lodge places in the top 20. The vitality of the German medtech industry, in this point, is clear. For example, the ranking for the years 2010–2014 includes a total of 10 specialized medtech companies, 5 of which were founded in the 1980s or later: the developer of software for medical technology Brainlab (founded in 1989), the manufacturer of devices for laser surgery Wavelight (1989), the producer of dialysis equipment Fresenius (1996), the producer of devices for the treatment of neurovascular disease Acadnis & Co. (2006) and the producer of dental equipment Sirona Dental Systems, a spin-off from Siemens (2007).

A focus on the top 10 largest companies applying for patents between 1960 and 2014 illuminates the presence of four kinds of firms (Table 6.1).

Table 6.1 Top 10 largest German firms by patent-application count in the medtech industry, 1960–2014

1960–1969	*1970–1979*	*1980–1989*	*1990–1999*	*2000–2009*	*2010–2014*
SIEMENS (171)	SIEMENS (572)	SIEMENS (753)	SIEMENS (964)	SIEMENS (3097)	SIEMENS (2152)
G. RODENSTOCK (62)	*RICHARD WOLF (86)*	*RICHARD WOLF (116)*	*AESCULAP (439)*	*AESCULAP (825)*	*AESCULAP (311)*
KOCH & STERZEL (43)	PHILIPS (67)	*AESCULAP (109)*	*KARL STORZ (186)*	PHILIPS (524)	CARL ZEISS (248)
HELLIGE (27)	*KARL STORZ (40)*	PHILIPS (101)	CARL ZEISS (155)	CARL ZEISS (408)	*KARL STORZ (223)*
RICHARD WOLF (27)	*AESCULAP (38)*	CARL ZEISS (69)	*RICHARD WOLF (152)*	*KARL STORZ (274)*	PHILIPS (199)
CARL ZEISS (20)	G. RODENSTOCK (38)	*DORNIER (67)*	PHILIPS (121)	ROCHE (252)	OLYMPUS (184)
KARL STORZ (17)	HELLIGE (34)	*KARL STORZ (43)*	OLYMPUS (84)	*BRAINLAB (200)*	ROCHE (111)
TELEFUNKEN (14)	ROBERT BOSCH (34)	*MECRON (32)*	*DORNIER (63)*	OLYMPUS (140)	FRAUNHOFER (76)
C. H. F. MUELLER (12)	ZEISS C (34)	*WALDEMAR LINK (31)*	*KAVO DENTAL (48)*	FRAUNHOFER (126)	*RICHARD WOLF (76)*
AUSTENAL EUROPA (10)	*DRAEGERWERK (33)*	*DRAEGERWERK (27)*	*B. BRAUN (47)*	*ERBE (124)*	*BIEDERMANN (71)*

Source: Centredoc, medtech database

Notes: (1) Numbers in parentheses correspond to numbers of patent applications. (2) Italic represent specialized German medtech companies

First, Siemens's growing domination over the German medtech industry is obvious. This multinational, whose development will be discussed in detail in the following section, not only ranks as the largest innovator in every decade since the 1960s but also maintains a very high share. For the whole period from 1960 to 2014, the 7709 patents applied for by Siemens represents 19.4% of all patents applied for by all companies, organizations, and individuals based in Germany. That type of dominance is exceptional, a phenomenon not found in any other major medtech country. In the United States, for example, General Electric—a giant in the field—has applied for 3.7% of all patents; in Japan, Toshiba comes to 13.1%.

Second, specialized medtech firms account for a substantial proportion of the patent-applicant population throughout the period (italics in the table): they represent about half of the top 10 innovators across the decades. These companies are, in most cases, long-lasting firms and innovators, as well. For example, Aesculap Werke, second after Siemens since the 1990s, has been a mainstay in the rankings since the 1970s. The company was founded in 1867 and remained consistently focused on the development and production of surgical instruments. Moreover, several of these veteran specialized medtech companies are independent, unlisted family firms; illustrative are the cases of the endoscope manufacturers Richard Wolf (founded in 1906, it has belonged to the Richard and Annemarie Wolf Foundation since 1968)[3] and Karl Storz (founded in 1945),[4] the respiratory device maker Dreager (founded in 1889),[5] Dornier MedTech, specializing in urology devices, and Biedermann Motech, specializing in spinal surgery (founded in 1916).[6] The independent, familial ownership structure prevented these highly specialized companies from becoming takeover targets due to their nature as unlisted firms and supported their development in their specialized niches over time.

Third, few manufacturing companies from other industrial sectors have engaged in medtech. Their diversification toward medicine relies essentially on technological convergence between their core businesses and medical devices. For examples, one can turn to the manufacturers of optical instruments Rodenstock and Carl Zeiss. Robert Bosch, Hellige, and Telefunken, meanwhile, come from the fields of precision mechanics and

[3] https://www.richard-wolf.com/en/company/.

[4] https://www.karlstorz.com/us/en/history.htm.

[5] https://www.draeger.com/en_corp/About-Draeger/History/Timeline.

[6] https://www.biedermann.com/company/.

electrical instruments. Finally, Fraunhofer, the largest research organization in Germany, has a broad range of divisions, one of which focuses exclusively on the development of medical technology. The presence of these companies even after 2000 is remarkable. In many other countries, after all, the growing specialization of the local medtech industry has given way to innovation domination by specialized firms.

Fourth, three major foreign-owned companies also dot the rankings. Notable, however, is the fact that none of them is American, even though US multinationals are major buyers of medtech firms around the world. All of the firms that have invested in Germany have done so to strengthen their core businesses through the acquisition of local firms. The first is the Dutch electronics multinational Philips, which began cooperating with the X-ray equipment manufacturer C.F. H. Müller in the early 1920s and eventually took it over in 1927 (Boersma, 2003, p. 82). Since that year, the German firm was integrated within the Philips R&D and manufacturing facilities and made the channel through which the Dutch multinational distributed its medical equipment in the German market (Donzé & Wubs, 2019). Since the 1970s, Philips has used Philips Intellectual Property & Standards, its subsidiary in charge of IP business around the world, for patent applications. The subsidiary has a German branch that applies for patents for innovations within Germany. The second foreign firm in the rankings is the Japanese optical-instrument company Olympus, which specializes in endoscopy and gastro-cameras. It is one of the two largest innovators in medtech in Japan since the 1960s. In 1975, it started a collaboration with the German company Winter & Ibe GmbH, an endoscope producer to which the Japanese company supplied optical systems. This small company was not a major innovator (applying for no patents in the 1960s and only three in the 1970s). Four years later, Olympus took over this firm and continues its R&D activities in Germany.[7] Finally, the Swiss pharmaceutical company Roche invested in Germany to develop its division for diagnostic equipment. In 1997, it took over Boehringer Mannheim GmbH, a pharmaceutical firm with a strong diagnostic-device division, in an effort to strengthen its global competitiveness in this specific field.[8] Consequently, the presence of these three foreign companies in Germany shows that their investment—a means of securing a better

[7] https://www.olympus.de/company/en/about-olympus/facts-milestones/milestones/ (accessed 28 May 2019).

[8] *Les Echos*, 27 May 1997.

competitive edge in the global market—resulted not from a market-seeking strategy but rather from a resource-seeking strategy.

Patent applications by individuals demonstrate the competitive advantage of a medtech industry based on a broad network of SMEs. The average number of patents by the top 10 patent grantees went from 6 in the 1960s to 17.6 in the 2000s. This development stems not from the growing presence of university-based researchers or medical doctors but on the increased activity of engineers (including technicians and mechanists). Among them are many entrepreneurs, like Lutz Biedermann (1990s), Erich Jaeger (1960s–1970s), Thomas Koehler (2000s), Norbert Lemke (1990s), Harald Maslanka (1980s), Peter Osypka (2010s), Rudolf Rodenstock (1960s), Blasius Speidel (1970s) and Dieter von Zeppelin (1970s–1980s). A shift toward engineers working at large corporations is evident after 2000, but the trend is less marked than it is in other countries. Medical doctors and university professors, meanwhile, have cooperated with small medtech companies; joint patent applications often point to this approach. One example is the case of Juergen Harms, a professor of orthopedics at Saarland University, who co-developed medical devices with Biedermann Motech in the 1990s.

5 The World's Largest Medtech Employer: Siemens

Siemens, a multinational enterprise, occupies a specific position in the German medtech industry. One could very well deem Siemens the world's most innovative company, at least in terms of patent applications (see above), and the company stands as the world's largest firm in the medtech sector. Although Siemens was in second place behind Fresenius in 2014 on the basis of gross sales (11.7 billion USD for Siemens healthcare business versus 16.7 billion for Fresenius, with all other Germany companies below 10 billion), it easily outspent every other company on R&D (4.5 billion USD in 2014 versus 351 million for Fresenius) and had far more employees, as well (348,000 employees compared to 35,000 at Fresenius). In 2014, Siemens was even the world's largest company in the medtech industry in terms of employee count (Medical Design, 2016). Siemens thus deserves special attention in properly understanding the dynamics of the German and global medtech industries.

5.1 Historical Roots (1900–1945)

Siemens started its medical business in the early twentieth century with the development, manufacture, and sale of X-ray equipment (von Weiher & Goetzeler, 1977; Feldenkirchen, 2000; Schraudolph, 1984; Kiuntke, 2006; Donzé, 2015). These devices remained its core technology and the basis for development until the 1980s. Siemens expanded first in the domestic market through M&As. In 1924, it took over Reiniger, Gebbert & Schall (RGS), an Erlangen-based electro-medical instrument company that traced its roots back to 1877 and dominated the world market at the beginning of the twentieth century (Vittinghoff & Vollertsen-Diewerge, 2008). Meanwhile, Siemens also purchased Industrie-Unternehmungen AG (Inag), a holding company belonging to RGS, which originated in 1921 and controlled around 20 companies involved in the manufacture of medical equipment. In 1924, S&H also founded a sales company called Siemens-Reiniger-Veifa (SRV), but the different production units of the group were still largely autonomous (Feldenkirchen, 1995, p. 312). SRV developed business abroad, especially through exports (which represented 51.8% of its sales between 1924 and 1930)[9] (Donzé, 2013).

The M&A consolidation process went further during the crisis of the 1930s. Siemens management decided in 1932 to merge RGS, SRV, and Phoenix-Röntgenröhren-Fabriken AG, an X-ray tube maker controlled by Inag, into Siemens-Reiniger-Werke (SRW), a new company based in Erlangen. The company also transferred most of its production of electro-medical equipment at Siemens' Berlin plant to Erlangen (Feldenkirchen, 1995, p. 313). As sales climbed from 21.3 million Reichsmark in 1924 to 39.1 million in 1938–1939, SRW became the world's largest X-ray machine producer, commanding a 36% share of world exports from 1936 through 1938.[10] Half of SRW's gross sales came from outside Germany in the 1930s.[11] Driving that global expansion was an active strategy in foreign direct investment (FDI). SRW had offices and sale subsidiaries throughout the world and, before WWII, had production centers in several countries (Argentina, Brazil, Hungary, Italy, Japan, Spain, and Sweden). Most of these subsidiaries were small companies purchased in the early 1920s by Inag (Bräuer, 1949).

[9] Siemens Med Archiv (SMA), Erlangen, 18500: Umsatz und Bestelleingang (Mappe 1).

[10] SMA 7615 4-2-05, Vortrag des Herrn Direktor Dr. Sehmer anlässlich der Bilanz- und Aufsichtsratssitzung, 15 November 1950.

[11] SMA 18500: Umsatz und Bestelleingang (Mappe 1).

The events of WWII essentially destroyed the connections between Germany and its foreign outlets, as Schroeter (1993) has discussed. SRW lost the property of its foreign subsidiaries and ceased to be a multinational enterprise until it recovered some of its holdings and founded other sale subsidiaries, mostly doing so during the second half of the 1950s. When SRW set up new production facilities in Erlangen in 1947, exports thus made up the key strategy for regaining footholds in world markets. SRW resumed exports as early as fiscal year 1946–1947,[12] while it took until 1948 for manufacturing capacity to recover fully (Feldenkirchen, 2000, p. 275). The objective was to find outlets outside the German market, where the economic system was still in disarray, but the beginnings of the export initiative were laborious. Theodor Sehmer, director of SRW, wrote in 1947 that "we re-established relations with some foreign customers and have already received some orders. The foreign gross sales during this fiscal year, however, are not important. The realization of business encountered huge obstacles, especially due to the absence of our own organization abroad."[13] In 1949, Germany accounted for a mere 5.3% of the world's exports of electro-medical instruments.[14]

5.2 *Post-World War II Growth (1945–1970)*

Nevertheless, SRW began a gradual growth process again after 1945. Gross sales went from 8.4 million DM in 1946–1947 to 25.5 million DM in 1950 and 103.3 million DM in 1960–1961. The Siemens group underwent a sweeping reorganization in 1966, with the formation of a single multidivisional organization, Siemens AG (Feldenkirchen, 2000, pp. 295–299). The company's healthcare business remained autonomous as a division, continued to develop, and reached sales of 885 million DM in 1969–1970.[15]

SRW became profitable again in 1947–1948. Unfortunately, SRW's archives make it impossible to compare the evolution of gross sales and exports perfectly, as the documents related to the former use fiscal years (from March to February) and the figures for the latter go by civil years.

[12] SMA 7615 1-5-02, Annual report, 1946–1947.

[13] SMA 7615 1-5-02, Annual report, 1946–1947.

[14] SMA 7615 4-2-05, Vortrag des Herrn Direktor Dr. Sehmer anlässlich der Bilanz- und Aufsichtsratssitzung, 15 November 1950.

[15] Siemens AG, annual reports.

However, a rough estimation shows that exports were essential for the reconstruction of the company: they represented about 70% of gross sales for the years 1949–1952. In subsequent years, the normalization and eventual growth of the German economy, as well as the reconstruction of hospitals in the country (Liesen, 2004), renewed the significance of the domestic market. Exports still represented about 48% of sales in 1960, but world markets were extremely competitive. SRW's share of world exports of electro-medical instruments gained steam at the beginning of the 1950s, growing from 7.9% in 1949 to 17.3% in 1952, but entered a phase of stagnation afterwards (19.2% in 1956 and 18.2% in 1961–1962). SRW never again enjoyed the robust export performance of the 1930s.[16]

Developing countries played a key role in SRW's comeback in the world markets. Despite the fact that the relative weight of developing countries was in constant decline since the mid-1950s (more than half of all foreign sales in 1950–1953; 32.9% in 1960–1963), their level was far from insignificant. Beginning in 1955, Western Europe became SRW's base for export growth (55.1% in 1955 and 62.7% in 1962) due to the rapid development of health systems. The United States accounted for a relatively low share, due in large part to an agreement with Westinghouse that prevented SRW from being present in the American market before WWII, but the US share began growing quickly after 1945 (going from 0.4% in 1950 to 7.3% in 1960). Acting on that trend, SRW opened a US-based subsidiary called Siemens Medical of America in 1963. The new organization specialized in the sales of X-ray equipment in the US and took over local companies engaged in the same business, such as Pacific Silver X-Ray (based in San Francisco) in 1965. It also launched into production on American soil (Feldenkirchen, 2002, pp. 94–95; Kreutzer, 2013, pp. 138–141).

For the entirety of the span from 1945 to 1970, Siemens focused on the development and sales of X-ray machines, electro-cardiographs, dental equipment, and hearing devices. Investments in hospital buildings, which it made through its subsidiaries Industrielle Anlangen für Krankenhäuser and Röntgen-Geratebau GmbH, were another line of activity. For example, Siemens had a 30% stake in the Deutsche Klinik für Diagnostic AG in Wiesbaden.[17] Moreover, it engaged in hospital buildings in emerging countries, especially in Latin America, through another informal

[16] SMA, Export Statistik Welt.

[17] Siemens AG, annual report, 1968–69, p. 39.

association (Deutsche Hospitalia) that was reorganized into a joint venture company (Hospitalia International) with Philips in 1964 (Donzé, 2015). Siemens's foreign expansion during this period also relied on FDI. In the early 1970s, the most important foreign subsidiary in medtech was Siemens-Elema AB, in Sweden, which specialized in the manufacture of cardiographs.

5.3 *Medical Imaging Fuels Rapid Development (1970–1993)*

The advent of the CT scanner strengthened Siemens's competitive advantage around the globe. For some twenty years, the company experienced rapid development, with sales going from 885 million DM in 1969–1970 to 2.2 billion DM in 1980 and a peak of 7.9 billion DM in 1993. The medtech division represented about 10% of the company's gross sales during the period. To pinpoint the sources of that dramatic growth, one can focus mainly on a specific technology (medical imaging equipment) and a specific market (the United States).

Siemens had built its competitive advantage on X-ray technology since the early twentieth century—and that meant that the CT scanner created a major challenge. In the early 1970s, Siemens engineers in charge of R&D visited the British company EMI, which had developed the first CT scanner. They started fundamental research in 1972 and presented a prototype two years later. In 1975, Siemens commercialized its CT scanner and entered the US market in 1977 (Zenger, 2015, pp. 9–10; Trajtenberg, 1990, p. 52). The acquisition of knowledge related to this technology thus resulted mostly from in-house R&D. Siemens successfully established itself as a leading manufacturer and sharpened its competitive edge in medical imaging; from 1975 to 1984, it had already delivered a total of 1200 CT scanners.[18]

At the same time, the company sought expansion in the US market. In 1974, Siemens communicated its ambition to open a new plant stateside and develop production in Belgium and Spain under the slogan of "Worldwide R&D, production and sales."[19] When the company opened its new American plant for X-ray devices and radiography equipment in October 1975, Siemens employed about 700 people in its US medtech division. Peter von Siemens, chairman of the group, explained that "the

[18] Siemens AG, annual report, 1984.
[19] Siemens AG, annual report, 1973–74, p. 27.

international importance of American medicine, the high standards of manufacturing technology, and the innovative spirit of the American economy as a whole are important reasons for establishing this manufacturing unit in the United States."[20] Moreover, Siemens continued to acquire local companies involved in medical-imaging services, like Applied Radiation Corporation, a firm based in Walnut Creek, California, in 1974.[21] The medical division's sales in the United States ballooned from 166 million USD in 1977–1978 to 316 million in 1980–1981.[22]

Siemens deepened its engagement in the US market during the 1980s through mergers of numerous manufacturing firms, which contributed to the technological development and diversification of the company's American subsidiary. In succession, it took over The Pelton & Crane Company (dental equipment; in 1985), Pacesetter Systems (pacemakers; 1985), Burdick Corporation (ECG recorders; 1988), the X-ray tubes division of Litton Industries (1988), and Quantum Medical Systems (ultrasound equipment; 1990). In 1987, Siemens Medical Systems and Analogic Corporation founded the joint venture Medical Electronics Laboratories, which specialized in patient-monitoring equipment.[23] The company's medtech sales in America grew to about 1.4 billion USD in 1990 (Kreutzer, 2013, p. 245), a continuing development that helped make Siemens a major player in the US medtech industry. During the 1990s, Siemens was the eighth-largest American-based company in terms of applications for medtech patents, a context in which it was basically non-existent in the previous decades. At the end of the 1980s, Siemens also invested in Japan, making the country its third-most important base for R&D and production. In 1988, it founded the joint venture Siemens Asahi Medical with the company Asahi Chemical, a small player in the medical imaging business.[24] Through this global expansion, Siemens became the world's largest medtech firm in 1987 (see Table 3.1, p. 50). The development of Japanese firms, however, would challenge Siemens's dominant position in the ensuing years.

[20] Siemens Archives, Berlin, 68 / 2i 262, Speech of Peter von Siemens at Cheshire, Connecticut, 3 October 1975.

[21] Siemens Archives, Berlin, 68 / 2i 262, *Siemens Presseinformation*, 27 May 1974.

[22] Siemens Archives, Berlin, 68 / 2i 262, Siemens in USA: Unternehmensbereiche in der Siemens Corporation und in den konsolidierten Beteiligungsgesellschaften, 1983.

[23] Siemens Archives, Berlin, 68 / 2i 262, annual reports of Siemens USA, 1985–1990.

[24] Siemens Archives, Berlin, 16091, *A History of Siemens Medical Equipment Business in Japan*, 2000, p. 5.

5.4 *The Crisis of the 1990s and the Shift Toward Healthcare IT Services*

Siemens's medical division experienced some difficulties during the 1990s, as Fig. 6.3 suggests. After sales peaked at 4 billion EUR (7.9 billion DM) in 1993, they declined to 3.5 billion in 1995 and stayed under 4 billion until 1998. As a result, the division was unprofitable from 1994 to 1997. Its share of the company's gross sales, meanwhile, dropped to a minimum of 6.1% in 1999. Siemens's medtech business was facing a crisis. It had lost its competitiveness against Japanese companies, particularly Toshiba, that had designed cheaper, simpler CT scanners. American companies, particularly GE, followed the same trend. The factors combined to prompt a sharp decrease in prices on the global market. Having focused on the development and manufacture of expensive, premium-quality equipment,

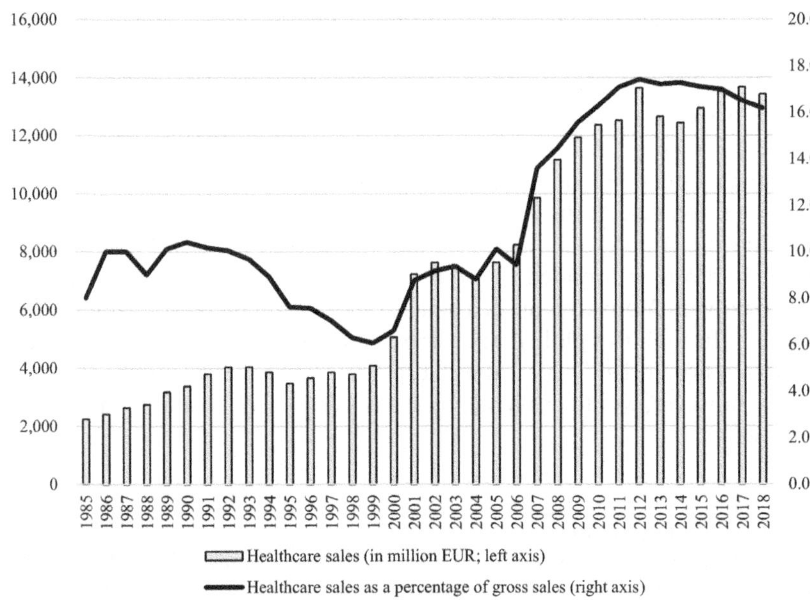

Fig. 6.3 Siemens healthcare division, sales growth in millions of EUR and share as a percentage of overall sales, 1985–2018. (Source: Siemens, annual reports, 1985–2018. Note: Fiscal years end on September 30)

Siemens saw its market shares dwindle dramatically.[25] In 1992, it decided to stop manufacturing MRI in Japan.[26]

To overcome this crisis, Siemens took various actions. First, it engaged in a strict policy of cutting production costs. It developed production centers outside Germany, bringing the proportion of its medtech production abroad from 20% in 1980 to 40% in 1994, and lowering costs by focusing on establishing operations in low-wage countries like China, India, and Indonesia. In 1997, the medical division cut 2000 jobs out a total of 24,000 and introduced flexible working hours.[27] Siemens also developed simpler and cheaper CT machines, learning from Japanese equipment through reverse engineering.[28] In addition, the company pursued in-house fundamental research to develop new diagnostic equipment and maintain its competitive advantage. Siemens thus became the world's first company to install MRI equipment for clinical use, which it did in Saint Louis (USA) in 1983 (Zenger, 2014, p. 13). In conjunction with that step, the company acquired foreign firms to internalize knowledge pertaining to the new technology; in 1989, for example, it purchased 51% of the capital of Oxford Magnet Technology, a division of the British group Oxford Instruments that specialized in the manufacture of medical magnets, a component of MRI equipment.[29]

However, the strategic change that allowed Siemens to recover its competitiveness was a drastic repositioning within the medtech industry. It disinvested from relatively low-technology and highly price-competitive segments, such as hospital construction (selling its related subsidiary to Fresenius in 1993) and dental equipment (selling its corresponding division in 1997), and refocused on a new, promising line of business: healthcare IT services. In 2000, the takeover of Shared Medical Systems, an American firm with a workforce of 7600, made Siemens the world's top company for IT solutions in the healthcare sphere and helped boost the sales of Siemens's medtech division by 24%.[30] The digitalization of medicine offered new opportunities, and Siemens decided to shift its identity from a pure manufacturer to an integrated medical diagnostic company

[25] *Financial Times*, 11 March 1994.

[26] Siemens Archives, Berlin, 16091, A History of Siemens Medical Equipment Business in Japan, 2000, pp. 51–52.

[27] *Financial Times*, 26 October 2001.

[28] *Financial Times*, 11 March 1994.

[29] *Financial Times*, 4 May 1989.

[30] Siemens AG, annual report, 2000, p. 45.

that offers imaging devices, laboratory testing, and clinical IT. Following this strategic move to medical services, Siemens took over several relevant companies, such as the medical-software companies CAD Vision Medical Tech in Israel (2004) and Medicalis in the United States (2017), as well as Pointshare Corporation, a provider of healthcare services to local communities in the United States (2001). The company's M&A strategy since 2000 has also leaned heavily toward the internalization of technology concerning diagnostic pharmaceuticals; acquisitions of the US firms Dade Behring Holdings in 2007 and New England Petmet in 2009 are illustrative cases. Finally, Siemens pursued the purchase of several medical-imaging companies to maintain and strengthen its traditional competitive advantage in the medtech industry (examples include Video Optics in the United States in 2004, Sensant in the United States in 2005, Meditel Electronics in Malaysia in 2006, Ultrasonic Technologies in South Korea in 2009, and Penrith in the United States in 2012).[31]

As Fig. 6.3 implies, Siemens's strategic realignment in 2000 had a positive impact on the growth of the medtech division. Siemens entered a fast-growth period, with sales swelling from 5.1 billion EUR in 2000 to 13.4 billion in 2018. Moreover, the medical division took on a growing importance within Siemens. While it had occupied a paltry share of just 6.6% in 2000, the percentage grew to 16.2% in 2018. Since 2009, the share stayed consistently above 15%, a level that the firm had never seen throughout its history.

6 The Case of Traditional Specialized Firms

In an international context, the presence of long-established specialized firms is a second important characteristic of the German medtech industry. Research on medtech SMEs in Germany has demonstrated that these firms converged into a single cluster, also gathering actors from universities and research centers. About 40% of these companies were founded before 1990. Steinle et al. (2007) argued that these SMEs carry out their own research within the cluster and do not cooperate intensively with outside multinational enterprises—they are rather the targets of M&A by foreign companies hoping to internalize knowledge. In looking at the internationalization of German medtech SMEs, Heiss (2017) also argued

[31] Thomson One database.

that these firms essentially focused on the domestic and European markets but stayed away from overseas markets and emerging countries.

The following section examines the cases of three major long-established firms and illuminates the reasons for their sustainability from a historical perspective. Three different paths of development come into view: Karl Storz Endoskope remained an independent family firm; Aesculap was taken over by a larger company (B. Braun) but stayed autonomous within it; and Fresenius developed into one of the world's largest medtech business through global M&A and diversification around its core businesses. Common to these three examples is the focus on a core technology over time, rather than a diversification into new, unrelated fields of medical technology, a pattern common in the United States and other locations.

6.1 An Independent Manufacturer: Karl Storz Endoskope

Karl Storz Endoskope (KSE), a family firm, inhabits a field of the medtech industry in which Germany has built and maintained a competitive advantage since the end of World War II. The application of optical technology—an area where German artisans have amassed substantial expertise over time—to medical instruments is the basis of lasting success for numerous firms, of which several have remained independent through today.

KSE was founded in 1945 as a producer of ENT instruments by Karl Storz, a mechanic trained to develop instruments for medical doctors. In 1960, Storz developed an endoscope with a fiber-optic light transmission that propelled his company to success and rapid growth (Linder et al., 1997). In 1971, the firm launched an internationalization initiative with the opening of a branch in the United States and a manufacturing company in Switzerland. However, KSE maintained its focus on its core technology and developed it, particularly through the integration of electronics. That was obviously the motivation for the opening of two manufacturing subsidiaries in the United States: KARL STORZ Endovision (1989) and KARL STORZ Imaging (1990), both of which regularly apply for patents. KSE's first sales subsidiary for the Asian market also opened in Singapore in 1990, followed by others in South Africa (2002) and Australia (2007).[32] The focus on its core business and technology enabled KSE to stay independent while growing as one of the world's leaders in endoscope

[32] https://www.karlstorz.com/us/en/history.htm (accessed 18 June 2019).

instruments. As of 2019, it was still an unlisted company operating under the management of its founder's grandson.

6.2 A Surgical-Instrument Maker Integrated within a Larger Group: Aesculap

The company Aesculap AG specializes in surgical instruments. Its roots go back to 1867, when Gottfried Jetter, a knifesmith based in Tuttlingen, opened a small workshop to manufacture instruments for surgeons. The operation grew quickly, employing more than 400 workers by 1890, and launched the trademark Aesculap in 1899 (Jetter, 1991). In the early twentieth century, the firm had sales agencies throughout Germany and in the world's major cities, from London and New York to Tokyo. The growth continued during the interwar years and after World War II, fueled by the competitiveness of the firm's traditional knowledge.

The internationalization of Aesculap started with the 1973 relocation of a production center to a low-wage country, Malaysia, owing to growing competition. Three years later, the manufacturer of hospital supplies and equipment B. Braun Melsungen AG took a stake in Aesculap—and later acquired full ownership in 1994. It provided capital to further the Aesculap's foreign expansion, which then centered on the creation of subsidiaries in the medtech giants of the United States (1977) and Japan (1986). Aesculap also purchased the German subsidiary of the British medical laser manufacturer Meditec (1988; sold to Jenoptik AG in 1999), the surgical-instrument manufacturers Skidmore and Downs Surgical, both in the United Kingdom (1989), as well as Chifa in Poland (1991). Finally, Aesculap diversified within the medtech field through the acquisitions of other firms, like the German software company Invitec (2008), US firm Aragon Surgical (2011), Swiss firm Advanced Osteotomy Tools (2016) and US company Dextera Surgical (2017). It opened a plant in China, too (2005).[33]

Despite operating under B. Braun's full ownership by since 1994, Aesculap AG still functions as an autonomous company from its position as a division of B. Braun group. It applies for its own patents and has its own board of directors. Its integration in a group provided it the capital

[33] https://www.bbraun.de/de/unternehmen/organisation-zahlen-und-fakten/aesculap-partner-der-chirurgie/150-jahre-aesculap-produkte/aesculap-meilensteine.html#20012009 (accessed 19 June 2019) and the Thomson One database.

necessary for pursuing R&D, diversifying through the acquisition of firms, and expanding into the global market.

6.3 A Pharma Company and Then a General Medtech Firm: Fresenius

Finally, Fresenius presents the case of a family firm from the pharmaceutical business that diversified into medical devices through M&A on a global scale and became one of the world's largest medtech companies. In 2014, the company was the world's fifth-largest medtech company in terms of gross sales (16.7 billion USD) and twentieth-largest in terms of workforce size (Medical Design, 2016). The company dates back to 1912, when a pharmacist named Eduard Fresenius established his own business in Frankfurt. The organization manufactured drugs during the interwar years and grew at a fast clip in the German and world markets after 1945, opening new related businesses for in nutrition-good manufacturing and infusion solutions, among others. This core business has developed until the present day, with takeovers of companies in Brazil in 1977 and later in the United States playing roles (Fresenius, 2012).

Diversification into medtech started in the 1960s, when Fresenius began importing dialysis devices from the United States and distributing its purchases in the German market. Fresenius then developed its own machinery and, in 1979, opened a plant to mass-produce the devices (Fresenius, 2012). This field further developed through the acquisition of the US firm National Medical Care (1996). Plants were subsequently opened throughout the world. The next step was the engagement in the hospital-construction business, which came through the acquisition of Hospitalia International (1994) and Vamed (1996) (Fresenius, 2012; Donzé, 2015). Next, it acquired clinics and hospitals in Eastern Europe and Asia. In 2001, Fresenius also started to purchase private hospitals in Germany and added healthcare-facility management to its portfolio. This was not only an opportunity to secure customers for the medical supplies and dialysis equipment but also a means of diversifying its revenue sources.

Fresenius thus represents the unique case of a medtech firm that emerged from the pharmaceutical industry and consolidated various businesses around a healthcare core, from drugs and medical devices to hospital construction and management (Korine, 2000). This development was made possible by a 1986 IPO, which provided capital for developing acquisitions and engaging in hospital construction and management. The company's gross sales went on to soar from 207 million EUR in 1985 (404 million DM) to 6.1 billion EUR in 2000.[34] From there, it grew to 16 billion in 2010 and 33.5 billion in 2018.[35] A small family firm had transformed into a giant healthcare-management organization through global M&A after making its way onto the stock exchange. The medtech division grounded itself in dialysis devices and continued to develop through global M&As (Glovik, 2017). Dialysis devices represented the largest division in 2000 (68.9% of gross sales), after which its relative weight declined due to takeovers of numerous clinics around the world. Still, however, it accounts for about half of turnover (49.3% in 2018).

7 Conclusion

The German medtech industry experienced rapid growth during the last third of the twentieth century, with significant acceleration coming after the year 2000. The coexistence of a large multinational company (Siemens) and numerous long-standing specialized firms is the key feature of this industry. The analysis in this chapter demonstrated that Siemens interacts very little with specialized firms. Unlike the conditions in models by Markusen (1996) and other scholars, the presence of a large multinational within the German medtech cluster is not a major engine of growth nor a significant mode of access to world markets.

On the one hand, Siemens developed from the end of World War II onward without intensive links to specialized medtech firms. It focused on medical imaging and strengthened its competitive advantage in the field through internal R&D (as its elevated levels of patent applications indicate). Siemens also worked closely with academics. Although the sources used for this study make it difficult to quantify joint research between a given company and other organizations to a high degree of precision, the available information does (albeit indirectly) point to relations between Siemens and universities. From 2000 to 2014, when patent applications by universities began to rise (3.6% of all applications), for example, the leading academic applicant was the Friedrich-Alexander-Universität Erlangen-Nürnberg (79 applications), located the exact same city where the medical division of Siemens has been based since the interwar years—and that suggests an important link between both organizations. In

[34] *Financial Times*, 5 December 1986 and *Annual report*, 2001.

[35] *Annual report*, 2010 and 2018.

addition, Siemens acquired very few domestic firms in medtech. When it decided to make its strategic move toward IT medical services in the late 1990s, Siemens took over a major US company and internalized the necessary knowledge through the acquisition of software and IT firms, both in Germany and abroad—outside the traditional field of medical devices.

On the other hand, specialized firms consistently trained their sights on their core technologies. Some of them became parts of larger groups or diversified into related businesses, but even while doing so, they maintained their autonomy and did not engage in unrelated diversification, unlike numerous US firms. Moreover, their M&A strategies aimed directly at strengthening their core technologies or accessing new markets with clear connections to their areas of specialization. From that perspective, the competitive advantage of the German firms specializing in medtech came from their own competencies; they did not need a large multinational like Siemens for development. The existence of a large number of specialized small firms attracted also foreign companies, particularly from the United States and Japan. For those investors, the objective of taking over a German company was not as much to access the European market (they acquired very few medical service companies, after all) but more to internalize specific knowledge in order to hone their own competitive edges.

References

Other Published Sources

Fresenius. (2012). *Fresenius: Forward Thinking Healthcare: 100 years*. Fresenius.

Medical Design. (2016). *Medtech's 100 Largest Players*. Retrieved May 18, 2019, from https://www.medicaldesignandoutsourcing.com/

Books and Academic Articles

Boersma, K. (2003). Tensions Within an Industrial Research Laboratory: The Philips Laboratory's x-ray Department Between the Wars. *Enterprise & Society, 4*(1), 65–98.

Bräuer, H. (1949). *Die Entwicklung der deutschen elektromedizinischen Industrie unter besonderer Berücksichtigung der Siemens-Reiniger-Werke AG Erlangen*. Friedrich-Alexander Universität Erlangen, Unpublished Dissertation.

Campagnolo, D., & Camuffo, A. (2011). Globalization and Low-Technology Industries: The Case of Italian Eyewear. In P. L. Robertson & D. Jacobson (Eds.), *Knowledge Transfer and Technology Diffusion* (pp. 138–161). Edward Elgar.

Catalan, J., & Ramon-Muñoz, R. (2013). Marshall in Iberia. Industrial Districts and Leading Firms in the Creation of Competitive Advantage in Fashion Products. *Enterprise & Society, 14*(2), 327–359.

Ciapetti, L. (2011). Technological Change, Knowledge Integration and Adaptive Processes: The Mechatronic Evolution of the Reggio Emilia District. In P. L. Robertson & D. Jacobson (Eds.), *Knowledge Transfer and Technology Diffusion* (pp. 107–137). Edward Elgar.

Donzé, P.-Y. (2013). Siemens and the Business of Medicine in Japan, 1900–1945. *Business History Review, 87*(2), 203–228.

Donzé, P.-Y. (2015). Siemens and the Construction of Hospitals in Latin America, 1949–1964. *Business History Review, 89*(3), 475–502.

Donzé, P. Y., & Wubs, B. (2019). Global Competition and Cooperation in the Electronics Industry: The Case of X-ray Equipment, 1900–1970. *Scandinavian Economic History Review, 67*(2), 210–225.

Feldenkirchen, W. (1995). *Siemens, 1918–1945*. Ohio State University Press.

Feldenkirchen, W. (2000). *Siemens: From Workshop to Global Player*. Piper.

Feldenkirchen, W. (2002). Siemens in the US. In G. Jones & L. Galvez-Munoz (Eds.), *Foreign Multinationals in the United States: Management and Performance* (pp. 94–95). Routledge.

Glovik, M. (2017). Case Study: Fresenius: Concentration Strategies in Healthcare Business. In M. Glovik (Ed.), *Global Strategy in the Service Industries: Dynamics, Analysis, Growth* (pp. 165–172). Routledge.

Heiss, G. (2017). Influencing Factors and the Effect of Organizational Capabilities on Internationalization Strategies for German SMEs in the MedTech Industry. *Management, 5*(4), 263–277.

Jetter, K. (1991). Tuttlingen und seine chirurgischen Instrumente unter besonderer Berücksichtigung der Aufbauleistung von Gottfried Jetter. *Tuttlinger Heimatblätter*. N.F. 54, 24–29.

Kiuntke, F. (2006). *Der Wiederaufbau der Siemens-Reiniger-Werke nach dem Zweiten Weltkrieg (1945–1950)*. Friedrich-Alexander-Universität Erlangen-Nürnberg, Unpublished Magisterarbeit.

Korine, H. (2000). Fresenius AG: High-speed Globalization. *Business Strategy Review, 11*(2), 47–57.

Kreutzer, U. (2013). *Von den Anfängen zum Milliardengeschäft. Die Unternehmensentwicklung von Siemens in den USA zwischen 1845 und 2001*. Franz Steiner Verlag.

Liesen, E. (2004). *Die Entwicklung der Patientenverpflegung im Krankenhaus seit den 50er Jahren in Deutschland*. Rheinische-Friedrich-Wilhelms-Universität.

Linder, T. E., Simmen, D., & Stool, S. E. (1997). Revolutionary Inventions in the 20th Century: The History of Endoscopy. *Archives Otolaryngology Head Neck Surgery, 123*(11), 1161–1163.

Markusen, A. (1996). Sticky Places in Slippery Space: A Typology of Industrial Districts. *Economic Geography, 72*(3), 293–313.

Schraudolph, E. (1984). *Die Entwicklung von RGS bzw. SRW zwischen 1877 und 1945 in Wechselwirkung zur Stadt Erlangen.* Friedrich-Alexander Universität Erlangen-Nürnberg, Unpublished Magisterarbeit.

Schroeter, H. G. (1993). Continuity and Change: German Multinationals Since 1850. In G. Jones & H. G. Schröter (Eds.), *The Rise of Multinationals in Continental Europe* (pp. 28–48). Edward Elgar.

Steinle, C., Schiele, H., & Mietzner, K. (2007). Merging a Firm-Centred and a Regional Policy Perspective for the Assessment of Regional Clusters: Concept and Application of a "dual" Approach to a Medical Technology Cluster. *European Planning Studies, 15*(2), 235–251.

Trajtenberg, M. (1990). *Economic Analysis of Product Innovation: The Case of CT Scanners.* Harvard University Press.

Vittinghoff, D. M., & Vollertsen-Diewerge, M. (2008). *Max Gebbert & the Pioneers of Medical Engineering.* Siemens Med Archives.

von Weiher, S., & Goetzeler, H. (1977). *The Siemens Company: Ist Historical Role in the Progress of Electrical Engineering, 1847–1980.* Siemens AG.

Zenger, I. (2014). *Magnetic Resonance Imaging at Siemens: A Success Story.* Siemens.

Zenger, I. (2015). *The History of Computed Tomography at Siemens: A Retrospective.* Siemens.

CHAPTER 7

Orthopedics SMEs and Pharmaceutical Giants in Switzerland

1 Introduction

Switzerland is, after the United States, Germany, and Japan, one of several European countries with a large number of competitive medtech companies. According to Medical Design (2016), the ranking of the world's top 100 largest medtech firms includes three Swiss companies, similar to the United Kingdom (with four companies), Denmark (three), France (two), and Sweden (two). I thus use Switzerland here as an example of a middle-size medtech competitor in Europe. According to the trade association Swiss MedTech (2018), the industry employed about 58,000 people and had a national production of about 15.8 billion francs in 2017. Its size is similar to that of the watch industry, which is one of the major sectors of the Swiss economy. Moreover, the medtech industry includes a broad variety of companies, from foreign multinationals to family enterprises and startups. Switzerland also has a long tradition of academic excellence in engineering and medicine. The Federal Institute of Technology (School of Zurich) regularly ranks as the world's best university outside the US and UK.

Literature on Swiss medtech companies is only nascent, however, and the competitive advantage of this industry remains unclear at this point. Most of scholarly works focused on specific firms, especially in the field of orthopedic equipment (Kuttruff, 1996; Schlich, 2002), or on the cooperation between universities and firms in developing new technology

P.-Y. Donzé, *Medtech*,
https://doi.org/10.1007/978-981-16-7174-6_7

(Weigel, 2011; Coffano et al., 2017; Bestetti, 2009). Moreover, Livi and Jeannerat (2014) have argued that medtech startups have played a key role in carrying out innovation thanks to their closeness with research centers and universities as well as their financial support from multinationals. However, their study is based on a small number of interviews and does not provide solid evidence. Finally, the only general analysis is the paper by Klöpper and Haisch (2008). It argues that the driving forces of the development of the Swiss medtech industry were the existence of the watchmaking industry, the availability of capital, and the presence of research centers. The authors also mention the contribution of multinational companies.

Understanding the dynamics of the Swiss medtech industry and the sources of its international competitiveness requires evidence-based answers to the following questions. What role has the watch industry played in the development of medtech companies (the issue of technological convergence, in other words)? Are Swiss medtech firms focused on specific fields or general medtech? Which is the impact of pharmaceutical giants? How have universities and startups contributed to the growth of this industry?

2 Foreign Trade

Similarly to Germany, there are no official statistics on the production of medtech goods in Switzerland. I therefore use foreign trade figures to highlight the dynamics of this sector since the early 1990s. The analysis in this section draws on the Comtrade database. As I did for other countries, I selected the three major types of medtech goods following the harmonized product classification (HS codes): instruments and appliances used in medical, surgical, dental, or veterinary sciences (HS 9018), orthopedic appliances (HS 9021), and apparatuses based on the use of X-rays or of alpha, beta or gamma radiations (HS 9022).

The main feature of the development of the Swiss medtech industry between 1991 and 2019 is the strong competitiveness of this sector (see Fig. 7.1). First, there has been an acceleration in the value of exports from 1.1 billion USD in 1991 to 2.1 billion USD in 2000 and a peak of 10.7 billion USD in 2019. Moreover, this tremendous increase is accompanied by a consistently positive trade balance. The value of exports is between double and triple that of imports over the entire period. The globalization of the Swiss medtech industry, in particular through waves of M&A and investments in Switzerland by American multinationals, strengthened its competitiveness after 2000.

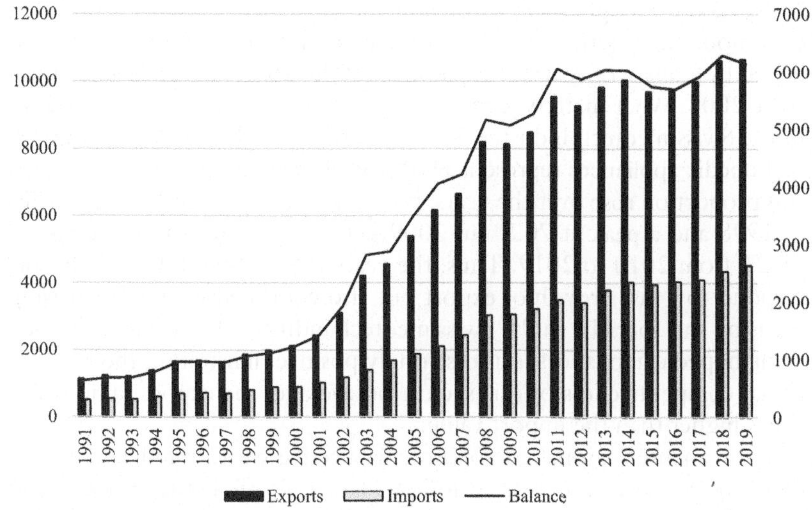

Fig. 7.1 Swiss foreign trade of medtech goods (million USD), 1991–2019. (Source: Comtrade, HS codes 9018, 9021 and 9022)

Which medtech fields are driving this expansion? First, the data on medical instruments and appliances shows a general rapid expansion of trade, which expresses the development of the Swiss medtech industry and the increase of the domestic consumption of medical technology. The growth of Swiss firms was not the mere outcome of the rising needs of domestic hospitals and doctors, however. Imports went from 286 million USD in 1991 to 2.3 billion USD in 2019, while growth accelerated at the end of the 1990s with the digitalization of medtech equipment. However, exports experienced a much larger development: they grew during these three decades from 540 million USD to more than 4 billion USD. Trade surplus increased constantly and amounted to more than 1 billion USD each year from 2008 onward. This does not, however, mean than Switzerland had a growing share of world market. In fact, it even slightly decreased from 3.6% of world's exports in 1995 to 3.2% in 2017. The burgeoning expansion of global the market was a growth opportunity not only for Swiss firms but also for companies based in newly emerging countries in the medtech business, such as China, Mexico, and Ireland. Consequently, the increasing shares of these countries brought Switzerland's relative share down.

Next, the foreign trade of orthopedic appliances presents a different evolution, characterized by a slow increase in exports (1991–1998) followed by a phase of very fast expansion (1998–2008) and then stagnation since 2008. What matters for this type of product is its important weight in the Swiss medtech industry. For the entire period from 1991 to 2019, orthopedic appliances represent 59.9% of all medtech exports. Moreover, this proportion rose over the years, growing from 45.1% in 1991 to 51.5% in 1998 and a peak at 70.3% in 2009 before stabilizing at an average of 63.2% from 2010 to 2019. Thus, the years 1992–2008 did not only correspond to a fast growth of export but also coincided with an increasing focus on this specialty in the Swiss medtech industry. The balance of trade of orthopedic appliances is also strongly positive, illustrating the international competitiveness of this sector: on average, the export value is 3.6 times higher than the import value.

From an international-comparison perspective, Switzerland has a strong competitive advantage despite losing market shares between 1995 and 2019. Between these two years, Switzerland shifted from second place behind the United States, with 15% of the global export total, to third place behind the United States and the Netherlands, with 11%. Although Switzerland lost some of its market share, it is still one of the top three largest nations in this business. Orthopedic appliances are one of the major specialties of the Swiss medtech industry, and numerous American firms have invested in Switzerland to acquire knowledge in the field (see below).

Finally, the field of X-ray and radiation devices constitutes only a small part of the Swiss medtech industry. At their maximum in 2012, exports totaled just 490 million USD, while medical instruments and appliances came to 2.7 billion USD and orthopedic appliances 6 billion USD that year. None of the giant electric appliance multinationals that dominate the X-ray device industry is based in Switzerland, as the field is largely controlled by American, German, and Japanese multinationals. Switzerland's market share is thus exceptionally low: it represented only 1.4% of world exports in 1995 and 1.5% in 2017. However, the balance of trade has improved over the years. It was still negative at the end of the 1980s, after which it reached a level close to equilibrium during the 1990s. After 2000, exports experienced a jump that led to a largely positive balance of trade despite a decrease in real value after 2012. This evolution does not stem from any development of production of complete X-ray equipment on Swiss territory by foreign multinationals, however. It is obviously the result of the emergence and growth of local suppliers to giant multinationals in a dual context: the integration of new electronic and digital technology on the one hand and the growing importance of MRI on the other.

Hence, this brief overview of the Swiss foreign trade of medtech products highlighted the presence of a competitive industry (a positive balance of trade) whose growth accelerated after 2000 and also underlined the substantial weight of orthopedic appliances in the sector. These features are significant factors shaping the M&A activities in this industry.

3 Mergers and Acquisitions

Data on mergers and acquisitions (M&As) in the Swiss medtech industry emphasizes two major characteristics of the sector: the strong international orientation of Swiss firms and their attractiveness for foreign investors. Between 1988 and 2017, a total of 199 other enterprises or company divisions have been acquired by Swiss medtech firms (Swiss firms as *buyers*), and 144 enterprises or company divisions in the Swiss medtech industry have been purchased by other firms (Swiss firms as *targets*) (see Fig. 7.2). Thus, there have been more acquisitions by Swiss medtech firms than acquisitions of Swiss firms. One can also observe an increase of M&As over time, with faster growth since the mid-1990s.

The international orientation of Swiss medtech firms is evident in the low proportion of domestic companies among the acquisitions. The domestic-acquisition share amounted to just 13.6% of the total in Switzerland, while the same rates over the same period came to 48.9% in Germany and 70.7% in Japan (Thomson One database). Of course, the sizes of these two countries are not similar to that of Switzerland, but size alone does not explain that gaping difference; a big factor is that the Swiss medtech industry has a relative global importance that far outweighs that of the Swiss economy as a whole. Swiss medtech firms are internationally competitive, and their objective is not to grow on the basis of gradual internalization of geographically close companies (either in Switzerland or transnationally) but rather to establish themselves as multinational firms. North America is the main region in which Swiss medtech firms invest (with North America accounting for 41.2% of acquisitions), followed by Europe (35.2%), while Asia represents only 5% of the total. Most acquisitions occur in the United States because Swiss firms seek both the new technologies emerging from the US and access to the world's largest medical market.

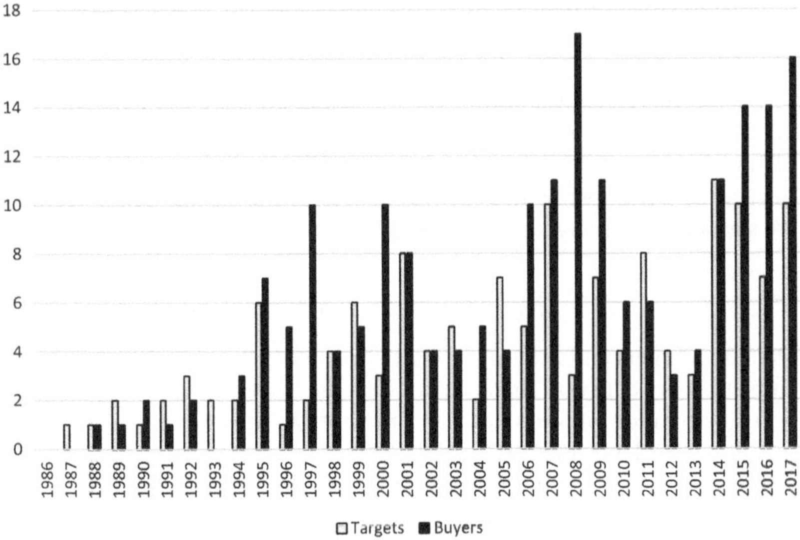

Fig. 7.2 Mergers and acquisitions in the Swiss medtech industry, 1988–2017. (Source: Thomson One)

The largest purchaser of American companies in the Swiss medtech industry is Hoffmann-La Roche (see below). It strengthened its diagnostic device, founded in 1968, through US acquisitions. For example, it acquired the equipment manufacturers Biomedical Reference Labs (1982) and American Diagnostic Corporation (1983), as well as the service supplier National Laboratories Holdings (1995). From the 1990s on, it expanded its network around the world. In 1997, the takeover of Corange Ltd., a company registered in Bermuda and headquartered in Germany, made Roche one of the largest diagnostic-products manufacturers in the world.[1] Acquisitions continued thereafter, particularly with the purchases of AVL Medical Instruments in Austria (2000), Thropgix SA in France (2005), Top Diagnostic in Rumania (2008), Innovatis in Germany (2009), and MTM Laboratories in Germany (2011).

Among the other firms active in the United States is the manufacturer of ophthalmological products and equipment Alcon (4 acquisitions in the US). Originally an American company, Alcon was taken over in 1978 by

[1] *New York Times*, 27 May 1997.

Nestlé, which then sold it to Novartis in 2008. It is thus difficult to consider Alcon as a Swiss company that expanded across the Atlantic. Other cases include Sulzer Medica (7 acquisitions in the US), Synthes (3), Sonova Holdings (2) and Straumann (2). All these Swiss medtech companies have based their international expansion on M&As.

Finally, most of the Swiss companies present in the US have been small, specialized firms that have only acquired a limited number of firms to strengthen their technological advantages. This was, for example, the case of Disetronic Holdings (acquisition of Micro Med in 1997), Comet AG (takeover of PCT Engineering Systems in 2015), Leman Cardiovascular (purchase of Hancock Jaffe Laboratories in 2006), laboratory-equipment manufacturer Buchi AG (takeover of the chromatographic division of Alltech Holdings in 2016), and surgical-material producer Codman Neuro Science (takeover of Pulsar Vascular Inc. in 2016).

This brief overview of the acquisitions of American companies by Swiss medtech firms highlights the twofold structure of the industry: it includes both large multinational enterprises that diversified into medtech (Roche and Nestlé) and a dense network of specialized SMEs.

As for the acquisitions of Swiss medtech firms (*targets*), the profile is more geographically balanced and also underlines the openness of the industry. Indeed, takeovers by other Swiss companies represent only 27.1% of the total cases. Other than Novartis (7 cases), most companies have only made one or two acquisitions of this type—but the same proportion comes to 48.9% in Germany and 89.3% in Japan. In Switzerland, however, foreign firms' interest in Swiss companies does not focus on access to the domestic market, due to its small size. What attracts FDI is technology and know-how developed by specialized companies. Most of these companies are European (34%) and American (29.9%), with Asian companies representing only 4.2% and the rest of the world 4.9%. The European companies are almost all French and German, mostly specialized firms that extend their R&D networks beyond national borders. The American companies, meanwhile, are essentially the giants of the global medtech industry (Baxter, Boston Scientific, Johnson & Johnson, etc.), with a high proportion of companies active in orthopedic appliances, like Stryker or Zimmer Holdings.

4 Innovation

An analysis of medtech patents applied for by enterprises, research organizations, and individuals established in Switzerland between 1960 and 2014 sheds light on the general evolution of innovation in the Swiss medtech industry. A total of 6657 applications were made over the course of the period, with enterprises (69.2%) and individuals (28.2%) filing the bulk of the submissions. Universities and hospitals accounted for only a paltry 2.6%—but numerous university scholars and medical doctors applied for patents as individuals. Change over time shows a rapid increase in applications since the 1990s, half of them being made after 2000 (see Fig. 7.3). However, the share of enterprises stayed relatively stable despite some fluctuations. From an international perspective, the enterprise share is relatively high. During the same period, the share of patent applications by firms was 82.9% in Japan, a country where R&D is strongly concentrated in the private sector, but only 59.3% in Germany and 40.7% in the United States. Among its counterparts in the West, Switzerland thus demonstrates a high level of R&D activity at private companies, a trend also apparent in other industries (Donzé, 2018a). In addition, research is concentrated in large enterprises: the top 10 largest patent applicants (all

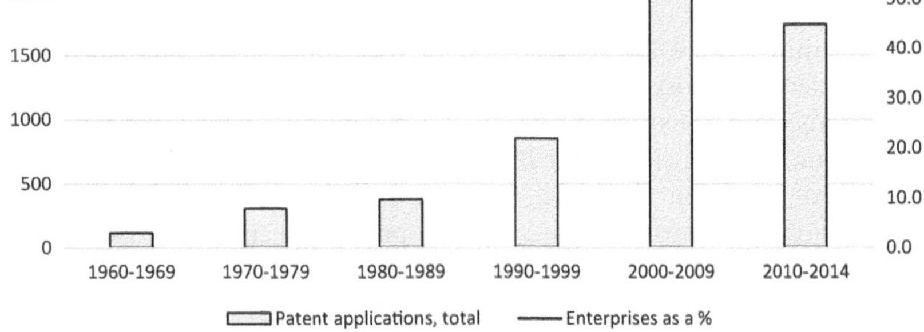

Fig. 7.3 Medtech patent applications made by assignees based in Switzerland, 1960–2014. (Source: PATSTAT)

companies) represent 42% of all applications and 61.2% of applications by companies. It is consequently necessary to focus on these actors.

Table 7.1 shows the top 10 largest Swiss firms by patent application and decade, highlighting the breakout in the 1990s and showing that the exponential growth since has relied on a new set of actors: specialized medtech companies, most of them with foreign capital. During the 1960s and the 1970s, the largest innovator was the pharmaceutical company Roche (particularly its diagnostic device division). One can also observe the presence of several firms outside the medtech specialization, such as the pharmaceutical company Sandoz, electrical-appliance manufacturer Brown, Boveri & Cie, and armament producer Contraves (formerly part of Oerlikon-Bührle). The watch companies Asulab and Lasag joined them in the 1980s. These types of companies dominated innovation in the Swiss medtech industry through the application of their technology in developing devices for medical doctors and hospitals. This technological convergence also explains the presence of Novartis in this ranking since 2000.

The period in question saw the emergence of just a few specialized medtech firms, most active in the fields of orthopedics, bone prosthetics, and implants. Synthes, founded in 1954, became the leading innovative firm in the Swiss medtech industry. It expanded successfully around the world and was taken over by the American group Johnson & Johnson in 2011.[2] The second major enterprise in this sector is Sulzer Medica, a division of the machine manufacturer Sulzer AG, which diversified after World War II into many other industrial sectors, including prosthetics. It was acquired in 2003 by the American company Zimmer.[3]

These takeovers of the "jewels" of the Swiss medtech industry point to a general trend that strengthened during the 1990s: the growth of inward FDI. Among the top 10 largest firms by patent application, the number of foreign firms went from two in the 1980s to six since 2000. The rapid increases in the Swiss medtech industry's application count since the 1990s thus appears to stem from the activities of large enterprises with foreign capital, a high proportion being active in orthopedic appliances.

The position of universities and research centers also merits attention. Indeed, the top-10 ranking for 2010–2014 includes a company specializing in R&D services for private partners, Centre suisse d'électronique et de microtechnique (CSEM). Founded in 1984, CSEM carries out research

[2] *Le Temps*, 24 April 2011.
[3] *Les Echos*, 7 August 2003.

Table 7.1 Top 10 largest Swiss firms in the medtech industry by patent application count and decade, 1960–2014

1960–1969	*1970–1979*	*1980–1989*	*1990–1999*	*2000–2009*	*2010–2014*
ROCHE (22)	ROCHE (53)	*SYNTHES (29)*	*SYNTHES (156)*	*SYNTHES (597)*	*SYNTHES (227)*
SYNTHES (6)	*SYNTHES (15)*	*SULZER (23)*	*SULZER (49)*	ROCHE (315)	ROCHE (113)
BROWN, BOVERI & CIE (5)	**STORZ ENDOSKOP (14)**	*JAQUET ORTHOPEDIE (14)*	**SHERWOOD (44)**	**ALCON (111)**	**KYPHON (92)**
	SULZER (14)	ASULAB (13)	SCHNEIDER (23)	***STRYKER (103)***	***STRYKER (74)***
	CONTRAVES (7)	**INTERMEDICAT (11)**	**LEICA AG (17)**	**BIOTRONIK CRM (79)**	NOVARTIS (58)
	BROWN, BOVERI & CIE (6)	**KONTRON HOLDING (11)**	**STORZ ENDOSKOP (15)**	**KYPHON (72)**	**LEICA (38)**
	SANDOZ (6)	*PROTEK (11)*	*FERTON HOLDING (14)*	**LEICA (70)**	**MEDOS (29)**
	INTERMEDICAT (5)	*S & T MARKETING (10)*	*PLUS ENDOPROTHETIK (14)*	**SHERWOOD (56)**	**SECA (20)**
	OSTEO (5)	LASAG (9)	*HAAG-STREIT (13)*	*PHONAK (32)*	**CELGEN (16)**
		CONTRAVES (7)	**STORZ MEDICAL (10)**	NOVARTIS (31)	CSEM (13)

Source: PATSTAT

Notes: (1) The table includes only firms with at least 5 applications. (2) Numbers in parentheses correspond to numbers of patent applications. (3) Italic represent firms specializing in orthopedic appliances, and companies in bold are foreign companies in a broad range of high-tech industries, from electronics to micromechanics, solar technology, and medical devices. This demonstrates the interest of research organizations in applied research in the medtech industry. What is the contribution of universities? Quantitative data suggests that universities have had an insignificant presence in the field of patent applications. All together, Swiss universities applied for only 177 patents in the period from 1960 to 2014. The largest assignees were the Federal Institute of Technology, School of Lausanne EPFL (50 patents) and School of Zurich ETHZ (22), and the University of Zurich (16)—these three accounted for about half of all applications by universities. If one considered EPFL as a company, it would even rank as the seventh-largest innovator in 2010–2014.

Moreover, the importance of universities goes beyond the volume of patents that they applied for in their own names. As major training centers, they have contributed to the competitiveness of Swiss medtech enterprises, whose many engineers and managers have graduated from the schools and with whom they continue to conduct joint research. This is the case of the Medical Engineering Laboratory (*Laboratoire de génie médical*) at EPFL, in particular, a spin-off from the Applied Physics Laboratory in the late 1970s (Cosandey, 1999, p. 140). Since the mid-1980s, the organization has cooperated with Lausanne Orthopedic Hospital (*Hôpital orthopédique de la Suisse romande*) and various private companies specializing in implants (Kaba, 2018, pp. 195–196). Finally, the numerous startups founded by EPFL and ETHZ illustrate the contribution of universities to the growth of the Swiss medtech industry since the 1990s (see below).

Beside private companies, what is the contribution of individual innovators? It is hard to make any relevant analysis until the 1980s due to their small numbers. Since the 1990s, the growing importance of engineers is striking (20% of top-10 largest individual applicants in the 1990s and 92.3% in 2010–2014). A major factor behind this change has been the development of departments and degrees in bioengineering at the Federal Institutes of Technology of Lausanne and Zurich. The career paths of these engineers indeed show that the graduates tend not to go on to become technical heads of R&D departments at large multinationals, like US and Japanese top innovators often do, but rather engage in a flexible medtech cluster focused on orthopedics. Belonging to a common community, they move between universities, startups, and larger enterprises. For example, Robert Frigg, the leading individual innovator between

1990 and 2014 (27 applications), started his career as a mechanist in 1978 at the research institute AO, specializing in orthopedics, and then worked during the 1980s as a project director at AO and the University of Bern. He was appointed chief technology officer at Synthes (2004) and served as a consultant, coach, and board member at several startups. He eventually became honorary professor in the Faculty of Medicine at the University of Zurich in 2008.[4] Human capital, as this example illustrates, is a major reason explaining the entry of foreign firms into the Swiss medtech industry.

5 The Main Actors in the Swiss Medtech Industry

The previous sections have laid out the most important features of the Swiss medtech industry. In the following section, I offer a detailed analysis of several cases that represent the general trends.

5.1 Orthopedic Appliance Makers

Equipment and implants related to orthopedic surgery have represented the main sector of the Swiss medtech industry since the post-World War II years. Numerous enterprises, some large, established themselves as competitors in world markets and attracted foreign investors. The roots of this competitiveness go back largely to the cooperation of a group of young and innovative surgeons and orthopedists with a few industrial companies (Schlich, 2002). The first set up a research group in 1958, *Arbeitsgemeinschaft für Osteosynthesefragen* (AO). Two years later, they founded a private company, Synthes AG, to which they transferred the rights to produce and sell equipment developed by AO, whose activities were in return funded by Synthes (Schlich, 2002, p. 57). This company then sold the manufacturing rights to two other firms, Straumann and Mathys AG, which signed a contract to share the world market between them (Schlich, 2002, p. 58). Hence Synthes focused on the management of patents and sales of goods. In 1960, Maurice E. Müller, head of the department of surgery at the Hospital of Sankt Gallen and a member of AO, created his own company, Protek AG, which specialized in the sales of hip prosthetics that he developed and were also manufactured by

[4] https://www.uzh.ch/de/about/portrait/awards/hc/2008/med2.html and https://www.linkedin.com/in/robert-frigg-7070088b/.

Mathys (Schlich, 2002, p. 289). This small network of firms is the basis on which the Swiss orthopedic appliance industry developed, through a process combining chains of spin-offs, outsourcing contracts, and the entry of a few new actors.

Sulzer, a manufacturer of machinery and mechanical equipment, secured a contract from Protek to manufacture implants in 1966. It internalized research capabilities, launched its own prosthetics, and finally took over Protek in 1989 (Kuttruff, 1996). Sulzer became a leading giant in the Swiss medtech industry and one of the world's largest producers of prosthetics. In 1998, the gross sales of Sulzer Medica came to 1.5 billion francs and centered largely on the American (46%) and European (42%) markets.[5] However, this subsidiary, renamed Centerpulse in 2002, was purchased by the American company Zimmer in 2003, following a scandal linked to defective products sold in the United States. Zimmer had a size similar to Sulzer Medica (gross sales of 1.2 billion USD in 2001), and the takeover of Sulzer Medica gave Zimmer an opportunity to strengthen its position in the European market, which represented only 11.2% of its sales in 2002.[6]

As for Mathys, it pursued its production for Protek and, later, for Sulzer until 1996. At that time, it launched its own prosthetics, which constitute the company's main activity. It consolidated its position through the takeover of Keramed Medizintechnik in Germany (2001). Mathys continued manufacturing equipment for AO until 2003, when it sold that portion of its operations to Stratec Medical, a spin-off of Straumann (founded in 1990) named Synthes—the same name as the company that marketed AO products. Although it was headquartered in Switzerland, this firm operated almost entirely in the United States during the 1990s (Schlich, 2002, p. 193). Synthes was purchased by Johnson & Johnson in 2011.

The rapid growth of these firms led to the accumulation of knowledge and technology related to orthopedic appliances on Swiss territory. A large number of smaller companies emerged, like Jaquet Orthopédie in Geneva or Precimed in canton Bern. Universities and the Federal Institute of Technology were also important training grounds for engineers and fertile environments for research on orthopedic technology. Finally, the specialization of the Swiss medtech industry in this field also attracted American

[5] Schweizerische Wirtschaftsarchiv (SWA), Basel, Bg885, Sulzer Medica, *Geschäftsbericht*, 1998.

[6] SWA, Bg885, Zimmer Holdings, Annual report, 2002.

investors, who took over not only the companies at the origin of this industry (Sulzer Medica and Synthes) but also smaller firms like the aforementioned Jaquet Orthopédie (purchased by Stryker) and Precimed (purchased by Greatbatch), resulting in a sector that today is largely controlled by American capital.

5.2 *Pharmaceutical Giants*

All large Swiss multinationals in the pharmaceutical industry have diversified into medtech, sometimes for a limited period, in the years since World War II. Although technology related to the development of drugs and medicine on the one hand and that concerning devices and instruments on the other hand are largely different, drugs and medtech circulate in markets controlled by the same actors (hospitals, clinics, and medical doctors). Thus, the diversification of pharmaceutical giants into medtech essentially comes down to marketing convergence. The process transpired basically through the acquisition of firms and divisions, as well as through some technical cooperation projects. For example, the pharmaceutical company Sandoz engaged actively in medtech during the 1970s, taking over two small Italian companies (1969), starting a joint-research collaboration with the Japanese company Sharp to develop measuring instruments for medical use (1973), and taking a stake in the American dialysis-device manufacturer Vital Assists (1974).[7] Ciba pursued a similar strategy. The diversification of these two firms represents the origins of the current presence of Novartis (a company born from the merger of Ciba-Geigy and Sandoz in 1996) in the medtech industry.

However, the Swiss pharmaceutical company that has shifted most intensively into medtech is Roche. In the mid-1960s, the firm adopted an all-out diversification policy that, in addition to fostering new organizations in other sectors, led to the creation of a medtech division after the acquisition of the diagnostic business of the Swiss chemical company Chemische Fabrik Schweizerhalle (1968) (Peyer, 1996). The same year, Roche signed a contract with another Swiss company, Société Genevoise d'Instruments de Physique (SIP), for the joint development of medical devices.[8] Roche also founded Tegimenta AG in Rotkreuz, Switzerland, specializing in instrument manufacturing, the following year. The

[7] *Le Journal de Genève*, 16 December 1969, 17 April 1973 and 29 January 1974.
[8] *Journal de Genève*, 3–4 Februray 1968.

investments in medtech extended past the domestic market, however. In 1970, Roche took over a diagnostic device company based in Denmark, Medi-Lab, and acquired the production rights for medical devices developed by the French industrial group Dassault.[9] These acquisitions formed the core of Roche's current diagnostic division. Launching a broad range of diagnostic devices during the 1970s and 1980s, Roche established itself as one of the world leaders in the field. The takeover of the group Corange in 1997 made Roche the first producer of diagnostic devices in the world. It again strengthened its position with the acquisition of the American company Ventana Medical Systems in 2008, followed by takeovers of other American and German microbiological diagnostic companies. The sales of Roche's diagnostic division have boomed, increasing from scratch in 1968 to 147 million francs in 1978 and 1.4 billion francs in 1989 (Peyer, 1996). In 2018, sales totaled 12.9 billion francs—22.7% of the gross sales of Roche Holdings.[10] That figure is close to the production value of the Swiss medtech industry, but it also includes activities in foreign countries. The total makes Roche one of the top ten largest medtech companies in the world.

5.3 *Startups*

Since the end of the 1990s, Switzerland has, like the United States and other European countries, seen a growing number of startups. Most have sprung up out of university campuses, not private enterprises. The Federal Institute of Technology (ETHZ and EPFL) and some other large universities have set up facilities to welcome startups and high-tech firms; Science Park in Lausanne (1991, today: EPFL Innovation Park) and Technopark in Zurich (1993) are two good examples (Donzé, 2018a).

Data from EPFL and ETHZ makes sheds light on the dynamics of these medtech startups.[11] Both organizations share two similarities: a fast-growing number of startups after 2010 and a very low percentage of companies that move out of startup status (through M&A or IPO). EPFL is the largest host of medtech startups, with 67 companies emerging out of

[9] *Traditionally Ahead of our Time*, Basel: Roche, 2016, p. 39 and *Journal de Genève*, 31 December 1970.

[10] Roche, *Annual Report*, 2018, p. 22.

[11] https://www.ethz.ch/en/industry-and-society/entrepreneurship/spin-offs/uebersicht-eth-spin-offs.html (accessed 10 October 2019). EPFL provided data to the author by email (25 May 2020).

the campus since 1989: 9 before 2000, 17 from 2000 to 2009, and 41 from 2010 to 2019. Among all these firms, only 4 were merged (EndoArt, Xitact, Aimago and KB Medical), and none became public. Moreover, 10 were discontinued—and 9 of those were startups founded before 2010; in total, 35% of all medtech startups founded before 2000 were discontinued. The overwhelming majority (53 companies) stayed private, either because they were aiming to grow as an independent SME or as a consequence of an inability to find investors. The number of medtech startups from ETHZ, meanwhile, came to just 23. The oldest (and the only one in the twentieth century) launched in 1999, while 5 were created in the 2000s and 17 in the 2010s. Only one, the developer of software and rehabilitation equipment YouRehab AG, has been merged. Occurring in 2017, the merger brought YouRehab AG together with a German company founded in 1999 to create Reha-Stim Medtec AG, a company headquartered in Switzerland with a subsidiary in the US.[12] None of ETHZ's medtech startups went public.

Therefore, unlike what companies tend to do in the United States and what the academic literature argues (Livi & Jeannerat, 2014), Swiss medtech startups have focused on neither M&A nor IPO. They developed mostly as private companies and contribute to the renewal of the strong network of SMEs that nurtures the sector.

6 Conclusion

This chapter's analysis of the dynamics of the Swiss medtech industry since the 1960s highlights some of the industry's features from an international comparative perspective, presenting three key specificities.

First, while the three dominant countries (the United States, Japan, and Germany) built their competitive advantages on the engagement of large multinationals from electric appliances and electronics (like General Electric, Toshiba, Hitachi, and Siemens) in developing medical devices, mostly since the interwar years, Switzerland has followed a distinct path (Gelijns & Rosenberg, 1999). The Swiss multinational Brown, Boveri & Cie (BBC, which merged with Asea to form ABB in 1988), a competitor of the aforementioned large companies, never invested massively in medtech. It developed some radiological equipment after World War II

[12] https://reha-stim.com/fr/la-societe/ (accessed 10 October 2019).

and pursued research in the field until the 1970s.[13] This was, however, only a side-business in comparison to what its competitors were doing (BBC applied for just 11 patents in medtech in the 1960s and 1970s), and the company withdrew from medtech in the 1970s (submitting only one patent application in the 1980s and another one between 2010 and 2014).

Rather than growing out of electric-appliance multinationals, then, the Swiss medtech industry started from a cluster of small companies involved in the development of orthopedic devices. Cooperation between medical doctors and small mechanical firms was the root of the industry in Switzerland. The orthopedics field remains today the largest and most competitive field of the Swiss medtech industry. It has benefited (albeit indirectly) from the know-how in fine mechanics and instrument-making that the watch industry has developed; companies like Straumann, which used to produce alloys for watches, have played an important role in the development of orthopedic equipment. However, only a scant few watch companies, including component suppliers, diversified into medtech. There is no direct link between the two sectors. The maintenance and development of Swiss firms' competitiveness results notably from research at the Federal Institute of Technology. Several startups founded in Lausanne are active in orthopedic devices.

A second field of medtech where Swiss companies have built a competitive advantage is the area of diagnostic devices, which is largely dominated by pharmaceutical giants that diversified into the business during the 1960s and 1970s due to the marketing convergence between their core businesses (drugs and medicine) and medtech. They strengthened their positions in the following decades via an active strategy of international M&As.

Second is the extremely open character of the Swiss medtech industry, which has been a crucial factor. Unlike other countries analyzed in this book, Switzerland sees exceptionally high levels of inward FDI. American medtech giants, as well as specialized firms in Europe and a few in Japan, are the main acquirers of Swiss medtech firms. The field of orthopedic devices in Switzerland is home to a substantial amount of American capital. Yet, in most cases, research activities take place on Swiss territory, as the ranking of the largest patent applicants in Switzerland indicates: the share of applications by foreign-owned companies is fast-growing since

[13] *Journal de Genève*, 29 November 1951.

the end of the twentieth century. The presence of high-quality academic centers provides direct support to the territorial roots of a global industry.

Third and finally, the general contribution of startups to the growth and diversification of the Swiss medtech industry remains unclear and merits further research. The engagement of universities and the Federal Institute of Technology in research and education related to medtech, as well as the presence of American medtech giants in the field of orthopedic devices, are certainly favorable to the creation and growth of startups. However, unlike the dynamics suggested by some scholars (Livi & Jeannerat, 2014) and observable in the United States, Swiss medtech startups do not usually end up merging into large corporations or going public. They developed as independent specialized firms and thus contribute to the renewal of the local medtech industry.

References

Other Published Sources

Medical Design. (2016). *Medtech's 100 Largest Players.* Retrieved May 18, 2019, from https://www.medicaldesignandoutsourcing.com/

Swiss Medtech. (2018). *The Swiss Medtech Industry 2018.* https://www.frn.swiss-medtech.ch/smti

Books and Academic Articles

Bestetti, G. (2009). Medtech: Potential for Innovation. *Swiss medical weekly, 139*(41–42), 587–590.

Coffano, M., Foray, D., & Pezzoni, M. (2017). Does Inventor Centrality Foster Regional Innovation? The Case of the Swiss Medical Devices Sector. *Regional Studies, 51*(8), 1206–1218.

Cosandey, M. (Ed.). (1999). *Histoire de l'Ecole polytechnique de Lausanne, 1953–1978.* PPUR.

Donzé, P.-Y. (2018a). Innovation. *Dictionnaire historique de la Suisse.* https://hls-dhs-dss.ch/fr/articles/055505/2018-12-17/

Gelijns, A. C., & Rosenberg, N. (1999). Diagnostic Devices: An Analysis of Comparative Advantages. In D. C. Mowery & R. R. Nelson (Eds.), *Sources of Industrial Leadership: Studies of Seven Industries* (pp. 312–358). Cambridge University Press.

Kaba, M. (2018). *Une histoire de l'orthopédie : l'Hôpital orthopédique de la Suisse romande dans le contexte international (18e–21e siècles).* BHMS.

Klöpper, C., & Haisch, T. (2008). Evolution de l'industrie biotech et medtech suisse et influence de l'industrie pharmaceutique sur le système d'innovation. *Revue Géographique de l'Est, 48*(3–4), 1–25.

Kuttruff, J. (1996). *Der vom Anwender induzierte strategische Prozess: eine empirische Längsschnittanalyse zum Innovationsprozess im Bereich der Medizinaltechnik*. Universität St. Gallen, Dissertation.

Livi, C., & Jeannerat, H. (2015). Born to Be Sold: Startups as Products and New Territorial Life Cycles of Industrialization. *European Planning Studies, 23*(10), 1953–1974.

Peyer, H. C. (1996). *Roche, Geschichte eines Unternehmens : 1896–1996*. Roche.

Schlich, T. (2002). *Surgery, Science and Industry*. Palgrave Macmillan.

Weigel, S. (2011). Medical Technology's Source of Innovation. *European Planning Studies, 19*(1), 43–61.

CHAPTER 8

The French Medtech Industry: A Lack of International Competitiveness

1 Introduction

The previous chapters specifically tackled two examples of European countries (Germany and Switzerland) that have experienced successful development of their respective medtech industries since the second part of the twentieth century. Although they share some similarities, particularly regarding the presence of numerous specialized SMEs that created a competitive advantage over the years, these two countries also present major specificities, such as the presence of one of the world's largest medtech multinationals located in Germany (i.e., Siemens), as well as the important role played by a pharmaceutical giant (Roche) and US firms in Switzerland. However, these two successful examples do not mean that all European countries were able to follow a similar path. The COVID-19 crisis has revealed the strong domination over the importing of the medical equipment of many European countries, France in particular.[1]

In reality, although the global rank of the one billion medtech firms also includes cases from Belgium, Denmark, France, Italy, the Netherlands, Spain, Sweden, and the UK (see Chap. 3), the medtech market in most of these countries is dominated by foreign goods. In 2018, while four major European countries had a medical device trade balance of over 5000 billion Euro (Ireland, Germany, Switzerland, and Netherlands), nearly all

[1] See, for example, *Le Monde*, 3 November 2020.

P.-Y. Donzé, *Medtech*,
https://doi.org/10.1007/978-981-16-7174-6_8

other countries were negative. Spain had the largest deficit (-2681 million Euros), followed by France (-2255 million Euros; MedTech Europe, 2020).

The French case is particularly intriguing. Although a large employer—with 89,000 people in 2018, consequently making it the third largest in Europe after Germany (227,700 employees) and the UK (97,600; MedTech Europe, 2020)—the French medtech industry is dominated by foreign firms. Yet, as the global medtech industry was formed and developed as a big business during the 1980s–1990s, precisely when the European Economic Community enforced its single-market policy, the large size of the French national market was not particularly important in its support of the development of domestic companies. Instead, it has attracted foreign companies to invest in Europe through France, as did GE in 1987 (see below, Sect. 5.1). In 2017, foreign companies represented 66% of the French medtech market and 50% of employment (SNITEM, 2017). Besides this, in 2011, 24% of all medtech firms active in France were foreign-owned companies with only a commercial activity (PIPAME, 2011). Moreover, domestic firms on average are small in comparison with those in other European countries. The share of medtech companies with less than 250 employees amounted to 94% of all firms in France in 2011, against 75% in Switzerland, 85% in Italy, 86% in Germany, 90% in Spain, and 98% in the UK (PIPAME, 2011).

Most recent publications on the French medtech industry by academic scholars (Andersson et al., 2013), authors from business (Moustial, 2019), and public organizations (PIPAME, 2011) emphasize the high quality of French medtech research and the numerous startups founded every year. Andersson et al. (2013) argue that the integration of French medtech SMEs in international networks makes it possible to connect them with major multinational enterprises and to support their internationalization. However, although this model can explain the development of a handful of SMEs, it fails to highlight the major weaknesses of medtech as an industry in France. In particular, the high volume of foreign companies must be discussed not only in terms of its ability to connect local SMEs with global markets but also in relation to the balance of trade (i.e., the production in France or import from foreign manufacturing centers) and R&D (i.e., where research is conducted). These issues are essential to achieving a proper understanding of the long-term dynamics of the French medtech industry.

Therefore, this chapter focuses on the example of France as the case of a European medtech industry that did not achieve global competitiveness and whose weaknesses had strengthened since the end of the twentieth century. The main questions addressed by this chapter are as follows: Why were French medtech companies unable to build and/or maintain a competitive advantage over the years? What are the sources of weakness in this industry?

2 Foreign Trade

The dependency of France on imported medical devices is not the mere result of the formation of giant medtech firms in the US, Japan, and Germany. Before these multinational companies began dominating the global market, France already had a negative balance for medtech goods. In 1980, medtech import (including electro-medical equipment, medical instruments, orthopedic aids, and X-ray devices) amounted to 518 million dollars, while export was only 355 million. Except for X-ray devices, which were slightly positive (+19 million) due to the presence of Compagnie Générale de Radiologie (CGR), one of the world's leaders in medical imaging (see below Sect. 5.1), import was largely more important than export for all other categories (United Nations [UN], 1980). The total deficit reached 163 million dollars in 1980 and developed continuously over the following decade (347 million in 1990). The successive devaluations of the Franc during the 1980s contributed to this increasing imbalance, as they made imports from the US and from Germany more expensive.

In this context of a growing dependency on imports, X-ray devices showed an impressive development. Between 1980 and 1990, the value of export increased from 125 million dollars to 278 million, and the positive balance for this division strengthened (+68 million in 1990). CGR had been acquired by GE, who decided to make it one of its major R&D and production centers for healthcare devices in the world. However, the competitiveness of this category of medical device was insufficient to improve the general balance. French medtech companies were largely lagging behind in other categories. This is particularly the case for two major sectors of the global medtech industry, electro-medical equipment and orthopedic aids. Between 1980 and 1990, the trade deficits for these two categories increased from 27 million dollars to 100 million, and from 61 million to 151 million, respectively (UN, 1980, 1990).

The general imbalance in French medtech trade developed in the early 1990s and established around 500 million dollars a year (see Fig. 8.1). A detailed analysis of this trade demonstrates that X-ray machines formed again the only division that was positive. However, the total export of such

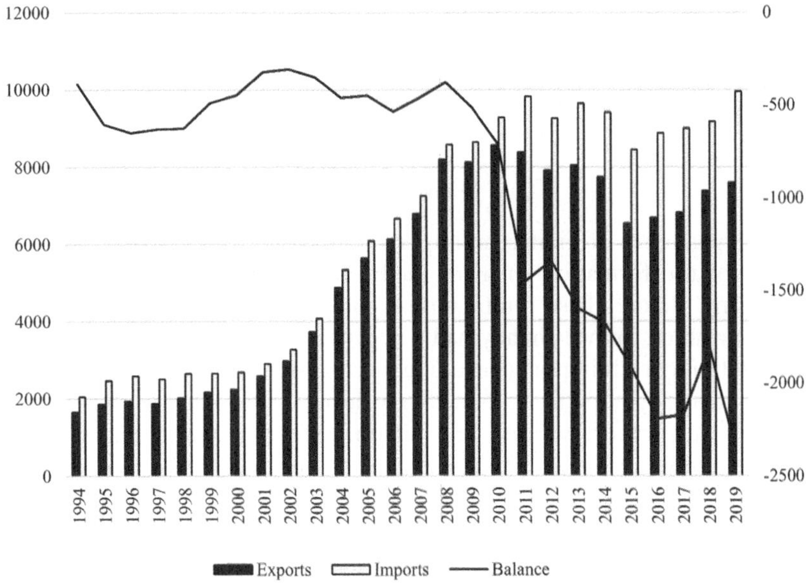

Fig. 8.1 French foreign trade of medtech goods (million USD), 1994–2019. (Source: Comtrade, HS codes 9018, 9021 and 9022)

devices only amounted to approximately 585 million a year, while it simultaneously exceeded 1.5 billion in neighboring Germany. Moreover, the balance was only slightly positive (126 million). France was not a giant in this business. As for other categories, they were largely negative. The deficit was over 130 million a year for orthopedic equipment and over 550 million for general medical and surgical devices. In the period 2000–2009, the rapid expansion of the trade had no significant impact on the deficit level. The development of X-ray device export, which grew from 630 million in 2000 to a peak at 1.7 billion in the period 2008–2012, supported the increasing deficits for other goods until 2009, but it was the rapid import of general devices and orthopedic equipment that has led to a larger deficit since 2010. In particular, the import of orthopedic devices was, on average, nearly three billion dollars in the period 2010–2019, against less than 500 million in 2000. Despite the existence of French small firms specialized in niche markets, such as Marle Orthopaedics and

Amplitude Surgical,[2] the market for implants is dominated by American and Swiss firms, which do not mainly produce in France. These two countries represented more than two-thirds of the value of French imports of orthopedic devices in the 2010s. Besides this, the export of X-ray devices began to decline in 2012. It was only 1.3 billion in 2019, and the positive balance for this equipment dropped from a peak at 702 million in 2010 to 366 million in 2019. The deterioration of France's most competitive equipment had a negative impact on the general balance of its medtech trade.

This brief analysis emphasized the weak foundations of the French medtech industry. First, it lacked competitiveness in orthopedic devices, which became (like in other countries) a major part of medtech consumption (18.2% of French medtech imports in 1994 and 35.7% in 2019). Second, the long-term growing deficit of general medical and surgical devices also represents a major weakness despite the existence of few leading companies in specific fields, such as in respiratory devices (L'Air Liquide) and diagnostic devices (BioMérieux). Third and finally, the rapid change in the condition of X-ray devices shows the degree of dependency against a foreign company that dominated this industry in France after a takeover. Once the company adopted a different strategy for its product development and production, export from France began to decline (see Sect. 5).

3 Mergers and Acquisitions

The M&A data related to the French medtech industry shows a slight increase from 1985 to 2017. It includes 470 cases of French medtech companies taken over by another firm ("target") and 338 cases of firms or divisions of firms acquired by a French medtech company ("buyers"). Like Germany, this means domestic companies were merged more by other companies versus merging themselves with other firms. However, unlike Germany, France presents a high proportion of domestic M&A. Over the 470 cases of the merged medtech firms, 59.6% were purchased by a French company. This is one of the highest levels in mainland Europe, as it is only 46.8% in Germany, 45.2% in Italy, 39.2% in the Netherlands, and less than 30% in Switzerland and Denmark. This is close to the UK (58.5%). These figures suggest that French medtech firms were generally not attractive for

[2] *Les Echos*, 30 January 2017 and 4 November 2019.

global companies, particularly giant firms from the US, Japan and Germany, or that large domestic firms actively acquired these companies.

A detailed analysis of these takeovers confirms the first assumption. Among the world's 10 largest medtech companies in 2014, GE was the only one to make a major acquisition in France (CGR, 1987), followed by the takeover of the small company Numeris (1997) and the ultrasound division of Thales (2003). As for Philips (Atek NC-Systems, 1986), Johnson & Johnson (Vania Expansion, 2008), Roche (ABX, 1990), and Siemens (Edap, 1997), each acquired only one firm. All in all, the world's 10 largest companies made only seven M&A cases in France. If one extends to the top 20 largest firms, total acquisition increases to 14 cases. Moreover, the breakdown by country certainly shows the domination of the US (81 cases), but with a lower number than in neighboring Germany (119 cases), as well as the near absence of Asian nations (three takeovers by companies based in China, three in Japan, and one in Singapore). Therefore, it is possible to assert that French medtech firms are not strategic targets for global companies that dominate this industry. This is likely related to a low level of innovation, as highlighted in the next section on patent data.

Next, let us look at the profile of French companies that acquired at least three domestic medtech firms. This includes a total of seven enterprises, all of which are small, specialized, and relatively uncompetitive internationally: Delta Plus Group, a manufacturer of professional protection equipment, including for medical use (four acquisitions); Diagnostic Medical Systems, a small company specialized in medical imaging (4); Bastide Le Confort Médical, a distributor of medical supplies and instruments on the French market (3); IMV Technologies, the French leader of artificial insemination and veterinary imaging (3), which also took over two companies in the Netherlands; Peters Surgical, a small producer of surgical instrument (3), which also acquired one company in India; and two investment funds, Midi Capital (3) and Turenne Capital (3). These examples clearly demonstrate that domestic M&A did not represent an effective way to build large and diversified French medtech conglomerates able to compete internationally (Fig. 8.2).

The analysis of the acquisitions made by French medtech firms ("buyers") offers a complementary look at this industry. It emphasizes that their development strategy was largely based on the domestic and European markets. These companies made a total of 338 acquisitions, among which nearly half in France (45.6%). The US is the second most important

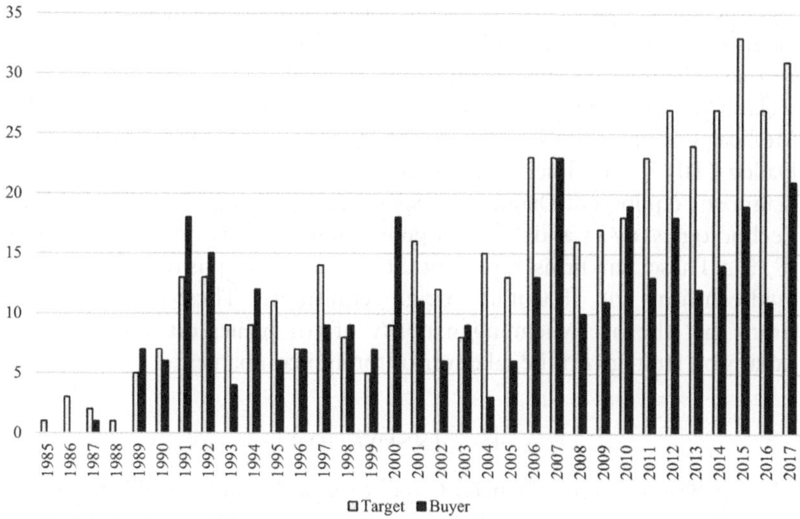

Fig. 8.2 M&A in the French medtech industry (number of cases), 1985–2017. (Source: Thomson-One database)

country, but only with a share of 11.5%, and close to Germany (10.4%). The UK (4.4%) and the Netherlands (3.6%) are next among the other major countries. Outside of Europe, one must stress the low number of acquisitions in Asia (four in India, two in China, two in Korea, one in Japan, and none in Taiwan). Besides this, the most striking feature of these takeovers is the strong domination by a handful of large companies. Air Liquide is the uncontested leader in acquisitions: it took over a total of 90 companies and divisions of firms—that is, more than a quarter of the total (26.6%). Moreover, this firm is the most internationally-oriented French medtech company: 69 of its acquisitions were realized abroad (37.5% of all foreign acquisitions). Yet, as Air Liquide is not a specialized medtech firm but an industrial gas manufacturer and distributor with a medtech division, not all of its acquisitions relate to its medtech business. Obviously, the company also took over companies to strengthen its other divisions. The Thomson-One database, however, does not allow for identification of the true M&A objective, but one must be conscious that the figures for medtech acquisitions by Air Liquide are overestimated. The development of this firm is analyzed in Sect. 5.

Other enterprises with five acquisitions or more include the in vitro diagnostic company BioMérieux (26 acquisitions, among which 19 are abroad), the pharmaceutical companies Synthelabo (14/10) and Roussel-Uclaf (13/11), the homecare service and respiratory assistance LVL Médical Groupe (11/7), the manufacturer of optical goods Christian Dalloz (10/7), the laser manufacturer Quantel (9/2), the producer of diagnostic equipment Diagnostica Stago (6/6), the abovementioned IMV Technologies (6/2), and the orthopedic equipment manufacturer Thuasne (5/5). These ten firms represent 56.2% of all acquisitions by French medtech firms and 75% of all foreign acquisitions. These figures demonstrate that the overwhelming majority of companies do not base their expansion strategy on the takeover of foreign companies.

4 Innovation

The analysis of medtech patent applications by individuals, firms and research organizations based in France between 1960 and 2014 sheds light on sources of weaknesses in the French medtech industry. First, one can stress the general decline of France's share in global applications. It decreased from 2.93% of the world's total in the 1960s to 2.63% in the 1990s and 1.11% in the period 2010–2014. The waning, therefore, became severe in the early twenty-first century, when large multinationals established themselves as dominant players in this industry.

A comparison with the leading nations in the medtech industry (see Chap. 2) makes it possible to emphasize the extremely low level of research activity conducted by the largest firms. This is the main feature of French R&D in the medtech industry. On average, firms represent only 35.8% of patent applications for the entire period, against 40.7% for the US, where applications by individuals are particularly high, and more than 60% for Germany and Switzerland. However, more than this general figure, the position of the top ten largest applicants among firms reveals a major weakness of the French medtech industry. On average, their applications amount to only 27.9% of all applications by firms, and the trend declined over the years (58.1% in the 1960s and 19.1% in the period 2010–2014). In the leading medtech nations, this share is either stable or has been increasing since the 1980s. The growth of the global medtech industry is based on large companies that have dominated this sector since the end of the twentieth century (see Chap. 3). Most of these do not conduct R&D in France. The weak position of large companies in R&D could be the result of a vibrant network of startups and small specialized firms. However, the domestic-oriented M&A trend demonstrates the low interest of global firms for the French medtech industry, where the argument of a large number of specialized medtech companies, like in the US where the top-ten firms have a relatively low position within applications by firms (however, higher than in France), is not relevant.

Table 8.1 shows who the largest French medtech innovators are. They include several firms specialized in medtech business, notably in X-ray devices and medical imaging (CGR), surgical instruments (Drapier, Porgès), diagnostic equipment (Spengler), orthopedic devices (Ceraver, Cousin Biotech, Dimso, Landos, LDR Medical, Safe Orthopaedics, Sofamor, Tornier), and other specialized medical devices (Ela Medical, Euros, FHI, JBS, Mauna Kea, Medicalex, Medinov, Sofradim, Technomed International).

One must also mention the presence of numerous non-medtech firms that diversified to this industry with few specific businesses, like the optical goods company Essilor or the industrial gas company L'Air Liquide. This is particularly the case of pharmaceutical companies with divisions of diagnostic and laboratory equipment (L'Oréal, Robert & Carrière, Synthelabo, Toraude) but also of manufacturers of electrical appliances that founded medtech subsidiaries such as GE or Siemens (Thales, Thomson Medical). Therefore, most of these firms are specialized medtech companies.

Until the 1980s, the medical imaging equipment maker CGR was the uncontested leader in French medtech research, although the number of patent applications, constantly below 100 for a decade, could not be compared with the large companies in leading nations, which often applied for thousands of patents. Moreover, following the takeover by GE, research activities have gradually decreased since the 1990s. The company disappeared from the top ten after 2000. This example embodies the French medtech industry excellently. A large number of the small firms mentioned in this ranking were taken over by foreign companies, which obviously used them as a market entry into the European market, but do conduct very few research in France. This is the case for Stryker, for example, a giant in orthopedic implants, who acquired Dimso in 1992 to make it its French subsidiary.[3] In 2020, it increased its presence in France with the purchase of Tornier. As for Zimmer Biomet, it merged LDR Medical in 2016, while Medtronic transferred the production activities of Sofamor to

[3] *L'Usine Nouvelle*, 10 March 1994.

Table 8.1 Top ten largest French firms for patent application in the medtech industry, 1960–2014

1960–1969	*1970–1979*	*1980–1989*	*1990–1999*	*2000–2009*	*2010–2014*
CGR (27)	CGR (50)	*GE-CGR (95)*	*GE-CGR (69)*	L'OREAL (29)	ESSILOR (29)
ROBERT & CARRIERE (13)	THALES (21)	THALES (41)	SOFAMOR (29)	ESSILOR (21)	*MEDICREA (13)*
LAB. TORAUDE (7)	ESSILOR (12)	ESSILOR (23)	JBS (25)	SOFRADIM (20)	L'AIR LIQUIDE (13)
DRAPIER (5)	THOMSON MEDICAL (8)	L'OREAL (15)	MEDINOV (24)	*STRYKER (20)*	COUSIN (11)
PORGES (3)	L'OREAL (7)	TECHNOMED (8)	TORNIER (22)	TORNIER (19)	L'OREAL (11)
BREVETS NOVO (3)	SYNTHELABO (5)	TORNIER (7)	DIMSO (19)	ELA MEDICAL (18)	ACES (10)
L'AIR LIQUIDE (3)	CERAVER (4)	LANDOS (6)	ELA MEDICAL (15)	MEDICREA (18)	OPHTIMALIA (10)
THOMSON MEDICAL (3)	SPENGLER (4)	SYNTHELABO (5)	EUROS (15)	FHI (16)	SAFE (10)
–	TORNIER (4)	MEDICALEX (4)	LANDOS (15)	LDR MEDICAL (14)	FHI (9)
–	PORGES (3)	MEDINOV (4)	STRYKER (15)	MAUNA KEA (14)	WITHINGS (9)

Source: Centredoc, medtech database

Note: This table includes firms with more than two patents, the number of applications is in brackets, and italic texts represent foreign companies its plants in the US after the takeover of the company in 1999.[4] These examples show that France is considered a place for marketing medical devices and sometimes also a place for manufacturing, but R&D is mostly conducted in other countries. This explains both the low presence of foreign companies in the top-ten ranking of patent applicants and the overall low level of patenting.

Besides this, the profile of the largest individual assignees in the 2000s confirms the low level of R&D activities in medtech companies based in France. During this decade, the ten largest individual assignees had a total of 121 patents, against 349 in the US, 176 in Germany, and 139 in Japan. Moreover, while these assignees were essentially engineers working in large companies in foreign countries, in France, it includes medical doctors, independent inventors and owners of small companies, together with only a few engineers working at GE Healthcare and Stryker.

Finally, universities and public research centers play an important role in France, with a share of 10.1% of all applications, which is twice as high as all other leading nations. However, this is still far from China where state-owned organizations are more important than private firms (see Chap. 9). The three most important research centers are not universities but public-funded organizations: Centre National de la Recherche Scientifique (CNRS), Commissariat à l'Energie Atomique (CEA), and Institut National de la Santé et de la Recherche Médicale (INSERM). They include approximately one third of all patents by research organizations. These centers are not only focused on fundamental research but also conduct applied research in cooperation with private companies.[5] For example, a total of 186 startups active in medtech were founded within CNRS between 1999 and 2019.[6] However, their future (IPO, M&A, closure) is unknown and there is presently no academic research that discusses the real contribution of research organizations to the development of the French medtech industry.

[4] *L'Usine Nouvelle*, 9 June 2016, and Les *Echos*, 28 April 1999.

[5] *Les Echos*, 10 April 2018.

[6] https://www.cnrs.fr/sites/default/files/press_info/2020-11/DP_StartUp_CNRS_VD_0.pdf (accessed 16 February 2021).

5 Varieties of Development Pathways for Large French Medtech Companies

Despite the existence of hundreds of SMEs active in medtech, these firms are unable to fulfill the needs of the domestic market. The French trade balance for medtech products has not only been negative at least since 1980, but the deficit has constantly increased over the last four decades. Data on M&A and patents has emphasized the difficulty most French medtech companies have to grow. Yet, the global market is increasingly dominated by large multinational enterprises (see Chap. 3). In this context, this section discusses the development pathway of two large French medtech companies: CGR, which was one of the world's leading X-ray companies until the 1990s, and Air Liquide, a company that diversified actively in medtech during the 1970s and 1980s. Both cases highlight the major importance of technological choices (the failure to invest in CT scanners for CGR, and the refocus on medical gases and respirators after 2000 for Air Liquide), as well as the impact of foreign ownership (the gradual decline in R&D in France for CGR).

5.1 *From the Pride of French Medtech to the Takeover by GE: CGR*

Compagnie Générale de Radiologie (CGR) was a joint stock company that specialized in X-ray devices and medical imaging equipment and was one of Siemens' and Philips' most important competitors on the European market during the post-war high-growth years. The roots of the company can be traced back to the foundation of a mechanical and optical instruments workshop in Paris by Adolphe Gaiffe in 1856. It developed a broad range of goods, among which were some medical instruments and X-ray devices in the early twentieth century. In 1919, it merged with a manufacturer of X-ray tubes, giving birth to the company Gaiffe-Gallot & Plon. In 1930, it was merged with two other producers of X-ray machines into the newly formed CGR (CGR, 1956; Racine, 1988).

CGR had some technical agreements with Siemens in its beginnings, but some financial disagreements led the French company to cooperate instead with GE.[7] In 1940, the former French subsidiary of GE,

[7] Bibliothèque nationale de France (BNF), Paris, WZ 1100, Annual Report and minutes of the general assembly of CGR, 26 June 1939.

nationalized in 1936, Compagnie Française pour l'Exploitation des Procédés Thomson-Houston (CFTH), became CGR's largest shareholder with 34.3% of the capital.[8] This firm experienced rapid growth after World War II but focused essentially on the domestic market, where it was established as the leading X-ray manufacturer through the absorption of numerous small competitors (Racine, 1988). Export represented only 16% of gross sales in 1963.[9] Consequently, to improve its international presence, CGR took stakes in companies in Belgium, Germany, Italy and Spain between 1963 and 1968.[10] It also began its expansion on the US market with a majority stake in Keleket (1968) and the acquisition of Westinghouse Electric's medical division in Baltimore (1970). It finally opened sales subsidiaries in Canada (1968), Venezuela (1968), Brazil (1970) and Mexico (1972). Finally, in 1975, it took over the European medical business of GE, an event that embodied the successful development of CGR. This wave of acquisitions made the French company the world's third largest X-ray producer after Siemens and Philips, while it was ranked only 25th in 1963 (Racine, 1988).[11]

However, despite this fast-growing expansion, CGR missed the technological turn towards CT scanners and MRI. Consequently, a decrease in sales began during the second part of the 1970s and led to the firm facing severe difficulties, as it had been in debt to finance its international expansion. In 1980, CGR was absorbed by its main shareholder, Thomson CSF (a company formed in 1966 by the merger of three firms, among which was CFTH), and reorganized as Thomson-CGR.[12] However, the cooperation with another firm was necessary in the development of competitive CT scanners. During the first part of the 1980s, Thomson-CGR negotiated with various British and US firms. An agreement was found with GE, as the French company had strong sales networks in Europe and Latin America, where the US multinational was weak (Racine, 1988). In 1987, GCR was taken over by GE, which exchanged it with Thomson against the TV business of its subsidiary RCA Music.

In the 1980s, GE Medical Systems (GEMS) adopted a new strategy to establish itself as the new global leader in medical imaging equipment (see

[8] Ibidem, 13 September 1940.

[9] Ibidem, Annual Report, 1963.

[10] Ibidem, Annual Report, 1963–1968.

[11] *Le Monde*, 11 October 1975.

[12] *Le Monde*, 17 March 1980.

Chap. 4). It positioned France as its main R&D and manufacturing base in Europe and specialized in X-ray equipment. Therefore, GE-CGR kept its position as the largest applicant of patents in the French medtech industry in the 1980s and 1990s (see Table 8.1). However, the shift toward the digitalization of medicine and to diagnostic services led GE to drastically reduce its research activities in France. The French subsidiary only applied for 12 patents in the 2000s (ranked 13th) and none in the period 2010–2014. It is still one of the largest employers in the French medtech industry, with approximately 2700 workers in 2018, but most high value-add activities are conducted outside France.[13]

5.2 *Air Liquide Healthcare*

The COVID-19 crisis has revealed to the general public the presence in France of one of the world's largest manufacturers of respirators: Air Liquide Healthcare.[14] Founded in 1902, this company is among the leaders of the industrial gas industry. It has developed on an international scale since the interwar years through the production and sales of acetylene, oxygen, and other gases used by the manufacturing industry (Jemain, 2002). Hospitals and clinics have also been customers of the producers of oxygen since the beginning of the twentieth century, but this was a minor market with regard to metalworking companies that used gas for cutting and welding (Stokes & Blanken, 2016). However, the arrival of US industrial producers in Europe during the 1960s and 1970s made the business much more competitive, where European companies engaged more actively to develop new markets outside of the manufacturing industry. Healthcare was one of these.

Therefore, Air Liquide began to invest significantly in medtech to strengthen its position as a provider of oxygen for medical use. In 1975, it opened a division that specialized in the development of respirators and equipment to distribute oxygen in hospitals. Three years later, in 1978, it founded Air Liquide Medical (ALM), a company that specialized in the manufacturing of lighting systems for operating rooms, with a sales network throughout Europe.[15]

[13] *L'Usine Nouvelle*, 12 October 2018.

[14] *Les Echos*, 18 April 2020.

[15] *L'Usine Nouvelle*, 6 June 1996.

Moreover, it acquired several home medical care enterprises and was able to achieve a 90% market share in medical gas business in France in 1991 (Stokes & Blanken, 2016, pp. 354–355). The engagement of the company in the medtech industry took a step forward during the latter half of the 1990s. In 1995, it founded a new subsidiary, Air Liquide Santé (ALS), for the supervision of all activities related to healthcare, from gases to respirators and other equipment.[16] It diversified from lighting systems (ALM was sold in 2001)[17] and took over several manufacturers of respirators abroad, particularly in Italy (1996 and 2000) and India (2008). These acquisitions enabled Air Liquide to come back to its core competence (medical gases) and build a strong competitive advantage in this area of technology. In the period 2010–2014, it was the second largest applicant of medtech patents in France (see Table 8.1). The sales of the medical gas division grew from 1.1 billion Euros in 2000 to 1.9 billion in 2010 and 3.7 billion in 2019.[18]

6 Conclusion

The analysis of the evolution of the French medtech industry conducted in this chapter makes it possible to emphasize the most important causes of its lack of international competitiveness. Despite the existence of numerous SMEs, France was unable to establish itself as a leading nation in the global medtech industry. Two main reasons for this were highlighted.

The low level of research activity by private companies appeared as the first major weakness. Data on patent applications demonstrated that French companies have one of the lowest levels in mainland Europe. Moreover, this feature also includes the largest firms. This likely explains why foreign companies did not take over a large number of French medtech firms. Public research centers play a major role in R&D in French medtech, but their ability to transfer technology to private firms and to contribute to nurturing competitive players should be discussed by scholars in a large-scale study.

The lack of investment in R&D also constitutes a major reason for the failure of CGR to maintain its competitive advantage and to transform

[16] *L'Usine Nouvelle*, 6 June 1996.

[17] *L'Usine Nouvelle*, 1 February 2001.

[18] L'Air Liquide, Annual Report, 2000–2019.

into a diversified medtech giant, as GE and Siemens did. During the 1970s, when the CT scanner was developed, CGR only applied to a total of 50 patents, while Toshiba had 797 applications in Japan, Siemens 572 in Germany, and GE 119 in the US—the latter was still lagging behind in the healthcare business at that time (see Chap. 4). Medical imaging equipment was—and still is—a major pillar of any national medtech industry and the failure of CGR contributed to the decline in the competitiveness of the French medtech industry.

Second, French medtech companies did not extensively use M&A as a way to internationalize. The number of acquisitions is rather low and mostly related to other domestic companies. The difference here with Germany and Switzerland is striking. French companies have remained small and domestic-oriented but have had to face competition by giant medtech companies that dominate their national market. Here also, CGR was an exception, but its takeover by GE in 1987 put a gradual end to the internationalization of the French medical imaging business.

These weaknesses clarify the strategy adopted by US and German medtech giants in France—their presence is not a problem per se. The case of Switzerland, where the domestic orthopedic device sector is dominated by US multinationals, demonstrates that foreign multinationals can continue investing in R&D and production locally (see Chap. 7). The presence of an environment to support these activities, such as dedicated research facilities at the world's top-level universities and innovative SMEs, is necessary. Yet, foreign companies have a completely different attitude in France, where they conduct negligible R&D and tend not to take over local firms. This has resulted from the features of the French medtech industry revealed in this chapter.

References

Other Published Sources

CGR. (1956). *Compagnie générale de radiologie, 1856–1956*. Compagnie Générale de Radiologie.

MedTech Europe. (2020). *The European Medical Technology Industry in Figures 2020*. Retrieved February 20, 2021, from https://www.medtecheurope.org/wp-content/uploads/2020/05/The-European-Medical-Technology-Industry-in-figures-2020.pdf

PIPAME. (2011). *Dispositifs médicaux : diagnostic et potentialités de développement de la filière française dans la concurrence internationale*. Pôle interministériel de prospective et d'anticipation des mutations économiques.

SNITEM. (2017). *De la filière industrielle des dispositifs médicaux en France en 2017*. Syndicat National de l'Industrie des Technologies Médicales.

United Nations. (1980). *International Trade Statistics Yearbook*. United Nations.

United Nations. (1990). *International Trade Statistics Yearbook*. United Nations.

Books and Academic Articles

Andersson, S., Evers, N., & Griot, C. (2013). Local and International Networks in Small Firm Internationalization: Cases from the Rhône-Alpes Medical Technology Regional Cluster. *Entrepreneurship & Regional Development, 25*(9–10), 867–888.

Jemain, A. (2002). *Les conquérants de l'invisible: Air Liquide, 100 ans d'histoire*. Fayard.

Moustial, P. (2019). La France dans la compétition mondiale des technologies médicales? *Les Tribunes de la sante, 2*, 67–72.

Racine, B. (1988). *Le syndicalisme et la modernisation: étude d'un cas type de modernisation démocratique: contribution à l'étude de la dynamique de transformation du rapport salarial dans la mutation*. [Rapport de recherche] Centre national de l'entrepreneuriat(CNE); Ministère des affaires sociales et de l'emploi.

Stokes, R., & Blanken, R. (2016). *Building on Air*. Cambridge University Press.

CHAPTER 9

The Rise of a New Medtech Giant: China

1 Introduction

During the last 20 years, China has established itself as one of the most important manufacturers of medtech equipment. Although there is only one Chinese firm among the world's largest companies in this industry (see Chap. 3), macroeconomic data on foreign trade, patent applications and M&A has emphasized the growing presence of China (see Chap. 2). Meanwhile, the COVID-19 crisis has revealed this position to a large public around the world. China has simultaneously not only become one the world's largest medtech markets, but also a fast-growing one. Its size was evaluated at 27.8 billion USD in 2011 and 75.9 billion in 2017 (Bao, 2019).

The conditions of formation and development of this national industry, however, are largely unknown. There is almost no academic research that explores the dynamics of the Chinese medtech industry. Cheong et al.'s (2020) research represents a rare exploration of the evolution of this sector, approached through the theory of innovation systems. It is, however, an overview that underestimates the weight of foreign firms. The objective of this chapter is therefore to analyze how this industry emerged, who are its main actors, and how it has changed over time.

Data published in the Chinese Statistical Yearbook (http://www.stats.gov.cn/tjsj/ndsj/) makes it possible to understand the overall development of domestic medtech companies since 2001. Figure 9.1 shows the

P.-Y. Donzé, *Medtech*,
https://doi.org/10.1007/978-981-16-7174-6_9

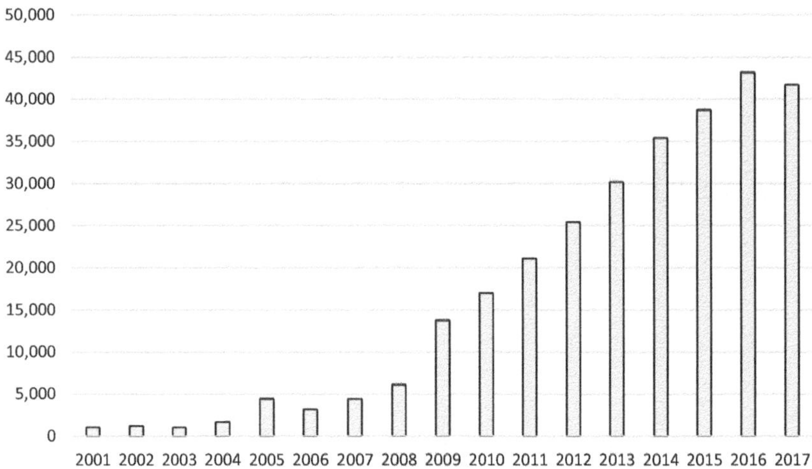

Fig. 9.1 Revenue from principal business by Chinese medtech companies (million USD), 2001–2017. (Source: Chinese Statistical Yearbook, 2002–2020. Note: Conversion in USD realized on the basis of exchange rates published on the website Measuring Growth (https://www.measuringworth.com))

value, in million USD, of the principal business of all companies engaged in the development and production of medtech equipment. It therefore excludes sales from other activities. These numbers demonstrate that this industry was still in a formational stage in the period 2001–2003. Revenues amounted only to an average of 1.1 billion USD, while the value of medtech production was over 60 billion in the US (see Chap. 4) and more than 12 billion in Japan (see Chap. 5) during the same years. Yet, the situation began to improve with a phase of slow growth that led to 6 billion sales in 2008, followed by an acceleration of the development during one decade, which led to a peak at more than 43 billion USD in 2016. China was still lagging behind the US, the largest producer in this industry (112 billion USD in 2016) but it had reduced the difference to less than one third within a decade. It had also become twice as large as Japanese medtech production and was obviously above Germany and other European countries, although the lack of data regarding national production in Europe means it is not possible to properly estimate this relation.

Moreover, the production by Chinese companies does not answer all the growing needs of the domestic healthcare market. Local manufacturers focus on low-end products, while the consumption of high-end equipment relies on import or local production by foreign companies.

What are the key characteristics and main drivers of this impressive development? First, the major factor is undoubtedly the improvement of the learning facilities of Chinese medtech companies. While the first manufacturers of medical equipment essentially focused on the copy of foreign products in the 1980s and 1990s (Cheong et al., 2020), medtech companies after 2000 gradually internalized knowledge related to engineering and medicine, and then engaged massively in R&D (see below Sect. 5). The number of full-time equivalent employees in R&D departments increased from 637 persons in 2001 to more than 7300 in 2010 and more than 30,000 in 2019, and the number of new products launched on the market increased from 673 in 2001 to more than 9200 in 2019 (China Statistical Yearbook, 2001–2020). These developments are not the mere result of an increasing demand for healthcare and medtech. The new policy adopted after the mid-2000s by the central government to promote high-tech industries played a major role. Investment in the development of universities made it possible to train a growing number of highly-educated engineers. The number of Chinese universities (including Hong Kong) ranked among the world's top 100 best universities in engineering and computer science increased from only 6 in 2007 to a total of 24 in 2017 (ARWU, 2007–2016). This gave companies in many industries the human resources necessary for their development. Moreover, several sectoral policies were adopted to support the formation of competitive companies in the medtech industry. For example, in 2009, the Ministry of Science and Technology organized the China Strategic Alliance of Medical Device Innovation, which promotes the formation of networks connecting various actors engaged in the development of specific products (private companies, universities, and hospitals). Regulation for the approvement of medical devices was also reformed and became stricter to avoid risks after 2000 (Cheong et al., 2020).

Second, one must stress the fast expansion of the domestic healthcare market, resulting from both the development of hospital infrastructure and an increase in individual consumption (Wang et al., 2019). The total number of general hospitals in China was only 14,377 in 1990, but it grew to 20,918 in 2010 and to 34,354 in 2019 (China Health Statistics Yearbook, 2020). Besides this, since 2005, the government has adopted various policies to promote the development of private clinics and introduce market mechanisms in hospital management. For example, the central state set prices that healthcare providers can charge patients at a lower level than real cost to make them affordable. Hence, to balance their accounts, hospitals and clinics needed to obtain revenue from other sources, such as selling drugs and diagnostic tests not included in state regulation. This provided private investors with the opportunity to develop diagnostic testing centers to offer these services to wealthy patients (Khanna & Raabe, 2007).

The development of China's national healthcare infrastructure represents an increasing demand for medtech equipment and an excellent opportunity of growth for numerous private enterprises. At the same time, Chinese people's growing income (the GDP per capita increased from 318 current USD in 1990 to 4550 in 2010 and 10,217 in 2019), as well as the trend regarding the ageing population (the share of population above 65 years grew from 5.6% in 1990 to 8.1% in 2010 and 11.5% in 2019) had an impact on medtech consumption.[1] The increasing demand from institutional and individual consumers has represented a major driver of the fast development of the Chinese medtech industry during the last decade.

Consequently, one can argue that the Chinese medtech industry is one of the sectors that benefited largely from the development of the domestic market as a strategic objective of the government after SARS and the global financial crisis (GFC; Wang et al., 2019). A remaining question, which is addressed below, is to estimate to what extent foreign companies benefited from this expanding demand in China. As we have seen throughout this book, the global medtech industry since the 1990s has largely been dominated by large multinational enterprises, mostly from the US, Japan and Germany. Their participation in the development of the Chinese medtech industry is discussed in Sect. 3. Moreover, another issue to clarify is the competitiveness of Chinese medtech companies. Their ability to reach beyond their borders, through export and M&A, is analyzed in Sects. 2 and 3.

[1] https://data.worldbank.org (accessed 20 May 2021).

2 Foreign Trade

Medtech foreign trade statistics perfectly illustrate that China became a major competitive manufacturer in this industry during the first two decades of the twenty-first century. The annual export was under 300 million USD during the second part of the 1990s—against more than 10 billion for the US, more than 5 billion for Germany and more than 3 billion for Japan. China, therefore, lagged far behind the medtech industry's leading nations. However, in 2000, Chinese export amounted to 445 million and entered a period of rapid expansion, reaching 4.9 billion in 2010 and 11.1 billion in 2019 (see Fig. 9.2). In 2019, China had established itself as one of the world's largest exporters of medtech goods. It had reduced the difference with the US (44.5 billion USD in 2019) and Germany (27.6 billion), and had overcome Japan (7.3 billion). A major issue, which is not possible to discuss on a quantitative basis, is to estimate the share of export by companies with foreign capital. To what extent the growing competitiveness of the Chinese medtech industry results from the presence of leading global firms remains an open question. Qualitative

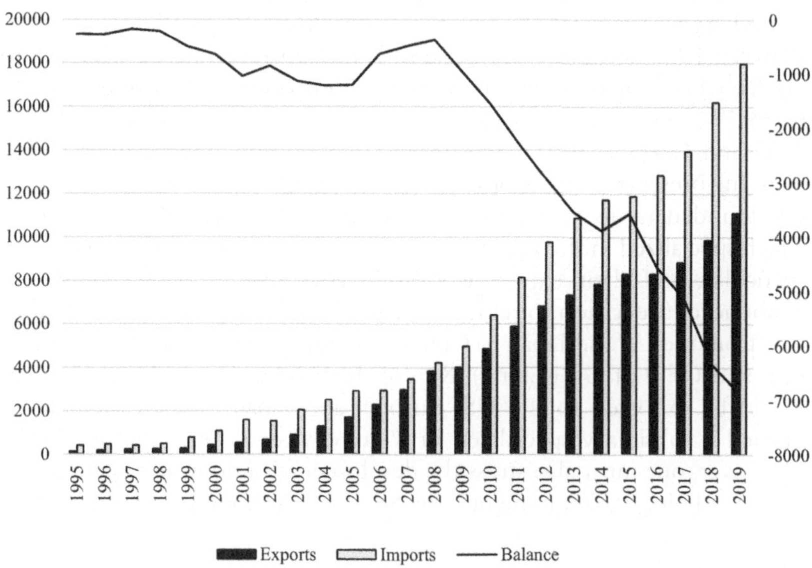

Fig. 9.2 Chinese foreign trade of medtech goods (million USD), 1995–2019. (Source: Comtrade, HS codes 9018, 9021 and 9022)

evidence provided below suggests that foreign firms contributed to this development, but only partially.

However, although this development is impressive, it was not enough to compensate the even faster-growing import of medtech products. The development of the national healthcare system led to a massive expansion of the needs for medical devices. Despite the growth of a domestic industry, China had to rely increasingly heavily on imports to equip its healthcare facilities with high-tech equipment. Moreover, the increasing disposable income and ageing population impacted the demand for individual medtech products. For example, the import of pacemakers grew from 6.6 million USD in 2000 to 81 million in 2010 and 189.4 million in 2019. Consequently, the deficit of the trade balance worsened over the years. It first decreased slightly, from—269 million USD in 1995 to—1.2 billion in 2005. Then, the rapid surge of export led to a short-term recovery to—379 million, before an acceleration of the trade deficit, which reached—6.7 billion in 2019.

A more detailed analysis of the composition of this trade makes it possible to stress several major features of the Chinese medtech industry. First, regarding the structure of export, there was a clear shift during the second part of the 1990s, followed by nearly two decades of stability. Between 1995 and 2001, the share of X-ray apparatuses grew from 8.8 to 26.7%, while general medical and surgical instrument decreased from 85 to 59.7%, and orthopedic devices experienced stable growth (6.3% in 1995 and 13.6% in 2001). The growth of X-ray equipment export results from the presence of the world's major manufacturers of such equipment. GE founded in 1991 a joint venture, Hangwei Medical Systems Co., which specialized in the production of X-ray machines and CT scanners in particular, and their export worldwide (see Sect. 5.2). In 1999, GE announced its decision to relocate the R&D and manufacture of CT scanners from the US and Japan to China. According to David C. Wang, chairman and CEO of GE (China), 80% of the production of this equipment would be exported to the US, Europe, and Japan.[2] As for Siemens, it opened a subsidiary specialized in X-ray devices in Shanghai in 1992.[3] Moreover, one must also stress the development of domestic manufacturers of radiological equipment (see Sect. 4). Although it is difficult to

[2] *BBC Monitoring Asia Pacific*, 27 December 1999.

[3] Website of Siemens China, https://www.healthcare.siemens.com.cn/about/ssme-cn (accessed 14 April 2021.).

estimate the share of foreign companies in the increase of X-ray equipment export, the fact that the two largest markets for Chinese export in 2000 and 2019 were the US and Japan, rather than emerging countries, suggests a domination of global firms in this trade—they produce in China for their home markets.

Second, the main characteristic of the structure of imports is the rapid increase in the share of orthopedic devices (1.5% in 1995; 17.8% in 2020; and 24% in 2019). This expresses the development of healthcare consumption related to the ageing population in China. The main suppliers were the US (32% of import in 2019), Ireland (13.5%), Switzerland (10.2%), Germany (10.1%) and Mexico (7.5%)—that is, countries where the multinationals dominating this business have their main manufacturing centers. For other equipment, the GFC appears to be a turning point. The share of general medical and surgical instruments declined from 59% in 1995 to 44.1% in 2007, then entered a period of steady growth to 54.6% in 2019. In the meantime, X-ray apparatuses shifted from a phase of stability (average of 38.5% in the period 1995–2007) to a decline to 21.4% in 2019. This was obviously the consequence of the development of production in China.

3 Mergers and Acquisitions

M&A statistics also emphasize the turning point of the mid-2000s (see Fig. 9.3). Before 2000, there was nearly no mergers including medtech firms, because this industry was still in a formative period, and because of the low number of private companies large enough to acquire other firms in this business. M&A was used in particular for the consolidation of the domestic industry, much more than for its insertion in the global economy. A total of 477 Chinese medtech firms were acquired (targets), among which 80.9% by another Chinese company. Moreover, Chinese medtech companies (buyers) took over a total of 379 companies, in medtech or in other industries, among which 88.7% were in China.

Details about this M&A data show that the consolidation process of the national medtech industry through mergers did not lead to the emergence of a few dominant players but, rather, to the general development of numerous firms. Indeed, among the 386 Chinese medtech firms merged by another Chinese company, only a small proportion were acquired by an enterprise who had a large-scale M&A strategy. Guangdong Biolight Meditech (7 acquisitions), Lepu Medical Technology (7), Mindray (6),

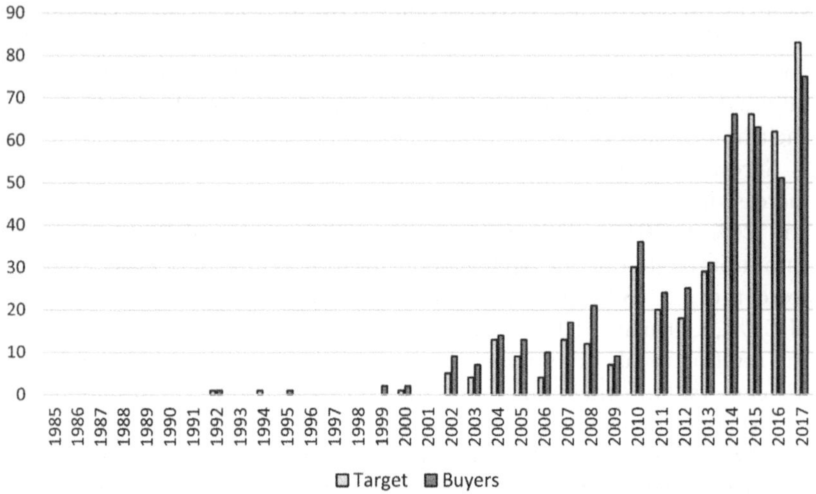

Fig. 9.3 M&A in the Chinese medtech industry (number of cases), 1986–2017. (Source: Thomson One database)

Wuhan Thalys Medical Technology (5), Hunan China Sun Pharma Mach (4), Shinwa Medical Instrument (3), Ningbo Xinhai (3) and Zhuhai Hokai Medical Instruments (3) represent the rare companies that had more than two acquisitions. This means that more than 90% of the acquisitions by domestic firms were realized by companies with only one or two acquisitions. This dispersion expresses the dramatic expansion of the Chinese healthcare market, which made it possible for numerous medtech firms to experience organic growth without focusing on an intense M&A strategy. There was, however, a weakness for the national industry, as no large conglomerate or company emerged from M&A, unlike in the US.

The foreign acquisitions by Chinese medtech firms confirm this lack of global expansion. Companies that fostered their expansion abroad are exceptions rather than the major manufacturers of medtech equipment. For example, Concord Medical Services Holdings, which was founded in 1993, is a provider of cancer medical imaging services. It was listed in New York Stock Exchange in 2009, launched a cooperation with GE Healthcare in 2011, and held five major hospitals in China in 2020. Despite that it took a minority stake in the US company MD Anderson Proton in 2015, the objective was not to expand business internationally.

The 2015 Annual Report explained that this company was "a leading proton treatment center in the world. As we plan to invest and operate two proton centers in China in the future, this transaction will enable us to expand our expertise and knowledge base in preparation for the operation of future proton centers" (CMS, 2015, p. 45). Similarly, in 2017, Shandong Weigao purchased two medtech firms in the US, among them was Argon Medical Devices. In the following year, it exposed in its annual report that one of the objectives was to "expand sales of Argon products in the PRC [People's Republic of China] market" (Weigao Group, 2018, p. 10). These two examples embody the fact that Chinese medtech firms focus on their fast-growing domestic market and realize acquisitions abroad to essentially internalize knowledge that will be useful at home. Even Mindray, the largest and most international Chinese medtech company, took over only three foreign companies (Datascope and Zonare Medical Systems in the US in 2008 and 2013, respectively, and Ulco Medical in Australia in 2013), and developed mostly on the domestic market (see Sect. 5.1).

Finally, one must discuss if M&A is used as an important market entry by foreign medtech companies. Although the overall number of cases of cross-border acquisitions is limited, several medtech giants merged Chinese companies. This is notably the case of US companies Medtronic (the acquisition of the medical polymer division of Shandong Weigao, 2007; China Kanghui Holdings and Lifetech Scientific Co. in 2012), Stryker (Trauson Holdings, 2013) and Zimmer (Beijing Montagne Medical, 2010), the British Smiths Group (Zhejiang Zheda Medical Instruments, 2008), the Dutch multinational Philips (Shenzhen Goldway Industrial, 2008), and the Japanese company Terumo (Shanghai Angiocare Medical, 2012). M&A, however, was not the only way to enter China. Many other foreign companies founded wholly-owned subsidiaries or joint-ventures.

4 Innovation

The medtech patent database, realized on the basis of PATSTAT, makes it possible to identify the assignees of patent applications since the 1980s. The top-ten largest medtech firms by patent applications are presented in Table 9.1. Like for other countries, I selected companies with a minimum of three applications per decade. However, for the 1980s, it was impossible to select any firm, as none had more than two applications. R&D in

Table 9.1 Top 10 largest Chinese firms by patent-application count in the medtech industry, 1960–2014

1990–1999	*2000–2009*	*2010–2014*
ANKE HIGH TECH (14)	TOUCHSTONE (200)	**BAODAN MEDICAL INSTRUMENT (399)**
ANSHAN IRON & STEEL (11)	MINDRAY (197)	RUNZE PHARMACEUTICAL (306)
AOWO INTERNATIONAL (10)	LANDWIND MEDICAL (129)	UNITED IMAGING HEALTHCARE (275)
SUZHOU MEDICAL (7)	TIANCHEN INTERNATIONAL (101)	TIANCHEN INTERNATIONAL (268)
HAOKE OPTOELECTRONIC APPARATUS (6)	*SIEMENS SHANGAI (70)*	*SIEMENS SHANGHAI (221)*
WEIDA MEDICAL APPARATUS AND INSTRUMENTS GROUP (4)	LEISHUO (53)	EDAN INSTRUMENTS (210)
TANGSHAN IRON & STEEL (4)	KANGJI MEDICAL (52)	MINDRAY (202)
WUJIN MEDICAL (4)	SHANGHAI LASER MEDICAL INSTRUMENT (49)	PANTHER MEDICAL EQUIPMENT (191)
LANZHOU MEMORY ALLOY (3)	*PHILIPS AND NEUSOFT MEDICAL SYSTEMS (33)*	NEUSOFT MEDICAL SYSTEMS (114)
–	TONGLU ACME ENDOSCOPE (32)	BEIJING CHOICE ELECTRONIC TECHNOLOGY (113)

Source: Centredoc, medtech database

Notes: (1) Numbers in parentheses correspond to numbers of patent applications. (2) Italic text represent companies with foreign capital. (3) Bold characters represent state-owned companies

the Chinese medtech industry during this decade was mostly carried out by state-owned organizations (see Chap. 2) and focused on copying and adapting foreign technology (Cheong et al., 2020).

During the 1980s, no firm filled out three or more patent applications. The emergence of innovative enterprises began in the 1990s. There were still only a few companies above the three-patent application mark, as only nine firms were identified. Their number grew to more than 300 in the

2000s and more than 400 in the period 2010–2014. Therefore, innovation in the Chinese medtech industry developed rapidly after 2000, and this growth relied on the development of private companies.

The profile of the largest patent applicants in the 1990s expresses the strong weight of the state in this industry at that time. There were two large diversified state-owned conglomerates, which owned a small medtech division (Anshan Iron & Steel and Tangshan Iron & Steel), and two producers of medical instruments belonging to local governments (Suzhou Medical and Wujin Medical). Moreover, the largest innovator, Anke High-tech, was a private company founded in Shenzhen in 1986 by the Chinese Academy of Science to manufacture medical imaging devices (Bai, 2016). It is a case of technology transfer from academics to industry, and confirms the impact of the state during the formative years of this industry, as universities are basically state-owned in China. Besides these firms, a handful of private companies applied for few patents.

This first generation of innovative enterprises, however, was not the basis of the growth of a medtech industry in China. The aforementioned four state-owned companies have an insignificant position in the ranking of patent applications after 2000, and Anke High-tech pursued its development thanks to a joint-venture agreement with the US company Analogic Corporation, signed in 2000.[4] It experienced a dramatic decline, however, in the ranking of innovative firms (16 patent applications in the 2000s and 12 in the period 2010–2014). The situation is similar for other private companies of the 1990s' ranking, none of which established themselves as a key actor in this industry after 2000.

Consequently, the enterprises that have dominated R&D in the Chinese medtech industry since 2000 are newcomers. This confirms quantitative data on the revenue, foreign trade and M&A that all emphasized the turning point of the mid-2000s. The largest patent applicants since 2000 have essentially been private companies founded in the 1990s onwards. Of course, these companies were not created from scratch. Knowledge largely came from universities, academic science parks, public research institutions, and state-owned companies, similar to Anke High-tech during the 1990s. Mindray Medical, one of the most competitive Chinese medtech firms and the only one in the global ranking of one billion medtech firms, resulted from a transfer of knowledge from state-owned organizations (see Sect. 5.1, below). For example, Kangji Medical explains on its website that

[4] Analogic Corporation, Annual Report (10-K Form), 2001.

it "has been stationed in Tonglu Economic Development Zone, Zhejiang Province, and has set up R&D centers for enterprises."[5] As for Hangzhou Kangji, it mentions that it "was recognized as a state-supported high-tech enterprise."[6] Although such assertions are rather vague about the nature of support by the state, they suggest a cooperation between public and private spheres toward developing a competitive medtech industry. Private entrepreneurship contributed to the building of profitable organizations for the development, the manufacture and the distribution of medtech products, while universities and hospitals supported knowledge development. For the entire period of 1980–2014, the total number of patent applications made by universities, hospitals, and other state-owned organizations amounted to 16,335, against only 12,692 for private enterprises. During the 2000s, 39 universities and 6 hospitals had more than 15 patent applications, against 22 private companies. The trend is similar for the period 2010–2014. In particular, the Chinese Academy of Sciences (305 applications in the 2000s), Shanghai Jiao Tong University (204), Zhejiang University (179), Tsinghua University (171) and Fudan University (106) were major innovators. The conditions of the transfer of technology to the private sector are unknown, but academic innovation undoubtedly contributed to the development of private firms.

Moreover, the growth of private companies does not mean that state-owned firms have disappeared from the medtech industry. In the period 2010–2014, the largest patent applicant was Baodan Medical Instrument, a manufacturer of optical instruments founded in 2008 in Guangzhou by the local government and a hospital of the city. The purpose was to create a company for marketing the innovations carried out by doctors and engineers in the field of endoscopy and diagnostic devices.[7] This was an exception, however. All other firms were private companies in the period 2010–2014.

The second feature of the largest patent applicants after 2000 is the presence of firms with foreign capital, essentially in the field of medical imaging devices (CT scanners and MRI). Siemens Shanghai Medical Technology is the fifth largest innovator in the Chinese medtech industry.

[5] https://www.hzkangji.com/En/about/index.html (accessed 5 May 2021).

[6] https://www.hzkangji.com/En/about/index.html (accessed 5 May 2021).

[7] Website from the Guangzhou Association for Promotion of Science & Technology and Finance, http://www.gzkjjr.cn/huiyuan/shownews.php?lang=cn&id=135 (accessed 5 May 2021).

It began in 1992 as an assembler of medical devices and shifted gradually to R&D. In 2012, it employed approximately 1000 people, among whom one third were in R&D, and exported 70% of its products to overseas markets.[8] The presence of Siemens in the Chinese medtech industry also led to the foundation of other joint ventures such as Siemens (Shenzhen) Magnetic Resonance Company (29 patent applications in the period 2010–2014). This example clearly shows the transition from manufacturing to development after 2000. A similar path led in some cases to the empowerment of the Chinese partner. For example, the Dutch multinational Philips founded in 2005 a majority-owned joint venture with the Chinese software company Neusoft for the development and production of medical imaging devices.[9] Although the company became one of the largest innovators in the Chinese medtech industry, Philips decided to withdraw from the joint venture in 2013.[10] Neusoft Medical kept its position as a major player in the medical imaging business.

5 Case Studies

Domestic private companies and foreign multinationals are major actors in the rapid development of a medtech industry in China since 2000. According to an official survey, the number of medtech firms listed in China (including on the Hong Kong Stock Exchange) went from a total of only 22 companies in 2014 to 74 in 2019, with total revenue growing from 3.4 billion USD to 21.2 billion between these two years (CAMDI, 2020).[11] If one considers that the total revenue of Chinese medtech companies amounted to approximately 34 billion USD in 2014 and was estimated to be roughly 45–50 billion in 2019 (see Fig. 9.1),[12] the growing weight of these listed firms is clear: it shifted from approximately 10% to more than 45%. This general trend aptly expresses the growing

[8] https://w1.siemens.com.cn/news_en/news_articles_en/2088.aspx (accessed 5 May 2021).

[9] https://www.neusoft.com/News/html/20051029/4638194234.html (accessed 5 May 2021).

[10] https://www.neusoft.com/News/html/20130705/4545143227.html (accessed 5 May 2021).

[11] Conversion in USD realized on the basis of exchange rates published on the website, Measuring Growth (https://www.measuringworth.com).

[12] The source used for Figure 8.1 has not published the total value since 2018.

importance of private Chinese companies in the domestic medtech industry—against state-owned organizations and foreign firms.

However, these largest Chinese companies are still small in comparison with other countries and other sectors. As discussed in Chap. 3, Mindray is the only one to be ranked among the world's largest medtech firms, with gross sales above one billion USD in 2014. Moreover, with 1.3 billion that year, it was ranked only 61st and lagged far behind the dominant firms (9 of them with more than 10 billion). Besides this, medtech companies are also relatively small within the Chinese economy. In 2018, only three of the listed medtech firms were among the ranking of the top-500 listed firms in China. These were Mindray, Lepu Medical and Weigao. However, Lepu Medical (318th rank) and Weigao (498th) were much less important than Mindray (88th; Wang & Geng, 2019).

Table 9.2 provides details on the 15 largest medtech firms listed in China in 2019. It therefore offers an excellent overview of the private firms that established themselves as major actors in this industry. Except for Weigao, all these companies were founded after 1990 and most are owned and controlled by private entrepreneurs. Few firms, among them Lepu Medical and Microport Scientific, have state-owned companies among their minority shareholders. Shinva Medical Instrument is the only company that can be considered state-owned. Its largest shareholder is the state-owned conglomerate Zibo Mining Group, which had 28.8% of its capital in 2019. Next, if one considers Hong Kong investors as Chinese, there are only a few firms with foreign capital, more specifically from medtech firms. Lepu Medical and Autobio Diagnostics have foreign shareholders with more than 5% of the capital, but these are companies founded in the US and in New Zealand, respectively, by their Chinese owners. This cannot really be considered foreign ownership from the perspective of technology transfer and global expansion in the medtech industry. The only Chinese company among the top-15 listed medtech firms with capital from a foreign medtech company is MicroPort Scientific. Otsuka Medical Devices, a Japanese diversified medtech firm, owned 23.6% of the capital in 2019.

However, although most of the largest listed medtech companies are owned by Chinese private entrepreneurs and investors, they present a broad dispersion in terms of size. Mindray, the largest, had gross sales of nearly 2.4 billion USD in 2019, followed by five companies with more than 1 billion. Two-thirds of these biggest companies were below the billion-dollar mark and four had less than 500 million USD. This confirms

Table 9.2 Top 15 largest Chinese-listed medtech companies, 2019

Company name	*Foundation*	*Gross sales (million USD)*	*State-owned (Y/N)*	*Foreign capital (Y/N)*	*Main products*
Shenzhen Mindray Bio-Medical Electronics	1991	2396	N	N	Patient monitoring devices, diagnostic laboratory instruments, ultrasound imaging systems
Shandong Weigao Group Medical Polymer	1988	1499	N	N	Medical disposable and consumables products
Shinva Medical Instrument	1993	1269	Y	N	Surgical instruments, diagnostic laboratory instruments, orthopedic products, pharmaceutical equipment and consumables series
Zhejiang DIAN Diagnostics	2001	1223	N	N	Diagnostic laboratory instruments and services
Lepu Medical Technology	1999	1129	N	Y	Cardiovascular medicines, cardiovascular diagnostic and treatment equipment
Shanghai Runda Medical Technology	1999	1021	N	N	Diagnostic laboratory reagent and instruments
MicroPort Scientific	1998	803	N	Y	Cardiovascular and other vascular devices and diabetic devices
Xiamen Comfort Science & Technology Group	1996	764	N	N	Rehabilitation devices
Jiangsu Yuyue Medical Equipment & Supply	1998	671	N	N	Patient monitoring devices, ultrasound imaging system, medical surgical equipment, consumables and household-use medical devices
Shanghai Fosun Pharmaceutical	1998	541	N	N	Diagnostic laboratory instruments

(*continued*)

Table 9.2 (continued)

Company name	*Foundation*	*Gross sales (million USD)*	*State-owned (Y/N)*	*Foreign capital (Y/N)*	*Main products*
Blue Sail Medical	2002	503	N	N	Medical disposable and consumables products
Maccura Biotechnology	1994	466	N	N	Diagnostic laboratory reagent and instruments
Medical System Biotechnology	2003	453	N	N	Diagnostic laboratory reagent and instruments
BGI Genomics	2010	405	N	N	Diagnostic laboratory instruments and services
Autobio Diagnostics	1999	388	N	Y	Diagnostic laboratory instruments

Source: CAMDI (2020), National Enterprise Credit Information Publicity System (http://www.gsxt.gov.cn) and annual reports of the firms

Note: Gross sales were converted to USD on the basis of average closing price of 6.91 Yuan for 1 USD; foreign capital includes shareholders with more than 5% of the capital

the trend of a medtech industry that is increasingly reliant on a handful of large companies.

Finally, regarding the fields of specialization of these firms, beyond the diversity of products, one can observe that many companies are engaged in diagnostic laboratory equipment, patient monitoring devices and consumable products. The rapid development of healthcare infrastructure and consumption leads to a massive demand for this basic equipment. Yet, medical imaging devices and orthopedic implants, which are major products in the global medtech industry, do not appear as special items within the product portfolio of the major Chinese medtech firms. Their production and sales are particularly overseen and regulated by foreign multinationals. Therefore, to shed light on the growth process of the private companies that dominate the Chinese medtech industry, I explore below the cases of the largest domestic company (Mindray) and of one of the major foreign firms (GE).

5.1 *The Largest Chinese Medtech Company: Mindray*

Mindray is the embodiment of the successful development of a private company in the Chinese medtech industry. However, its size and rapid growth make it particular and non-representative of the majority of private firms in this industry (see Table 9.2). As it represents today the only company that succeeded in establishing itself among the world's largest firms, it is worth exploring the sources of its competitiveness.

The company was founded in Shenzhen in 1991 by former employees of Anke High-tech, a firm founded in the same city five years before by the Chinese Academy of Science to manufacture medical imaging devices (see Sect. 5). It was not formally a state-owned company but benefited directly from the support by governmental organizations. Mindray began its business as an agent of GE, Hitachi, HP and Siemens (Bao & Hu, 2011). The main agency products were life-support monitors (Liu, 2008). China did not have any domestic players capable of making these devices at that time and the global brands were too expensive for the small county hospitals to afford (Liu, 2008). The founders had a strong background in technology and established their own R&D in 1992 with a loan of one million Yuan (approximately 180,000 USD) from the Shenzhen Government (Liu, 2008). Although they were experts in the development of ultrasound imaging systems, they predominantly focused on mid- and low-range devices at the beginning, such as life-support monitors and clinical laboratory reagents (Bao & Hu, 2011). These devices not only have a large market demand but also required at the time lower capital investments compared with the high-end medtech products.

In the early stages, Mindray did not have any brand awareness; nevertheless, it was able to expand its market share by innovating and improving the quality and design of the agency's products with a much lower price. It released an oxygen saturation monitor in 1992 and a color transcranial doppler instrument for cerebral blood flow diagnostics in 1993 (Bao & Hu, 2011). Its revenue reached 60 million Yuan in 1997 (approximately 7.2 million USD) and half of it was from its own developed products (An, 2003). In 1997, the Shenzhen Government established within Mindray the Shenzhen Medical Electronics Engineering Technology R&D Center (Bao & Hu, 2011). This action not only demonstrated Mindray's leading technological position in Shenzhen, but also the importance of local government support for its further development.

However, state support was insufficient to finance the expansion of Mindray. In 1997, it opened its capital to foreign investors and acquired two million USD from Walden Venture Capital, a US company (An, 2003). With this money, it was able to focus more on the development of its own products and to expand R&D to higher-end products. Research on ultrasound imaging systems was launched in 1997 and their product range was expanded to laboratory diagnostic instruments, such as the hematology analyzer (Liu, 2018). At the same time, as advised by its investor, Mindray hired a professional manager who had extensive work experience at Siemens (An, 2003). It also strengthened its distribution network (Bao & Hu, 2011). Two years later, in 1999, Mindray's promising development attracted new foreign investors (e.g., Japanese firms Softbank Finance Group and Japan Asia Investment) for a second-round investment of six million USD. This enabled Mindray to pursue the growth of its R&D and to establish overseas sales subsidiaries in 2000 (An, 2003). New ultrasound imaging systems were released in 2001 (Bao & Hu, 2011).

To raise more capital from foreign investors, a non-operating holding company, Mindray Medical International, was founded in 2005 in Cayman Islands, which held at that time 91% of the capital of Shenzhen Mindray Bio-Medical Electronics.[13] The company was listed in New York (2006–2016) and in Shenzhen (2018).

Mindray developed with a focus on the production of patient monitoring devices, diagnostic laboratory instruments and ultrasound imaging systems.[14] These three divisions were strengthened by in-house R&D and by the acquisitions of competitors, in China and abroad. Mindray is indeed one of the largest applicants of medtech patents (see Table 9.1). In 2014, it had R&D centers in China, in Sweden and in the US, and employed more than 2000 engineers and staff in R&D, against 600 in 2006.[15]

It also acquired several companies active in its fields of specialization, particularly the US developer of patient monitoring equipment Datascope Corporation (2008); several small Chinese companies, such as Shenzhen Shenke Medical Instrument, who are specialized in the production of injection systems and syringes (2011); Suzhou Hyssen Electronics, a

[13] Mindray Medical International, *Registration statement under the Securities Act of 1933* (SEC Form F-1), 2006, Retrieved from: https://www.sec.gov.

[14] Mindray Medical International, *Registration statement under the Securities Act of 1933* (SEC Form F-1), 2006, Retrieved from: https://www.sec.gov.

[15] Mindray Medical International, Annual Report (Form 20-K), 2007 and 2015.

manufacturer of automated urine sediment analyzers (2011); Hunan Changsha Tiandiren, which produces microbial diagnostic instruments (2011); the endoscope manufacturers Hangzhou Optcla (2012) and Shanghai Medical Optical Instruments Factory (2012); as well as another US firm, Zonare Medical Systems, who is specialized in ultrasound devices (2013). Mindray took over only two firms engaged in other fields of medtech, namely the developer of implants Wuhan Dragonbio Surgical (2012), and Shanghai Long Island Biotec, a maker of thrombotic and hemostatic reagent products (2014). This shows a will to maintain a focus on original core competences and to limit diversification.

Mindray International also founded two subsidiaries in the US and in UK to support sales, then expanded their number throughout Asia and Europe. In 2011, it had sales subsidiaries in Brazil, Canada, Colombia, Egypt, France, Germany, India, Italy, Mexico, the Netherlands, Singapore, Spain, Sweden, Turkey, and the US.[16] This geographical expansion was supported by the verticalization of Ulco Medical, Mindray's main distributor in Oceania (2013). This expanding sales network led to the growth of foreign sales. In 2003, foreign sales already amounted to 24.7% of the revenue, with a balance between North America (7.7%), Asia (7.3%) and Europe (6.7%). They expanded to 58.3% of the revenue in 2010 and decreased to 50% in 2018, due to the rapid growth of the domestic market.

Consequently, Mindray's development process since 1991 highlights the major factors that helped the firm build a competitive advantage over time. First, the financial and academic support of local government and state-owned organizations was essential during the company's formative years. Second, the control of a nationwide distribution network in China enabled Mindray to work with foreign medtech companies as an agent. Third, the company acted as an intermediary that adapted foreign goods to the local market. Finally, capital from foreign investors made it possible to enter into a new phase characterized by technological upgrade and global expansion.

5.2 *Foreign Firms: The Development of GE Healthcare in China*

Despite the impressive development of Mindray and other private companies, the Chinese medtech industry still strongly relies on foreign

[16] Mindray Medical International, Annual Report (Form 20-K), 2011.

companies for the supply of high-end goods. According to Bao (2019), the high-end product market, which accounts for approximately 25% of the overall medtech market in China, is dominated by foreign firms, with a 70-% market share. Moreover, devices with high technical barriers, like medical imaging equipment and in-vitro diagnosis products, have a share of more than 80% of foreign companies.

However, although foreign companies dominate the high-end medtech market in China, their strategy has changed drastically over the years. They gradually shifted manufacturing facilities in the country, and started later to carry out R&D, contributing to the growth of the Chinese medtech industry. to analyze the entry of foreign medtech companies and the evolution of their expansion in China, I focus here on the case of GE. Like in most countries, this enterprise is a major player in the Chinese medtech industry. In 2019, it was the dominant firm in one of the most important markets related to medical technology, CT scanners. It had a share of 30% and was followed by Siemens (23.5%), Philip (12.8%), and the domestic company Neusoft (10.4%).[17] The global strategy adopted by GE in the 1980s helped establish it as the leader in the diagnostic imaging equipment business (see Chap. 4). In 2005, its share of the global market was estimated at 34% (Khanna & Raabe, 2007).

GE Healthcare has been present in China since 1979.[18] That year it sold a CT unit to a Chinese hospital. Sales in China were first supervised through Hong Kong, until GE established a first office in Beijing in 1986. At first, the objective was to sell medical equipment to Chinese hospitals. In 1991, GE had to found a manufacturing joint venture to be able to make some import, subjected to quota at that time (Khanna & Raabe, 2007). Assembling medtech equipment, then, first followed state regulation. It was the only way to access the domestic market.

Since the mid-1990s, after quota were eliminated, GE multiplied its joint ventures in China and moved the production of several kinds of medtech devices. The objective was to develop equipment suitable to emerging countries—that is, low-end versions GE's products. Mike Jones, GEMS' global business and market development manager, declared that "People in the US can't design a low-end product for China [...]" (Khanna

[17] Survey of the consulting company Frost & Sullivan, mentioned on the business news website.

[18] *China Medical Devices Multinational Manufacturers*, Business Monitor Online, 14 September 2020 (Nexis Uni database).

& Raabe, 2007, p. 4). Three main joint ventures were made with local partners close to regulating authorities: GE Hangwei Medical Systems with a state-owned company belonging to the Ministry of Health; China National Equipment & Supplies Import & Export, for the production of medical imaging devices; GE Medical Systems China with a state-owned shipbuilding company in Wuxi, for manufacturing ultrasound devices; and a last joint venture with Xinan Medical Equipment Company in Chengdu, Sichuan Province, specializing in X-ray equipment.[19]

In the early twenty-first century, GE had acquired full or majority ownership of all these three joint ventures. It strengthened its presence in China, gradually moving production from Tokyo and making China a major production place for the global market. In 2005, 65% of medtech equipment manufactured in China was exported (Khanna & Raabe). In 2009, GE founded a new joint venture with Shinva Medical Instrument, a company listed at Shanghai Stock Exchange and for which the largest shareholder is the state-owned company Zibo Mining Group.[20] It focuses on the R&D, manufacturing and sales of diagnostic X-ray equipment. Finally, in July 2011, GE Healthcare moved its X-ray division's global headquarters to Beijing to enable an entire in-country X-ray business cycle, from engineering and development to sales and service.

6 Conclusion

China is a newcomer in the global medtech industry. It has experienced dramatic development since the mid-2000s. The dynamics of the Chinese medtech industry analyzed in this chapter are characterized as involving three major specificities.

First, the state is a major actor, although not always visible. It played a major role during the formative years of this industry, with state-owned enterprises as major innovators. Its most important contribution, however, is represented by the transfer of knowledge from academics to private firms. The example of Mindray, the largest private medtech company in China, has demonstrated that engineers and managers trained in state-owned organizations established a private company to create a business

[19] *China Medical Devices Multinational Manufacturers*, Business Monitor Online, 14 September 2020 (Nexis Uni database).

[20] This group owned 28.8% of the capital in 2019. Sinva Medical, Annual Report (2019, p. 59).

from their knowledge. Moreover, data on patent applications shows that universities are much larger patent applicants than private companies. The knowledge acquired by universities is undoubtedly transferred to the fast-growing private sector, but the conditions of this transfer remain unclear. Further research should investigate this issue.

Second, the development of the Chinese medtech industry relies on a large number of private companies, among which only a handful had gross sales of over a billion USD in 2019. These companies are largely focused on low-end products (especially patient monitoring and laboratory diagnostic devices) for the domestic market. M&A is not used to expand internationally but rather to strengthen the position of these companies in China. They answer a growing domestic demand, develop their export, but they have largely failed to establish themselves as major actors in high-end equipment, as expressed by the increasing trade deficit. For all high-tech industries, domestic firms had a 63% market share in China in 2005 but only 20% in the high-end medtech industry (Boyer et al., 2015).

Third, like in other countries, foreign multinationals dominate the Chinese medtech market. They have implemented two major strategies to strengthen their position. For the producers of large equipment such as CT scanners and other medical imaging devices, the development of specific machines for the Chinese market—cheaper and more affordable—was necessary and led to the transfer of production and R&D in China. They subsequently used China as a manufacturing basis for world markets. This was the way followed by GE and Siemens, for example. However, for companies specialized in consumer medtech products like implants and pacemakers, adaptation is less important. These goods are not an investment made by a healthcare organization but, instead, consumer goods used by individuals. Their producers privilege an export strategy.

Consequently, the major challenge faced by Chinese medtech firms is their ability to transform themselves into competitive global firms. This is definitely one of the major issues inherent in the current medtech industry, although the refocus of Mindray on the domestic market during the last decade demonstrates how difficult such a change can be.

References

Other Published Sources

ARWU. (2007–2016). *Academic Ranking of World Universities.* Retrieved April 20, 2021, from http://www.shanghairanking.com/index.html

CAMDI. (2020). *China Medical Device Industry Development Report (2020).* Economy & Management Publishing House.

Books and Academic Articles

An, J. (2003). How Does Shenzhen Mindray Gain the Venture Capital. *Technology Entrepreneurship, February, 2003,* 68–69. [in Chinese].

Bai, L. (2016). *Shenzhen Anke's Large Imaging Medical Equipment Marketing Strategy Research.* Lanzhou University of Technology, MBA Thesis (unpublished).

Bao, F. F., & Hu, H. (2011). From Local Agents to International Competitors: Experience and Implications of Shenzhen Mindray. *Enterprise Vitality, 5,* 30–34. [in Chinese].

Bao, Y. (2019). Brief Talking About the Development of Medical Device Industry in China. *Journal of Advances in Medicine Science| Volume, 2*(04), 24–28.

Boyer, P., Morshed, B. I., & Mussivand, T. (2015). Medical Device Market in China. *Artificial Organs, 39*(6), 520–525.

Cheong, S. T., Li, J., Ung, C. O. L., Tang, D., & Hu, H. (2020). Building an Innovation System of Medical Devices in China: Drivers, Barriers, and Strategies for Sustainability. *SAGE Open Medicine, 8,* 1–14.

Khanna, T., & Raabe, E. A. (2007). *General Electric Healthcare, 2006.* Harvard Business School. Case Study No. 9-706-478.

Liu, X. D. (2008). *Strategy Analysis of Shenzhen Mindray Company.* Master's Thesis, Capital University of Economics and Business [in Chinese].

Wang, B. T., & Geng, H. W. (2019). *Annual Report on the Development of Medical Device Industry in China.* Social Sciences Academic Press [in Chinese].

Wang, L., Wang, Z., Ma, Q., Fang, G., & Yang, J. (2019). The Development and Reform of Public Health in China from 1949 to 2019. *Globalization and Health, 15*(1), 1–21.

CHAPTER 10

Conclusion

This book has presented an analysis of the medtech industry's formation and transformation over the last half century. It has demonstrated that a process of diversification led to the emergence of large companies, mostly in the US, but also to some extent in Japan and Germany. These firms have dominated the world market since the early twenty-first century.

The medtech industry did not exist in the 1960s. A broad variety of companies developed, manufactured, and distributed a diverse range of equipment, devices and instruments, all of which had been used by medical doctors and hospitals for healthcare purposes. These companies were usually focused on specific goods such as surgical instruments, equipment for dentists, hearing aids, patient monitoring devices, and orthopedic appliances. Innovation by doctors and engineers led to the creation of new companies for the production and marketing of these goods. This was the case for Medtronic, for example, with its pacemakers in the US, as well as for Terumo with its thermometers in Japan. The market of all these firms was originally national, and even local. Several of them grew via export, which created competitiveness with other firms worldwide, such as the Swiss manufacturers of implants and orthopedic appliances, and German endoscope manufacturers.

The only large-scale MNEs engaged in the medical devices market were companies in the electrical appliance and pharmaceutical industries. The first of these included GE, Siemens, Toshiba and Philips. They established a competitive advantage for themselves in their development of X-ray

P.-Y. Donzé, *Medtech*,
https://doi.org/10.1007/978-981-16-7174-6_10

machines during the interwar years and maintained it through substantial R&D expenditure toward improving their goods. This was in addition to their development of CT scanners in the 1970s and MRI equipment in the 1980s. Despite medical imaging being their core competence, they diversified into neighboring fields, applying electronic technology to develop patient monitoring devices. As for pharmaceutical companies, several of them (e.g., Abbott, Baxter and Roche) developed divisions that specialized in diagnostic devices and patient monitoring, essentially as activities related to the development of diagnostic agents.

Whatever the size of these companies, however, they did not form part of a medtech industry. Due to their focus on specific devices and equipment, they did not compete with each other. A process of diversification began in the 1970s and 1980s. This was not based on technological convergence but on market convergence. Although based on different technologies (e.g., computer science, electronics, micromechanics, material science), medical devices shared similar clients: they were essentially sold to medical doctors and hospitals. It was therefore possible to build a portfolio of healthcare-related equipment to approach customers. M&A became a driving force for product diversification and the creation of diversified companies. The existence of hundreds of small specialized firms and the establishment of new startups annually enabled diversification through M&A. One of the first movers was Johnson & Johnson. They were followed by many firms, each of whom began to compete fiercely with each other. Thus, the medtech industry was born.

The growth of diversified medtech companies co-occurred with the globalization of their organization. Although export continues to represent an important driver of the internationalization of markets, cross-border M&A enabled firms to strengthen their competitive advantage. Since the 1990s, takeovers have developed dramatically. Some companies took over firms and founded joint ventures worldwide to access the local knowledge necessary to adapt their equipment to some countries. This was the case for GE, whose investments in Japan, and later on in China, were made to develop new generations of CT scanners. Other companies, such as the US orthopedic appliance manufacturers Stryker and Zimmer, maintained a focus on their core technology and acquired firms around the world to access local markets (like in France), or to internalize R&D capabilities (like in Switzerland). Finally, companies like Siemens used cross-border M&A to diversify and acquire new technologies related to digitalization and ICT.

The globalization of the medtech industry challenges the conventional national-based approach. The overwhelming majority of scholarly works on this sector has tackled national cases (see Introduction). The existence of SME clusters, of university-industry relations, and of localized knowledge has often been stressed as a major reason for the development of national medtech industries. I have shown in this book that, although local knowledge is important and SMEs continue to be competitive (notably in Germany and Switzerland), large MNEs established themselves as dominant actors in the medtech industry. The different chapters in this book based on national medtech industries emphasize a variety of trajectories regarding the formation and growth of a global medtech industry. The US appears as a special case, as the home country of the majority of the most powerful firms in this industry and of the constant creation of startups thanks to innovative universities and the presence of a developed financial market for capital risk. In other countries, medtech companies were able to continue their growth where they benefited from established competitive advantages in specific fields, such as electronics (Japan), micromechanics (Germany and Switzerland), optical technology (Germany and Japan), and orthopedic appliances (Switzerland). As demonstrated by the cases of Germany and Switzerland, the strong presence of foreign firms is not a disadvantage for local industry as long as local R&D capabilities maintain their presence in a country. On the contrary, the case of France shows that a low level of R&D can lead foreign firms to takeover local companies but with a focus essentially on marketing and sales, in turn giving way to a decline in local manufacturing capabilities. Finally, China appears to be the embodiment of emerging countries whose large domestic market benefits both local firms specialized in low-tech equipment as well as the industry's largest global firms in high-tech equipment.

Beyond the specific case of the medtech industry, this book contributes to literature in the fields of industry studies and industrial history. Considering "industry" the "fundamental arena in which competition occurs" (Porter, 1985, p. 1), the analysis presented in this book confirms the model proposed by Stokes and Blanken (2016) in their work on the industrial gas industry. They demonstrated that "industry" is the consequence of the action of firms, which began to invest outside of their core business and consequently began to encounter competitors. A new arena for competition can then result from this process and lead to the formation of a new industry. Its definition and boundaries, however, evolve over time (Stokes & Blanken, 2015). The current medtech industry is the outcome of a process of diversification and consolidation of companies engaged in the development, manufacturing and sales of devices used by medical doctors and hospitals. The limits of this industry, however, are not fixed forever. Technological innovation and the transformation of markets—for example, a growing integration between medtech, biotechnology and life sciences—will impact the nature of this industry in the future.

Another important contribution of this book is to the field of global health and the global history of medicine. Although some medtech firms based their international expansion on the localization of their equipment, like some medical imaging devices, one can argue that the result of the formation of a global medtech industry is the existence of standardized medical equipment worldwide. Companies offer similar devices to doctors and hospitals throughout the world. They contribute deeply, therefore, to the globalization of medicine, like the pharmaceutical industry or medical science itself. A proper understanding of the dynamics of the global healthcare system would require, however, more of a focus on factors that lead to divergence between nations. The role of governments and regulation, the varieties of health insurance systems, as well as demographic and geographic specificities should be taken into consideration to offer a more balanced view. Despite the globalization of medtech equipment, the practice of healthcare and of medicine differs between nations. Providing a narrative of the historical development of the global healthcare system that integrates global actors, such as medtech companies, and local specificities is the next major step of my research.

References

Books and Academic Articles

Porter, M. (1985). *Competitive Advantage: Creating and Sustaining Superior Performance*. The Free Press.

Stokes, R., & Blanken, R. (2015). Constructing an 'industry': The Case of Industrial Gases, 1886–2006. *Business History, 57*(5), 688–704.

Stokes, R., & Blanken, R. (2016). *Building on Air*. Cambridge University Press.

References

Archives

Bibliothèque nationale de France (BNF), Paris, WZ 1100, Compagnie générale de radiologie (CGR).
Schweizerische Wirtschaftsarchiv (SWA), Basel, Files on Swiss Medtech Companies.
Siemens Archives, Berlin.
Siemens Med Archiv (SMA), Erlangen.
Taniguchi Collection, Tokyo, Copies of General Electric Archives.

Annual Reports of Listed Companies

Abbott Laboratories, Air Liquide, Analogic Corporation, Bard, Baxter Laboratories, Bristol Myers, Canon, CMS, General Electric, Hitachi Medical, IBM, Intuitive Surgical, Johnson & Johnson, Medtronic, Mindray Medical International, Nipro, Olympus, Roche, Siemens, Sinva Medical, Steris, Stryker, Terumo, Weigao Group, and Zimmer.

Newspapers

China Daily, Beijing, 1981–.
Financial Times, London, 1888–.
Journal de Genève, Geneva, 1826–1998.
L'Agefi, Paris, 1911–.

P.-Y. Donzé, *Medtech*,
https://doi.org/10.1007/978-981-16-7174-6

Les Echos, Paris, 1908–.
Le Monde, Paris, 1944–.
L'Usine Nouvelle, Paris, 1891–.
New York Times, New York, 1851–.
Nikkei (Nihon Keizai Shimbun), Tokyo, 1879–.
The Irish Times, Dublin, 1859–.

Other Published Sources

ARWU. (2007–2016). *Academic Ranking of World Universities*. Retrieved April 20, 2021, from http://www.shanghairanking.com/index.html

Bay Area Council. (2016). *Entrepreneurs, Startups, and Innovation at the University of California*. Bay Area Council Economic Institute. Retrieved November 10, 2020, from http://www.bayareaeconomy.org/report/entrepreneurs-startups-innovation-at-uc/

CAMDI. (2020). *China Medical Device Industry Development Report (2020)*. Economy & Management Publishing House.

CGR. (1956). *Compagnie générale de radiologie, 1856–1956*. Compagnie Générale de Radiologie.

CHSY. (2020). *China's Health Statistics Yearbook 2020*. Peking Union Medical College Press.

CSY. (2001–2020). *China Statistical Yearbook*. China Statistics Press.

Donahoe, G. (2018). *Estimates of Medical Device Spending in the United States*. Advanced Medical Technology Association. Retrieved June 20, 2020, from https://www.advamed.org/sites/default/files/resource/estimates_of_medical_device_spending_in_the_united_states_november_2018.pdf

Evaluate. (2014). *Welcome to the Evaluate MedTech: World Preview 2014, Outlook to 2020*. Evaluate Ltd. Retrieved February 2, 2021, from http://info.evaluategroup.com/rs/evaluatepharmaltd/images/2014WPM.pdf

Fresenius. (2012). *Fresenius: Forward Thinking Healthcare: 100 years*. Fresenius.

IDCH. (1988–2014). *International Directory of Company Histories* (150 vols.). St. James Press.

IDCH. (1998). Ethicon. *International Directory of Company Histories, 23*. St. James Press, 1998, pp. 188–190.

IDCH. (1999a). Steris Corporation. *International Directory of Company Histories, 29*. St. James Press, 1999, pp. 449–451.

IDCH. (1999b). Strkyer Corporation. *International Directory of Company Histories, 29*. St. James Press, pp. 453–455.

IDCH. (2001a). Abbott Laboratories. *International Directory of Company Histories, 40*. St. James Press, 2001, pp. 9–13.

IDCH. (2001b). Johnson & Johnson. *International Directory of Company Histories, 36*. St. James Press, 2001, pp. 302–307.

IDCH. (2001c). Bristol Myers Squibb. *International Directory of Company Histories, 37*. St. James Press, 2001, pp. 41–43.

IDCH. (2002). Zimmer Holdings. *International Directory of Company Histories, 45*. St. James Press, pp. 455–457.

IDCH. (2003). Terumo. *International Directory of Company Histories, 48*. St. James Press, 2003, pp. 393–395.

IDCH. (2005). Medtronic. *International Directory of Company Histories, 67*. St. James Press, 2005, pp. 252–254.

Medical Design. (2016). *Medtech's 100 Largest Players*. Retrieved May 18, 2019, from https://www.medicaldesignandoutsourcing.com/

MedTech Europe. (2020). *The European Medical Technology Industry in Figures 2020*. Retrieved February 20, 2021, from https://www.medtecheurope.org/wp-content/uploads/2020/05/The-European-Medical-Technology-Industry-in-figures-2020.pdf

MHLW. (1960–2020). *Yakuji kogyo seisan jotai tokei nenpo*. Ministry of Health, Labor and Welfare.

National Venture Capital Association. (2015). *Yearbook 2015*.

Nikkei. (1950–2000). *Kaisha yoran*. Nikkei.

Nikkei. (2017, February 10). Geka shujutsu ni idomu Sony. *Nikkei bijinesu*, p. 17.

Nipro. (2017). *Sano minoru to nipuro no 70 nen*. Nipro.

OECD. (2018a). Hospitals (Indicator). Retrieved December 12, 2018, from https://stats.oecd.org/BrandedView.aspx?oecd_bv_id=health-data-en&doi=data-00541-en

OECD. (2018b). FDI stocks (Indicator). Retrieved December 12, 2018, from https://doi.org/10.1787/80eca1f9-en

OECD. (2018c). Computed Tomography (CT) Scanners (Indicator). Retrieved December 12, 2018, from https://doi.org/10.1787/bedece12-en

OECD. (2018d). Magnetic Resonance Imaging (MRI) Units (Indicator). Retrieved December 12, 2018, from https://doi.org/10.1787/1a72e7d1-en

OECD. (2020). *Health Care Resources: Medical Technology*. Retrieved December 10, 2020, from https://stats.oecd.org/#

Olympus. (1969). *50 nen no ayumi*. Olympus.

PIPAME. (2011). *Dispositifs médicaux : diagnostic et potentialités de développement de la filière française dans la concurrence internationale*. Pôle interministériel de prospective et d'anticipation des mutations économiques.

Radiology. (1930). Westinghouse Forms X-Ray Company. *Radiology, 15*(3), 402–403.

SNITEM. (2017). *De la filière industrielle des dispositifs médicaux en France en 2017*. Syndicat National de l'Industrie des Technologies Médicales.

Swiss Medtech. (2018). *The Swiss Medtech Industry 2018*. https://www.frn.swiss-medtech.ch/smti

Terumo. (1982). *Iryo to tomoni: terumo 60 nen no ayumi*. Terumo.

Toshiba Medical. (1998). *21 seiki he no kakehashi: Okyakusama totomoni ayunda Toshiba iyo kikai kaihatsu no rekishi*. Toshiba Medical.
United Nations. (1980). *International Trade Statistics Yearbook*. United Nations.
United Nations. (1990). *International Trade Statistics Yearbook*. United Nations.
USITC. (1981). *Automative trade statistics, 1964–1980*. USITC. Retrieved September 2, 2020, from https://www.usitc.gov/publications/332/pub1203.pdf

Books and Academic Articles

Aldridge, T. T., & Audretsch, D. (2011). The Bayh-Dole Act and Scientist Entrepreneurship. *Research Policy, 40*, 1058–1067.
Altenstetter, C. (2014). *Medical Technology in Japan: The Politics of Regulation*. Transaction Publishers.
An, J. (2003). How Does Shenzhen Mindray Gain the Venture Capital. *Technology Entrepreneurship, February, 2003*, 68–69. [in Chinese].
Anderson, J., Neary, F., & Pickstone, J. (2007). *Surgeons, Manufacturers and Patients: A Transatlantic History of Total Hip Replacement*. Palgrave Macmillan.
Andersson, S., Evers, N., & Griot, C. (2013). Local and International Networks in Small Firm Internationalization: Cases from the Rhône-Alpes Medical Technology Regional Cluster. *Entrepreneurship & Regional Development, 25*(9–10), 867–888.
Bai, L. (2016). *Shenzhen Anke's Large Imaging Medical Equipment Marketing Strategy Research*. Lanzhou University of Technology, MBA Thesis (unpublished).
Bao, F. F., & Hu, H. (2011). From Local Agents to International Competitors: Experience and Implications of Shenzhen Mindray. *Enterprise Vitality, 5*, 30–34. [in Chinese].
Bao, Y. (2019). Brief Talking About the Development of Medical Device Industry in China. *Journal of Advances in Medicine Science| Volume, 2*(04), 24–28.
Bartlett Foote Susan. (1992). *Managing the medical Arms Race: Innovation and Public Policy in the Medical Device Industry*. University of California Press.
Bestetti, G. (2009). Medtech: Potential for Innovation. *Swiss medical weekly, 139*(41–42), 587–590.
Blume, S. S. (1992). *Insight and Industry: On the Dynamics of Technological Change in Medicine*. MIT Press.
Blume, S. (2003). Medicine, Technology and Industry. In R. Cooter & J. Pickstone (Eds.), *Companion to Medicine in the Twentieth Century* (pp. 171–185). Routledge.
Boersma, K. (2003). Tensions Within an Industrial Research Laboratory: The Philips Laboratory's x-ray Department Between the Wars. *Enterprise & Society, 4*(1), 65–98.

Bouwens, B., Donzé, P. Y., & Kurosawa, T. (Eds.). (2018). *Industries and Global Competition: A History of Business Beyond Borders.* Routledge.

Boyer, P., Morshed, B. I., & Mussivand, T. (2015). Medical Device Market in China. *Artificial Organs, 39*(6), 520–525.

Bräuer, H. (1949). *Die Entwicklung der deutschen elektromedizinischen Industrie unter besonderer Berücksichtigung der Siemens-Reiniger-Werke AG Erlangen.* Friedrich-Alexander Universität Erlangen, Unpublished Dissertation.

Burfitt, A., Macneill, S., & Gibney, J. (2007). The Dilemmas of Operationalizing Cluster Policy: The Medical Technology Cluster in the West Midlands. *European Planning Studies, 15*(9), 1273–1290.

Campagnolo, D., & Camuffo, A. (2011). Globalization and Low-Technology Industries: The Case of Italian Eyewear. In P. L. Robertson & D. Jacobson (Eds.), *Knowledge Transfer and Technology Diffusion* (pp. 138–161). Edward Elgar.

Cantwell, J. A. (1995). The Globalization of Technology: What Remains of the Product Cycle Model. *Cambridge Journal of Economics, 19*(1), 154–174.

Catalan, J., & Ramon-Munoz, R. (2012). Marshall in Iberia. Industrial Districts and Leading Firms in the Creation of Competitive Advantage in Fashion Products. *Enterprise & Society, 14*(2), 327–359.

Chandler, A. D. (1990). *Scale and Scope: The Dynamics of Industrial Capitalism.* The Belknap Press of Harvard University Press.

Chandler, A. D. (2009). *Shaping the Industrial Century: The Remarkable Story of the Evolution of the Modern Chemical and Pharmaceutical Industries.* Harvard University Press.

Chang, H. J. (2001). Intellectual Property Rights and Economic Development: Historical Lessons and Emerging Issues. *Journal of Human Development, 2*(2), 287–309.

Chatterji, A. K. (2009). Spawned with a Silver Spoon? Entrepreneurial Performance and Innovation in the Medical Device Industry. *Strategic Management Journal, 30*(2), 185–206.

Chatterji, A. K., & Fabrizio, K. (2007). *Professional Users as a Source of Innovation: The Role of Physician Innovation in the Medical Device Industry.* Working Paper, Duke University, https://faculty.fuqua.duke.edu/~ronnie/bio/ChatterjiFabrizio_July2nd.pdf

Chatterji, A. K., Fabrizio, K. R., Mitchell, W., & Schulman, K. A. (2008). Physician-Industry Cooperation in the Medical Device Industry. *Health Affairs, 27*(6), 1532–1543.

Chen, X. (2021). *The Development of the Chinese Medical Device Industry Since 2000.* Osaka University, Graduate School of Economics: Unpublished Master Thesis.

Cheong, S. T., Li, J., Ung, C. O. L., Tang, D., & Hu, H. (2020). Building an Innovation System of Medical Devices in China: Drivers, Barriers, and Strategies for Sustainability. *SAGE Open Medicine, 8*, 1–14.

Christensen, C. (2013). *The Innovator's Dilemma: When New Technologies Cause Great Firms to Fail*. Harvard Business Review Press.

Christensen, C., & Raynor, M. (2013). *The Innovator's Solution: Creating and Sustaining Successful Growth*. Harvard Business Review Press.

Ciapetti, L. (2011). Technological Change, Knowledge Integration and Adaptive Processes: The Mechatronic Evolution of the Reggio Emilia District. In P. L. Robertson & D. Jacobson (Eds.), *Knowledge Transfer and Technology Diffusion* (pp. 107–137). Edward Elgar.

Clayton-Matthews, A. (2001). *The Medical Device Industry in Massachusetts*. University of Massachusetts, Donahue Institute.

Cody, T. G. (1990). *Strategy of a Megamerger: An Insider's Account of the Baxter Travenol-American Hospital Supply Combination*. Quorum Books.

Coffano, M., Foray, D., & Pezzoni, M. (2017). Does Inventor Centrality Foster Regional Innovation? The Case of the Swiss Medical Devices Sector. *Regional Studies, 51*(8), 1206–1218.

Cosandey, M. (Ed.). (1999). *Histoire de l'Ecole polytechnique de Lausanne, 1953–1978*. PPUR.

Craven, M. P., Allsop, M. J., Morgan, S. P., & Martin, J. L. (2012). Engaging with Economic Evaluation Methods: Insights from Small and Medium Enterprises in the UK Medical Devices Industry After Training Workshops. *Health Research Policy and Systems, 10*(1), 29.

Davis, A. B. (1978). Historical Studies of Medical Instruments. *History of Science, 16*(2), 107–133.

DiMaio, S., Hanuschik, M., & Kreaden, U. (2011). The da Vinci Surgical System. In J. Rosen, B. Hannaford, & R. M. Satava (Eds.), *Surgical Robotics* (pp. 199–217). Springer.

Donzé, P. Y. (2016). The Beginnings of the Japanese Medical Instruments Industry and the Adaptation of Western Medicine to Japan, 1880–1937. *Australian Economic History Review, 56*(3), 272–291.

Donzé, P. Y. (2018). *Making Medicine a Business: X-ray Technology, Global Competition, and the Transformation of the Japanese Medical System, 1895–1945*. Springer.

Donzé, P.-Y. (2013). Siemens and the Business of Medicine in Japan, 1900–1945. *Business History Review, 87*(2), 203–228.

Donzé, P.-Y. (2015). Siemens and the Construction of Hospitals in Latin America, 1949–1964. *Business History Review, 89*(3), 475–502.

Donzé, P.-Y. (2018a). Innovation. *Dictionnaire historique de la Suisse*. https://hls-dhs-dss.ch/fr/articles/055505/2018-12-17/

Donzé, P.-Y. (2018b). *Making Medicine a Business: X-ray Technology and the Transformation of the Japanese Medical System (1895–1945)*. Basingstoke: Palgrave Macmillan.

Donzé, P.-Y., & Fernandez Perez, P. (2019). Health Industries in the Twentieth Century. *Business History, 61*(3), 385–403.

Donzé, P.-Y., & Imer, R. (2020). Innovation in the Global Medtech Industry: An Empirical Analysis of Patent Applications, 1960–2014. *Osaka Economic Papers, 69*(4), 18–42.

Donzé, P. Y., & Wubs, B. (2019). Global Competition and Cooperation in the Electronics Industry: The Case of X-ray Equipment, 1900–1970. *Scandinavian Economic History Review, 67*(2), 210–225.

Estrin, N. F. (Ed.). (1990). *The Medical Device Industry: Science: Technology, and Regulation in a Competitive Environment.* CRC Press.

Feldenkirchen, W. (1995). *Siemens, 1918–1945.* Ohio State University Press.

Feldenkirchen, W. (2000). *Siemens: From Workshop to Global Player.* Piper.

Feldenkirchen, W. (2002). Siemens in the US. In G. Jones & L. Galvez-Munoz (Eds.), *Foreign Multinationals in the United States: Management and Performance* (pp. 94–95). Routledge.

Fennelly, D., & Cormican, K. (2006). Value Chain Migration from Production to Product Centred Operations: An Analysis of the Irish Medical Device Industry. *Technovation, 26*(1), 86–94.

Folland, S., Goodman, A., & Stano, M. (2013). *The Economics of Health and Health Care.* Pearson.

Fontana, R., Nuvolari, A., Shimizu, H., & Vezzulli, A. (2013). Reassessing Patent Propensity: Evidence from a Dataset of R&D awards, 1977–2004. *Research Policy, 42*(10), 1780–1792.

Foote, S. B. (1992). *Managing the Medical Arms Race: Public Policy and Medical Device Innovation.* University of California Press.

Foote, S. B., & Mitchell, W. (1989). Selling American Medical Equipment in Japan. *California Management Review, 31*(4), 146–161.

Foray, D. (2014). *Smart Specialisation: Opportunities and Challenges for Regional Innovation Policy.* Routledge.

Foster, L. G. (1986). *A Company That Cares: One Hundred Years Illustrated History of Johnson & Johnson.* Johnson & Johnson.

Frost & Sullivan. (2017). *Global Medical Device Industry Snapshot.* Retrieved October 31, 2018, from https://store.frost.com/

Gardner, K. E. (2000). Hiding the Scars: A History of Post-Mastectomy Breast Prostheses, 1945–2000. *Enterprise & Society, 1*(3), 565–590.

Gelijns, A. C., & Rosenberg, N. (1999). Diagnostic Devices: An Analysis of Comparative Advantages. In D. C. Mowery & R. R. Nelson (Eds.), *Sources of Industrial Leadership: Studies of Seven Industries* (pp. 312–358). Cambridge University Press.

Gelijns, A. C., & Thier, S. O. (2002). Medical Innovation and Institutional Interdependence: Rethinking University-Industry Connections. *Jama, 287*(1), 72–77.

Glovik, M. (2017). Case Study: Fresenius: Concentration Strategies in Healthcare Business. In M. Glovik (Ed.), *Global Strategy in the Service Industries: Dynamics, Analysis, Growth* (pp. 165–172). Routledge.

Godelier, E. (2007). "Do You Have a Garage?" Discussion of Some Myths about Entrepreneurship. *Business and Economic History On-line*, vol. 5, https://thebhc.org/sites/default/files/godelier_0.pdf

Grossman, J. S. (2006). *Innovative Doctoring: Solutions Lie Within Us*. Innovative Doctoring.

Harrington, P. R. (1988). The History and Development of Harrington Instrumentation. *Clinical Orthopaedics and Related Research, 227*, 3–5.

Heiss, G. (2017). Influencing Factors and the Effect of Organizational Capabilities on Internationalization Strategies for German SMEs in the MedTech Industry. *Management, 5*(4), 263–277.

Hogle, L. (2008). Emerging Medical Technologies. In E. J. Hackett, O. Amsterdamska, M. Lynch, & J. Wajcman (Eds.), *The Handbook of Science and Technology Studies* (pp. 841–873). MIT Press.

Hoshi, T. (2018). Has Abenomics Succeeded in Raising Japan's Inward Foreign Direct Investment? *Asian Economic Policy Review, 13*(1), 149–168.

IDCH. (2005). Medtronic. *International Directory of Company Histories, 67*. St. James Press, 2005, pp. 252–254.

Ikegami, N. (Ed.). (2014). *Universal Health Coverage for Inclusive and Sustainable Development: Lessons from Japan*. The World Bank.

Janssen, L., & Medford, G. (2009). *Envision: A History of the GE Healthcare Business*. Meadow Brook Farm.

Jemain, A. (2002). *Les conquérants de l'invisible: Air Liquide, 100 ans d'histoire*. Fayard.

Jetter, K. (1991). Tuttlingen und seine chirurgischen Instrumente unter besonderer Berücksichtigung der Aufbauleistung von Gottfried Jetter. *Tuttlinger Heimatblätter*. N.F. 54, 24–29.

Jones, C. L. (2018). Surgical Instruments: History and Historiography. In *The Palgrave Handbook of the History of Surgery* (pp. 235–257).

Kaba, M. (2018). *Une histoire de l'orthopédie : l'Hôpital orthopédique de la Suisse romande dans le contexte international (18e–21e siècles)*. BHMS.

Kawashima, J., & Shimizu, M. (1989). Kokusai tokkyo bunrui. *Joho to kagaku to gijutsu, 9*(11), 503–510.

Khanna, T., & Raabe, E. A. (2007). *General Electric Healthcare, 2006*. Harvard Business School. Case Study No. 9-706-478.

Kimura, H. (2012). *Kakkai toppu chousen suru: iryo herusukea sangyo bijinesu moderu*. Kanki shuppan.

Kiuntke, F. (2006). *Der Wiederaufbau der Siemens-Reiniger-Werke nach dem Zweiten Weltkrieg (1945–1950)*. Friedrich-Alexander-Universität Erlangen-Nürnberg, Unpublished Magisterarbeit.

Klöpper, C., & Haisch, T. (2008). Evolution de l'industrie biotech et medtech suisse et influence de l'industrie pharmaceutique sur le système d'innovation. *Revue Géographique de l'Est, 48*(3–4), 1–25.

Korine, H. (2000). Fresenius AG: High-speed Globalization. *Business Strategy Review, 11*(2), 47–57.

Kreutzer, U. (2013). *Von den Anfängen zum Milliardengeschäft. Die Unternehmensentwicklung von Siemens in den USA zwischen 1845 und 2001.* Franz Steiner Verlag.

Kruger, K., & Kruger, M. (2005). The Medical Device Sector. *The Business of Healthcare Innovation*, 271–321.

Kurosawa, T. (2018). Industry History: Its Concepts and Methods. In B. Bouwens, P.-Y. Donzé, & T. Kurosawa (Eds.), *Industries and Global Competition: A History of Business Beyond Borders* (pp. 1–24). Routledge.

Kuttruff, J. (1996). *Der vom Anwender induzierte strategische Prozess: eine empirische Längsschnittanalyse zum Innovationsprozess im Bereich der Medizinaltechnik.* Universität St. Gallen, Dissertation.

Lawyer, P., & Alford, R. (2005). Industrial Revolution: The New Medical Device Acquirers. *In Vivo-New York Then Norwalk, 23*(6), 47.

Le Vine, H. (2010). *Medical Imaging*. Greenwood.

Li, N. (2007). Mindray Trilogy. *IT Management World, 2007*, 32–33. [in Chinese].

Liesen, E. (2004). *Die Entwicklung der Patientenverpflegung im Krankenhaus seit den 50er Jahren in Deutschland.* Rheinische-Friedrich-Wilhelms-Universität.

Linder, T. E., Simmen, D., & Stool, S. E. (1997). Revolutionary Inventions in the 20th Century: The History of Endoscopy. *Archives Otolaryngology Head Neck Surgery, 123*(11), 1161–1163.

Liu, X. D. (2008). *Strategy Analysis of Shenzhen Mindray Company.* Master's Thesis, Capital University of Economics and Business [in Chinese].

Livi, C., & Jeannerat, H. (2015). Born to Be Sold: Startups as Products and New Territorial Life Cycles of Industrialization. *European Planning Studies, 23*(10), 1953–1974.

Llobrera, J. T., Meyer, D. R., & Nammacher, G. (2000). Trajectories of Industrial Districts: Impact of Strategic Intervention in Medical Districts. *Economic Geography, 76*(1), 68–98.

Maresova, P., & Kuca, K. (2014). Porters Five Forces on Medical Device Industry in Europe. *Military Medical Science Letters, 83*(4), 134–144.

Markusen, A. (1996). Sticky Places in Slippery Space: A Typology of Industrial Districts. *Economic Geography, 72*(3), 293–313.

Mason, M. (1995). Japan's Low Levels of Inward Direct Investment: Causes, Consequences and Remedies. In *Corporate Links and Foreign Direct Investment in Asia and the Pacific* (pp. 129–152). Westview Press.

MHLW. (2020). *Yakuji kogyo seisan jotai tokei nenpo.* Tokyo: Ministry of Health, Labour and Welfare.

Miyajima, H. (Ed.). (2007). *Nihon no M&A: kigyo touji, soshiki kouritsu, kigyo kachi heno inpakuto*. Toyo keiyai hosha.

Moustial, P. (2019). La France dans la compétition mondiale des technologies médicales? *Les Tribunes de la sante, 2*, 67–72.

Mowery, D. C., & Rosenberg, N. (1998). *Paths of Innovation: Technological Change in 20th-Century America*. Cambridge University Press.

Mowery, D. C., & Sampat, B. N. (2001). Patenting and Licensing University Inventions: Lessons from the History of the Research Corporation. *Industrial and Corporate Change, 10*(2), 317–355.

Mowery, D. C., Nelson, R. R., Sampat, B. N., & Ziedonis, A. A. (2001). The Growth of Patenting and Licensing by US Universities: An Assessment of the Effects of the Bayh–Dole Act of 1980. *Research Policy, 30*(1), 99–119.

Nishimura, S. (2010). Gurobaru keiei to chiteki zaisan manejimento. In U. Okura, K. Suyama, & K. Ito (Eds.), *Gurobaru keizai ni okeru keiei to kaikaei no kenkyu* (pp. 95–134). Kansai University Press.

Onuma, M. (2010). Shinkyu sumiwake wo jikken suru seihin tenkai: shuyo kakusha ni yoru X-sen CT to MRI he no shigen haifu to seihin tenkai. In Hitotsubashi University (Ed.), *Nihon kigyo kenkyu no furonteiya, vol. 6* (pp. 47–63). Yuhikaku.

Oshita, H., & Ikeno, F. (2016). *Iryo kikai kaihatsu to bencha kapitaru*. Gentosha Media Consulting.

Palermo, A. (1995). A Legacy of Caring-the History of Picker International. *GEC Review, 10*(2), 103–119.

Panescu, D. (2006). Medical Device Industry. In *Wiley Encyclopedia of Biomedical Engineering*.

Peyer, H. C. (1996). *Roche, Geschichte eines Unternehmens : 1896–1996*. Roche.

Porter, M. (1985). *Competitive Advantage: Creating and Sustaining Superior Performance*. The Free Press.

Rabier, C. (2013). Introduction: The Crafting of Medicine in the Early Industrial Age. *Technology and Culture, 54*(3), 437–459.

R&D Co. (2014). *Iryo kiki youhin nenkan*. R&D Co.

Racine, B. (1988). *Le syndicalisme et la modernisation: étude d'un cas type de modernisation démocratique: contribution à l'étude de la dynamique de transformation du rapport salarial dans la mutation*. [Rapport de recherche] Centre national de l'entrepreneuriat(CNE); Ministère des affaires sociales et de l'emploi.

Reiser, S. J. (1978). *Medicine and the Reign of Technology*. Cambridge University Press.

Rodengen, J. L. (2001). *The Ship in the Balloon: The Story of Boston Scientific and the Development of Less-Invasive Medicine*. Write Stuff Enterprises.

Romeo, A. A., Wagner, J. L., & Lee, R. H. (1984). Prospective Reimbursement and the Diffusion of New Technologies in Hospitals. *Journal of Health Economics, 3*(1), 1–24.

Rosenberg, N. (2009). Some Critical Episodes in the Progress of Medical Innovation: An Anglo-American Perspective. *Research Policy, 38*(2), 234–242.

Rossiter, L. F., & Wilensky, G. R. (1984). Identification of Physician-Induced Demand. *Journal of Human Resources*, 231–244.

Russell, L. (2017). The Current State of Japanese Inbound FDI: Deterrents and Initiatives. *Hannan Ronshu, 52*(2), 13–35.

Sakai, K. (2018). Thriving in the Shadow of Giants: The Success of the Japanese Surgical Needle Producer MANI, 1956–2016. *Business History, 61*(3), 1–27.

Sawai, M. (2012). *Kindai nihon no kenkyu kaihatsu taisei*. Nagoya University Press.

Schlich, T. (2002). *Surgery, Science and Industry*. Palgrave Macmillan.

Schlich, T., & Tröhler, U. (Eds.). (2006). *The Risks of Medical Innovation: Risk Perception and Assessment in Historical Context*. Routledge.

Schraudolph, E. (1984). *Die Entwicklung von RGS bzw. SRW zwischen 1877 und 1945 in Wechselwirkung zur Stadt Erlangen*. Friedrich-Alexander Universität Erlangen-Nürnberg, Unpublished Magisterarbeit.

Schroeter, H. G. (1993). Continuity and Change: German Multinationals Since 1850. In G. Jones & H. G. Schröter (Eds.), *The Rise of Multinationals in Continental Europe* (pp. 28–48). Edward Elgar.

Shah, S. G. S., & Robinson, I. (2007). Benefits of and Barriers to Involving Users in Medical Device Technology Development and Evaluation. *International Journal of Technology Assessment in Health Care, 23*(1), 131–137.

Shaw, B. (1998). Innovation and New Product Development in the UK Medical Equipment Industry. *International Journal of Technology Management, 15*(3–5), 433–445.

Shimizu, H. (2019). Patterns of Spin-Outs and Innovation. In *General Purpose Technology, Spin-Out, and Innovation* (pp. 221–245). Springer.

Shioji, H., & Tanaka, A. (Eds.). (2020). *Higashi ajia yui sangyo: tagenka suru kokusai seisan netowaku*. Tokyo: Chuo keizaisha.

Slade, E. P., & Anderson, G. F. (2001). The Relationship Between Per Capita Income and Diffusion of Medical Technologies. *Health Policy, 58*(1), 1–14.

Steinle, C., Schiele, H., & Mietzner, K. (2007). Merging a Firm-Centred and a Regional Policy Perspective for the Assessment of Regional Clusters: Concept and Application of a "dual" Approach to a Medical Technology Cluster. *European Planning Studies, 15*(2), 235–251.

Stokes, R., & Blanken, R. (2015). Constructing an 'industry': The Case of Industrial Gases, 1886–2006. *Business History, 57*(5), 688–704.

Stokes, R., & Blanken, R. (2016). *Building on Air*. Cambridge University Press.

Takenaka, T. (2005). Technology Licensing and University Research in Japan. *International Journal of Intellectual Property-Law, Economy and Management, 1*(1), 27–36.

Takeuchi, A. (1974). Tokyo ni okeru iryo kikai kogyo shudan no kosei. *Jinbun chiri, 26*, 658–673.

Tamura, A. (2013). Japan: Medical Device Regulatory System. *Handbook of Medical Device Regulatory Affairs in Asia*, 459–474.

Teixeira, M. B. (2013). *Design Controls for the Medical Device Industry*. CRC Press.

Tichy, N. M., & Sherman, S. (1993). *Control Your Destiny or Someone Else Will: Lessons in Mastering Change – The Principles Jack Welch Is Using to Revolutionize General Electric*. Doubleday.

Timmermann, C., & Anderson, J. (Eds.). (2006). *Devices and Designs: Medical Technologies in Historical Perspective*. Palgrave Macmillan.

Trajtenberg, M. (1990). *Economic Analysis of Product Innovation: The Case of CT Scanners*. Harvard University Press.

de Vet, J. M., & Scott, A. J. (1992). The Southern Californian Medical Device Industry: Innovation, New Firm Formation, and Location. *Research Policy, 21*(2), 145–161.

Vittinghoff, D. M., & Vollertsen-Diewerge, M. (2008). *Max Gebbert & the Pioneers of Medical Engineering*. Siemens Med Archives.

Vlckova, J., & Thakur-Weigold, B. S. (2019). Global Value Chains in the MedTech Industry. *International Journal of Emerging Markets, 15*(1), 70–62.

von Weiher, S., & Goetzeler, H. (1977). *The Siemens Company: Ist Historical Role in the Progress of Electrical Engineering, 1847–1980*. Siemens AG.

Wang, B. T., & Geng, H. W. (2019). *Annual Report on the Development of Medical Device Industry in China*. Social Sciences Academic Press [in Chinese].

Wang, L., Wang, Z., Ma, Q., Fang, G., & Yang, J. (2019). The Development and Reform of Public Health in China from 1949 to 2019. *Globalization and Health, 15*(1), 1–21.

Weigel, S. (2011). Medical Technology's Source of Innovation. *European Planning Studies, 19*(1), 43–61.

Wu, B. (2013). Opportunity Costs, Industry Dynamics, and Corporate Diversification: Evidence from the Cardiovascular Medical Device Industry, 1976–2004. *Strategic Management Journal, 34*(11), 1265–1287.

Xu, N. N., & Xu, Y. S. (2015). Research on the Path of Reverse Innovation of Latecomer Enterprises: Based on Grounded Theory Analysis of Longitudinal Cases. *Chinese Journal of Management, 12*(11), 1579–1587. [in Chinese].

Yamaguchi, S., & Shimizu, H. (2015). Orinpasu: ikamera to faiba sukopu no kaihatsu. *Hitotsubashi Business Review, 3*, 100–112.

Zenger, I. (2014). *Magnetic Resonance Imaging at Siemens: A Success Story*. Siemens.

Zenger, I. (2015). *The History of Computed Tomography at Siemens: A Retrospective*. Siemens.

The manufacturer's authorised representative in the EU is Springer Nature Customer Service Centre GmbH, Europaplatz 3, 69115 Heidelberg, Germany. If you have any concerns regarding our products, please contact ProductSafety@springernature.com

Printed and bound by CPI Group (UK) Ltd, Croydon, CR0 4YY

30/09/2026

02225311-0005